W9-BBC-257
20686

Victor Hugo

Napoleon
the
Little

New York

HOWARD FERTIG

1992

Published in 1992 by Howard Fertig, Inc.
80 East 11th Street, New York, N.Y. 10003
All rights reserved.

Library of Congress Cataloging-in-Publication Data
Hugo, Victor, 1802–1885.
  [Napoléon le Petit. English]
  Napoleon the Little / Victor Hugo.
    p. cm.
  ISBN 0-86527-408-8
  1. France—History—Coup d' état, 1851. 2. Napoleon III,
Emperor of the French, 1808–1873. 3. France—History—
Second Republic, 1848–1852. I. Title.
DC274.H913 1992
944.07—dc20   92–29403
                                           CIP

Printed in the United States of America

CONTENTS

NAPOLEON THE LITTLE

BOOK I.— The Man

Chapter		Page
I.	The 20th of December, 1848	1
II.	Mandate of the Representatives	7
III.	Demand in Due Form of Law	8
IV.	There will be an awakening	12
V.	Biography	15
VI.	A Portrait	18
VII.	The Panegyrics continue	24

BOOK II.— The Government

I.	The Constitution	32
II.	The Senate	33
III.	The Council of State and the Legislative Body	35
IV.	The Finances	37
V.	The Liberty of the Press	38
VI.	Innovations in Matters of Legality	40
VII.	The Adherents	42
VIII.	Mens Agitat Molem	46
IX.	Omnipotence	51
X.	The Two Profiles of Monsieur Bonaparte	54
XI.	Capitulation	57

BOOK III.— The Crime 65

BOOK IV.— The Other Crimes

I.	Sinister Questions	99
II.	Continuation of the Crimes	105
III.	What 1852 would have been	117
IV.	The Jacquerie	120

CONTENTS

BOOK V.— PARLIAMENTARISM.

CHAPTER   PAGE

I. 1789 127
II. MIRABEAU 128
III. THE TRIBUNE 129
IV. THE ORATORS 131
V. THE POWER OF SPEECH 134
VI. WHAT THE ORATOR IS 135
VII. WHAT THE TRIBUNE DID 136
VIII. PARLIAMENTARISM 138
IX. THE TRIBUNE DESTROYED 140

BOOK VI.— THE ABSOLUTION.

First Form

THE SEVEN MILLION FIVE HUNDRED THOUSAND VOTES

I. THE ABSOLUTION 142
II. THE DILIGENCE 143
III. EXAMINATION OF THE VOTE. RECALLING PRINCIPLES.
    FACTS 144
IV. WHO REALLY VOTED FOR MONSIEUR BONAPARTE 152
V. A CONCESSION 154
VI. THE MORAL SIDE OF THE QUESTION 155
VII. AN EXPLANATION TO MONSIEUR BONAPARTE 158
VIII. AXIOMS 162
IX. WHERE MONSIEUR BONAPARTE HAS BEEN MISTAKEN . . . 163

BOOK VII.— THE ABSOLUTION.

Second Form

THE OATH

I. TO AN OATH AND AN OATH AND A HALF 166
II. A DIFFERENCE IN VALUES 168
III. THE OATH OF THE LETTERED AND THE LEARNED 170
IV. SOME CURIOUS FEATURES 172
V. THE 5TH OF APRIL, 1852 175
VI. SWEARING ON ALL SIDES 178

CONTENTS

BOOK VIII.— Progress contained in the *Coup d'Etat*

Chapter		Page
I.	The Quantity of Good contained in the Evil	181
II.	The Four Institutions opposed to the Future	184
III.	Slowness of Normal Progress	185
IV.	What the Assembly might have done	187
V.	What Providence has done	189
VI.	What the Ministers, the Army, the Magistracy, and the Clergy have done	191
VII.	Forms of the Government of God	191

CONCLUSION

FIRST PART. Pettiness of the Master, Shabbiness of the Situation 192

SECOND PART. Mourning and Faith 207

BOOK I

THE MAN

CHAPTER I

THE 20TH OF DECEMBER, 1848

ON Friday the 20th of December, 1848, the Constituent Assembly was in session, surrounded by an imposing array of troops. It had met to hear the report of the Commission charged with the verification of the ballots read by Representative Waldeck Rousseau. The full significance of this report is summarized in the following sentence: —

"By this admirable execution of the fundamental law the nation places the sanction of its inviolable power on the Constitution, which it thereby renders sacred and inviolable."

Amid the profound silence of the crowded Chamber, almost at its full complement of nine hundred members, the President of the Constituent National Assembly rose and said,—

"In the name of the French People!
"Whereas Citizen Charles Louis Napoleon Bonaparte, born in Paris, possesses all the qualifications of eligibility required by the forty-fourth article of the Constitution,—
"Whereas in the election, open throughout the whole extent of the Republic, he has received the absolute majority of votes,—
"The National Assembly, by virtue of the forty-seventh and forty-

1

eighth articles of the Constitution, proclaims him President of the Republic from this day until the second Sunday of May, 1852."

There were signs of emotion among the people who thronged the benches and tribunes; the President of the Constituent Assembly added: —

" According to the terms of the decree, I invite the President of the Republic to ascend the tribune and take the oath."

The Representatives who were blocking up the lobby on the right returned to their seats and left the passage free. It was about four o'clock in the evening, night was coming on, the immense hall of the Assembly was half plunged in shadow; chandeliers hung from the ceiling, and the ushers had just placed the lamps on the tribune. At a sign from the President, the door on the right opened.

Then a man still young, dressed in black, with the badge and broad ribbon of the Legion of Honour on his breast, entered the hall and quickly took his place in the tribune.

All eyes were turned upon this man,— a pallid face whose spare angular lines were brought out with distinctness by the lamp-reflectors, a nose coarse and long, a lock of hair curled over a straight forehead, eyes small and dull, a timid and troubled demeanour, a likeness to the Emperor nowhere; it was Citizen Charles Louis Napoleon Bonaparte.

During the confused murmur that succeeded his entrance, he stood motionless for some moments, with his right hand in his buttoned coat, on the tribune which bore on its front the dates: 22, 23, 24 *fevrier*, and above, these three words: *Liberté, Egalité, Fraternité.*

Before his election as President of the Republic, Charles Louis Napoleon Bonaparte was a Representative of the People.   For several months he had a seat in the Assembly, and, although he was rarely present at entire sessions, he was seen not unfrequently in the place he had chosen on one of the upper benches of the Left, in the fifth gallery, in that zone commonly called the Mountain, behind his former tutor, Representative Vieillard.   His was no new face for the Assembly, and yet his entrance was the occasion of deep excitement. For friends, as well as for enemies, it was the future that was entering, and that future was an unknown one. In the low murmurs which the voices of the spectators contributed to swell into an enormous volume of sound, his name ran from lip to lip coupled with comments of the most diverse character. His antagonists told of his adventures, his turbulent outbreaks, Strasburg and Boulogne, the tame eagle, and the bit of meat in the little hat. His friends, in his favour, pleaded his exile, his proscription, his imprisonment, a good work on artillery, his writings at Ham, distinguished to some extent by a liberal, democratic, and socialist character, and that ripeness of thought advancing years develop; they recalled his misfortunes to those who revived his follies.

General Cavaignac, not having been elected President, had just surrendered the powers with which the Assembly had invested him, speaking with the quiet brevity so befitting in a Republic. Sitting with folded arms in his usual place on the left of the tribune at the head of the bench of Ministers, beside Marie, the Minister of Justice, he was a silent observer of the installation of the new man.

At length there was stillness. The President of the Assembly rapped the table with his gavel, the last murmurs died away, and the President of the Assembly rose and said:—

"I am about to read the formula of the oath."

The moment seemed to bring with it a sense of religious awe. The Assembly was no longer the Assembly, it was a temple. The immense import of this oath derived additional significance from one fact,— it was the only oath taken throughout the whole extent of the Republic. February had rightly abolished the political oath, and, with equal right, the Constitution had preserved no oath but that of the President. This oath had the twofold impress of necessity and grandeur. The executive power, which is a subordinate power, swore obedience to the legislative power, which is a

superior power, nay, it meant even more than this. Invert-
ing the monarchic fiction, in which the people swore allegiance
to the man invested with power, it was the man invested with
power who swore allegiance to the people. The President,
as a functionary and a servant, took the oath of fidelity to
the sovereign people. Bending before the national majesty
made manifest in the omnipotent Assembly, he received the
Constitution from the Assembly, and swore to obey it. The
Representatives were inviolable, and he was not. He was,
we repeat, a citizen responsible to his fellow-citizens, and the
only man in the nation controlled by such a bond. And
hence there was in this exceptional and supreme oath a solem-
nity that took entire possession of the heart. He who writes
these lines was in his place in the Assembly on the day
when this oath was taken. He is one of those who, in presence of the civilized world called to witness the act, received
that oath in the name of the people; he is one of those who
still hold it in their hands. It is worded thus: —

"In presence of God and before the French People, represented by
the National Assembly, I swear to remain faithful to the democratic
Republic, one and indivisible, and to fulfil all the duties imposed on me
by the Constitution."

The President of the Assembly, standing up, read this majestic formula.

Then, while the entire Assembly listened in impressive silence, Citizen Charles Louis Napoleon Bonaparte raised his
right hand and said in a loud and firm voice,—

"I swear!"

Boulay (de la Meurthe), then a Representative and afterwards Vice-President of the Republic, who knew Charles
Louis Napoleon Bonaparte from infancy, cried out: "He is
an honest man; he will keep his oath!"

The President of the Assembly, who had remained standing, spoke again, and we quote his words literally, as they
have been recorded in the "Moniteur."

"We take God and men to witness the oath that has been sworn. The National Assembly gives official acknowledgment of the act, and enjoins that it be inserted in the *procès-verbal* in the 'Moniteur,' and published and posted in the form prescribed for public acts."

It looked as if all was ended. It was expected that now Charles Louis Napoleon Bonaparte, henceforth President of the Republic until the second Sunday of May, 1852, would descend from the tribune. He did not descend. The noble necessity of binding himself still further, if that were possible, constrained him to add to the oath the Constitution demanded, in order to show to the world how free and spontaneous on his part was that oath. He asked permission to speak. "You have it," returned the President of the Assembly. The silence and attention of the spectators became more intense than ever. Citizen Louis Napoleon Bonaparte unfolded a paper and read a discourse. In this discourse he announced and installed the ministry he had called to his council and said: —

"Like you, Citizen Representatives, I desire to establish society on its true bases, to strengthen democratic institutions, and to adopt every method calculated to alleviate the sufferings of the intelligent and generous people who have given me so signal a proof of their confidence." [1]

He thanked his predecessor in the Executive Power,— that predecessor who was able to say later these fine words: "I have not fallen from power, I have descended,"— and eulogized him in the following terms: —

"The new administration, in entering upon business, feels bound to thank the preceding one for the efforts it has made to transmit the power intact, and to maintain public order.[2]
"The conduct of General Cavaignac has been worthy of the loyalty of his character and of that sentiment of duty which is the first qualification of the head of a state." [3]

These words were applauded by the Assembly; but it was the opening declaration,— a declaration, we repeat again,

[1] Très bien! très bien! — *Moniteur.*
[2] Manifestations of approval. — *Moniteur.*
[3] Renewed marks of approbation. — *Moniteur.*

altogether spontaneous,— which impressed every mind, was deeply engraved on every memory, and found an echo in every loyal conscience:—

"The suffrages of the nation, the oath I have just sworn, command my future conduct and indicate my duties.

"I shall regard as enemies of the country all who may endeavour by illegal means to change the form of government which France has established."

At the conclusion of his address the Constituent Assembly rose and with one voice uttered that grand cry: "Long live the Republic!"

Louis Napoleon Bonaparte descended from the tribune, moved deliberately towards General Cavaignac, and tendered him his hand. The General hesitated for some moments before he took that hand. All who had just heard the words of Louis Bonaparte delivered in tones that gave evidence of the sincerest loyalty, censured the demeanour of the General.

The Constitution to which Louis Napoleon Bonaparte swore obedience on the 20th of December, 1848, "in the face of God and of men" contained the following articles among others: —

"ARTICLE 36. The Representatives of the People are inviolable.

"ARTICLE 37. They cannot be arrested on a criminal charge, except taken in the very act, nor can they be prosecuted until the Assembly has permitted the prosecution.

"ARTICLE 68. Every measure by which the President of the Republic dissolves the National Assembly, prorogues it, or places an obstacle in the way of the exercise of the powers delegated to it by the people, is a crime of high treason.

"The President, by the very fact, forfeits his office; all citizens are bound to refuse him obedience, the executive power passes in full right to the National Assembly. The Judges of the High Court shall meet immediately, under penalty of forfeiture; they shall convoke juries in the place by them designated for the trial of the President and his accomplices; they shall themselves name the persons charged with the functions of the public ministry."

Less than three years after that memorable day, on the 2d of December, 1851, might be read at daybreak the subjoined proclamation posted on every street-corner of Paris:—

IN THE NAME OF THE FRENCH PEOPLE.

THE PRESIDENT OF THE REPUBLIC

DECREES:

ARTICLE 1. The National Assembly is dissolved.
ARTICLE 2. Universal suffrage is restored. The law of the 31st of May is repealed.
ARTICLE 3. The French people is convoked in its electoral districts.
ARTICLE 4. The state of siege is decreed throughout the first military division.
ARTICLE 5. The Council of State is dissolved.
ARTICLE 6. The Minister of the Interior is charged with the execution of the present decree.
Given at the Palace of the Elysée, the 2d of December, 1851.

LOUIS NAPOLEON BONAPARTE.

At the same time Paris was informed that fifteen of the Representatives of the People,— the inviolable Representatives,— had been arrested during the night, at their own homes, by order of Louis Napoleon Bonaparte.

CHAPTER II

MANDATE OF THE REPRESENTATIVES

THE Representatives of the People who on behalf of the people received in trust the oath of the 20th of December, 1848, above all, the Representatives of the People who, twice invested with the confidence of the nation, saw that oath sworn to as constituents and violated as legislators, had two duties imposed upon them by their mandate. The first was to rise on the very day when that oath was violated, to stake their lives, careless of the number of the enemy or of his strength, to cover with their bodies the sovereignty of the people, and to lay' hold of every arm for the overthrow of the usurper, from the law in the code to the paving-stones of the street. The second duty was, after accepting the struggle with all its vicissitudes, to accept proscription with all its miseries; to remain eternally erect before the traitor, with his oath in their hands; to forget their inward sufferings, their private sorrows, their families dispersed and mutilated, the ruin of their fortunes, the wounds of their affections and their bleeding hearts; to forget themselves, and henceforth feel but one wound,— the wound of France; to cry aloud for justice; to scorn the thought of submission or resignation; to be implacable; to seize the odious crowned perjurer, if not by the hand of the law, at least with the pincers of truth, and redden in the fires of history the letters of his oath and brand them on his face!

He who writes these lines is one of those whom no danger deterred from the fulfilment, on the 2d of December, of the first of these duties; by publishing this book he discharges the second.

CHAPTER III

DEMAND IN DUE FORM OF LAW

IT is time for the human conscience to awaken.
Since the 2d of December a successful ambuscade, an odious, abominable crime, an unheard-of crime, if we take into account the century in which it has been committed, reigns triumphant, has been exalted into a doctrine, and expands in the light of day. It makes laws, issues decrees, takes society, the family, and religion under its protection, tenders its hand to the kings of Europe, who accept it, and calls them " my brother " or " my cousin." This crime is controverted by none, not even by those who profit and live by it,— they merely say it was " necessary "; not even by him who has committed it,— he merely says that he, the criminal, has been " absolved." This crime is the embodiment of all crimes,— treason in its conception, perjury in

its execution, murder and assassination in the struggle, spoliation, knavery, and theft in the triumph.   This crime draws in its train, as integral parts of itself, the suppression of the laws, the violation of constitutional inviolability, arbitrary sequestration, confiscation of property, nocturnal massacres, secret fusilades, commissions substituted for tribunals, the deportation of ten thousand citizens, the proscription of forty thousand citizens, the ruin and despair of sixty thousand families.   These facts are notorious.

Well then, it is a bitter thing to have to say, men are silent on this crime!   It is before their eyes, they touch and see it, and pass by and attend to their several affairs.   The shop opens; the Bourse jobs; Commerce, seated on her bale of merchandise, rubs her hands; and we are almost at the point where this shall be considered a matter of course.   He who is measuring his cloth hears not the cry of the ell-wand in his hand; it is saying to him: " The ell-wand that governs you is false."   He who is weighing out his wares hears not the balance which raises its voice; it is saying to him: " The weight that reigns is false."   Strange order that, which has for its basis limitless disorder, the negation of all right!   An equilibrium resting on iniquity!

Add to this a fact, for that matter sufficiently obvious: the author of this crime is a malefactor of the most shameless and abandoned species.

Let all who wear a robe, a scarf, or a uniform, let all the servants of this man know the truth now; let them open their eyes if they think they are the agents of a power. They are the comrades of a pirate.   Since the 2d of December there are no more functionaries in France; there are only accomplices.   The time has come when each must render a clear account to himself of that which he has done and of that which he continues doing.   The gendarme who has arrested those whom the man of Strasburg and Boulogne calls " insurgents," has arrested the guardians of the Constitution.   The judge who has judged the combatants of Paris or the provinces has condemned and humiliated the

upholders of the law.   The officer who has confined the " condemned " in the depths of the ship's hold, has confined the
defenders of the Republic and of the State.   The African
general who imprisons the men banished to Lambessa, stoop-
ing under the sun, shivering with fever, digging in the
parched earth a trench that shall be their grave, that general
incarcerates, tortures, and murders the supporters of justice
and right.   And all, generals, officers, gendarmes, judges,
are directly guilty of felony.   The innocent men before whom
they stand are more than innocent, they are heroes! are more
than victims, they are martyrs!

Let every one, then, be aware of this, and at least make
haste to break the chains, to draw the bolts, to empty the
hulks, since no one has yet the courage to seize the sword.

If law, right, justice, equity, duty, reason, understanding,
do not avail, let men bethink themselves of the future.   If
remorse is dumb, let responsibility speak!   And let all who,
as land-holders, grasp the hand of a magistrate; as bankers,
entertain a general; as peasants, take off their caps to a
gendarme; let all who do not shun the *hôtel* of the minister,
the house of the prefect, as they would a lazaretto; let all who
attend, not as functionaries, but as private citizens, the balls
and banquets of Louis Bonaparte, not seeing that the black
flag waves over the Elysée,— let all those know too that this
species of infamy is contagious; if they escape material complicity, they do not escape moral complicity.

The crime of the 2d of December bespatters them.

The present situation, which seems calm to the unthink-
ing, is violent.   On this point there must be no misunderstanding.   When public morality suffers eclipse, the social
order is pervaded by an appalling shadow.   All guarantees
disappear, all supports fall to the ground.

From this forth there is not a tribunal or court in France,
there is not a judge who can give judgment and pronounce
sentence in the name of anything whatever, in connection
with anything whatever or respecting any person whatever.

Bring before the assize a malefactor,— it matters not of

whut kind.   The robber will say to his judges: " The Head of the State has robbed the Bank of France of twenty-five millions;" the false witness will say to his judges: " The Head of the State has sworn an oath before God and before men, and this oath he has violated;" the person accused of arbitrary detention will say: " The Head of the State has arrested and imprisoned contrary to all laws, the Representatives of the sovereign people;" the swindler will say : " The Head of the State has gained his election by swindling, has gained power by swindling, has gained the Tuileries by swindling;" the forger will say: " The Head of the State has forged ballots;" the bandit who lurks in a corner of the forest will say: " The Head of the State picked the pockets of the princes of Orleans;" the murderer will say: " The Head of the State has fusiladed, cannonaded, sabred, and butchered those who were peacefully walking along the streets."   And all, swindler, forger, false witness, bandit, robber, and assassin will add,—

" And you, judges, you have saluted this man, have lauded him for being a perjurer, have complimented him for being a forger, have eulogized him for being a swindler, have congratulated him on having robbed, and thanked him for having murdered!   What have you to do with us?"

Surely this is a grave state of things.   To allow one's self to fall asleep in such a situation is an added ignominy.

It is time, we repeat, for this monstrous sleep of the human conscience to come to an end.   After the horrible scandal of the triumph of the crime, mankind must not be confronted with a still more horrible scandal,— the indifference of the civilized world.

If this could be, history would some day appear as an avenger.   But till then, just as wounded lions hide themselves in solitudes, the righteous man, veiling his face in presence of this universal abasement would take refuge in the immensity of disdain.

CHAPTER IV

THERE WILL BE AN AWAKENING

BUT it will not be so; there will be an awakening.
The single aim of this book is to do away with this sleep.   France must not adhere to this Government even with the acquiescence of lethargy.   At certain times, in certain places, beneath certain shades, to sleep is to die.

Moreover, at the present moment — it is a strange thing to say, but yet the truth — France knows nothing of what took place on the 2d of December and on the ensuing days, and this is her excuse.   But thanks to several noble and courageous publications, the facts are becoming known.   It is the object of this work to shed light on some of them, and with God's help, depict them all in their true colours.   It is important that mankind should know what Monsieur Bonaparte is.   At present, thanks to the suppression of the tribune,' thanks to the suppression of the press, thanks to the suppression of free speech, of liberty, and of truth,— a suppression that, while it gives Monsieur Bonaparte the power of doing whatever it may seem his good pleasure to do, really nullifies every one of his acts, not excepting the utterly anomalous vote of the 20th of December,—thanks, we say, to this suppression of every protest, to this extinction of every ray of light, neither men nor things nor deeds appear under their real form and bear their real name.   The crime of Monsieur Bonaparte is not a crime, it is styled necessity; the ambuscade of Monsieur Bonaparte is not an ambuscade, it is styled the defence of order; the robberies of Monsieur Bonaparte are not robberies, they are styled measures of State; the murders of Monsieur Bonaparte are not murders, they are styled public safety; the accomplices of Monsieur Bonaparte are not malefactors, they are styled magistrates, senators, and councillors of State; the adversaries of Monsieur Bonaparte are not soldiers of law and right, they are styled lawless peasants (*Jacques*), demagogues, aiming at a universal division of property. In the eyes of France, in the eyes of Europe, the 2d of December still wears a mask. This book is a hand issuing from the darkness, and tearing off that mask.

Yes, we shall expose this triumph of order; we shall paint this vigorous Government,— this Government so firm, secure, and strong; this Government which has in its favour a crowd of poor young creatures, better supplied with ambition than with shoes, showy coxcombs and sorry paupers at the same time. We shall depict this Government, supported at the Bourse by Fould the Jew, and in the church by Montalembert the Catholic, esteemed by women who would be mistresses and by men who would be prefects, resting on a coalition of prostitutions, appointing cardinals, wearing a white tie, with opera-hat under its arm, with cream-coloured gloves like Morny, newly varnished like Maupas, fresh brushed like Persigny, rich, elegant, spruce, polished, and joyous,— born in a pool of blood!

Yes, there will be an awakening!

Yes, there will be an escape from that torpor which, for such a people, is shame; and when France shall have awakened, she opens her eyes and begins to distinguish what is before her and beside her, she will recoil with a terrible shudder in presence of the monstrous felony that dared to espouse her in the darkness and make her the sharer of its bed.

Then shall the last hour strike! The sceptics smile, and are very earnest and emphatic. They say: " Abandon hope. You tell us this *régime* is the shame of France. Granted. What then? This shame is quoted on 'Change. Abandon hope. You are poets and dreamers if you hope. Only consider; the tribune, the press, intelligence, eloquence, thought, everything that constituted liberty has disappeared. Yesterday these were living, moving forces; to-day they are struck dumb. Well, every one is satisfied, and reconciled to this insensibility, turns it to his advantage and finds his account in it, and none discovers that the ordinary course of life is thereby disturbed. Society goes on, and many worthy people believe that things as they are, are well. Why do you want this situation changed? Why do you want this situation to come to an end? Be under no illusion; it is solid and stable, it is the present and the future.

We are in Russia. The Neva is frozen. Houses are erected on it; heavy chariots roll along its surface. It is no longer water; it is rock. Men go and come across this marble floor that was once a river. In an instant a city is built on it; streets are laid out and shops are opened, and men buy and sell, and eat and drink, and light their fires above this water. All are free to do as they like. Pray, do not be afraid; do whatever it seems good to you to do. Laugh and dance, for this is more firm than the solid earth. Yes, really, it sounds like granite under one's feet. Hurrah for winter! hurrah for the ice! it will last to eternity. And then, look at the sky; is it day or is it night? A pale and silky streak of light shimmers along the snow; it seems as if the sun were dying.

No, thou art not dying, Liberty! Some day, at the very moment when thou art least looked for, at the very hour when thou art most forgotten, thou shalt rise! O dazzling spectacle! We shall see thy starry face mount upward on a sudden from the earth and shine in thy glorious splendour above the horizon. Over all this snow and ice, over this hard white plain, this water turned to stone, over all this hideous winter, thou wilt launch thy golden arrows, thy gleaming, burning rays, light, warmth, and life! and then, hark! do you hear that dull and rumbling sound? Do you hear that deep, tremendous report? It is the breaking up of the ice! It is the Neva that is sinking down! It is the river resuming her course! It is the living waters, joyous and terrible, upheaving the dead and ghastly ice and dashing it to pieces. It was granite, you said; see, it splits like glass! It is the breaking up of the ice; it is truth returning once more; it is progress renewing her work; it is humanity resuming her march and driving, tearing, hurling along in her course, striking, crushing, and drowning in her waves, as 't were no more than the wretched furniture of some poor hovel, not only the freshly constructed empire of Louis Bonaparte, but all the erections and all the works of ancient and eternal despotism! Look at all this as it passes away. It is disappearing forever. You shall never behold it again. That book, half submerged, is the hoary code of iniquity! That frame which is being fast ingulfed is the throne! That other frame which is vanishing from sight is the scaffold!

And for this immense ingulfment, for this supreme victory of life over death, what was needed? A glance of thine, O sun! One of thy rays, O Liberty!

CHAPTER V

BIOGRAPHY

CHARLES LOUIS NAPOLEON BONAPARTE, born in Paris on the 20th of April, 1808, is the son of Hortense de Beauharnais, married by the Emperor to Louis Napoleon, King of Holland. In 1831, Louis Bonaparte was involved in the insurrections in Italy, where his eldest brother was killed, and tried to overthrow the Papacy. On the 30th of October, 1835, he attempted to overthrow Louis Philippe. He failed at Strasburg, and having been pardoned by Louis' Philippe, embarked for America, leaving his accomplices behind him to be tried. On the 11th of November he wrote: " The King, *in his clemency* has ordered me to be sent to America; " he declared himself " deeply moved by *the generosity* of the King," adding: " Certainly we were all guilty of taking up arms against the Government, but I am the guiltiest of all." And he concludes thus: " I was guilty of attempting to overthrow the Government, and yet the Government has shown itself generous towards me." [1]   He returned to Switzerland from America, and was made captain of artillery at Berne and a burgher of Salenstein in Thurgau. Amid the diplomatic complications to which his presence in Switzerland gave rise, he was equally careful to avoid acknowledging a French or a Swiss nationality.   To reassure the French Government, he limited himself to a declaration, in a letter of the 20th of August, 1838, that he was living " almost alone " in the house " in which his mother died," and that his firm intention was " to remain tranquil."   On the 6th of August, 1840, he landed at Boulogne, parodying the landing at Cannes, with the traditional little hat on his head, bringing a gilt eagle on top of a flag, and a live eagle in a cage, a number of proclamations, sixty lackeys, cooks, and stable-boys disguised as French soldiers, with uniforms purchased in the Temple and buttons of the 42d of the line manufactured in London.[2]   He threw money to the people walking in the streets, raised his hat on the point of his sword, and shouted: " Vive l'Empereur; " fired a pistol at an officer,[3] but hit a soldier, breaking three of his teeth — and fled.   He is taken, and five hundred thousand francs in gold and banknotes are found on him.[4]   The *procureur-général* Franck-Carré says to him before the full Court of Peers: " You attempted to corrupt soldiers by the distribution of money."   The Peers condemn him to perpetual imprisonment, and he is sent to Ham.   There self-communion and reflection would seem to have ripened his mind; he wrote and published some works which, in spite of a certain ignorance of France and of the age, were imbued with a spirit of progress and democracy. Their titles are: " Extinction du Paupérisme," " Analyse de la Question des Sucres," and " Idées Napoliennes," in which he

[1] Letter read at the Court of Assizes by Parquin, one of the council for the accused, who, after reading it, exclaimed, " Among the numerous faults of Louis Napoleon we need not, at least, reckon ingratitude."

[2] Court of Peers.   Affair of the 6th of August, 1840, page 140; witness, Geoffroy, grenadier.

[3] Captain Col-Puygellier, who said to him, " You are a conspirator and a traitor."

[4] Court of Peers, witness, Adam, Mayor of Boulogne.

makes the Emperor out a " humanitarian." In the " Fragments Historiques " he wrote: " I am a citizen first, a Bonaparte after." He had already declared himself, in 1832, a republican in his " Rêvéries Politiques." After six years' captivity, he escaped from Ham, disguised as a mason, and took refuge in England. When February came, he hailed the Republic, took his seat as Representative of the People in the Constituent Assembly, mounted the tribune on the 21st of September, 1848, and said: " All my life will be devoted to the consolidation of the Republic," published a manifesto which may be summarized in two lines: liberty, progress, democracy, amnesty, abolition of decrees of proscription and of banishment; was elected President by five million five hundred thousand votes, swore fealty solemnly to the Constitution of the 20th of December, 1848, and destroyed it on the 2d of December, 1851. In the interval he had crushed the Roman Republic, and restored in 1849 that Papacy which in 1831 he had attempted to overthrow; he had moreover taken some part or other in the shady transaction called the " Lottery of the ingots of gold." In the weeks preceding the *coup d'état* this money-bag had become transparent, and a hand was perceived in it resembling his. On the 2d of December and the following days, he, the Executive Power, assailed the Legislative Power, arrested the Representatives, drove away the Assembly, dissolved the Council of State, expelled the High Court of Justice, suppressed the laws, took twenty-five millions from the Bank, gorged the army with gold, mowed down Paris with grape-shot, and struck terror into France. Since then, he has proscribed eighty-four Representatives of the People, robbed the Princes of Orleans of the property of their father, to whom he owed his life, decreed despotism in fifty-eight articles under the title of a constitution, garotted the Republic, turned the sword of France into a gag in the mouth of liberty, jobbed in railway shares, rifled the pockets of the people, regulated the budget by a ukase, deported ten thousand democrats to Africa and Cayenne, exiled forty thousand republicans to Belgium, Spain, Piedmont, Switzerland, and

2

England, and brought anguish to every soul and a blush to every brow.

Louis Bonaparte thinks he is ascending a throne; he does not perceive that he is climbing a gibbet.

CHAPTER VI

A PORTRAIT

LOUIS BONAPARTE is a man of middle height, cold, pale, and heavy. He has the look of a person who is not quite awake. He has published, as we have already related, a work of some value on artillery, and has a thorough acquaintance with the management of cannon. He rides well. There is a slight German drawl in his words. As to his histrionic abilities, he gave an exhibition of them in the Eglinton tournament. He wears a thick moustache, hiding a smile like the duke of Alba's, and has the lacklustre eye of Charles IX.

Judged outside of what he calls " his necessary acts " or " his great acts," he is a vulgar fellow, childish, theatrical, and vain. The persons invited by him to Saint-Cloud in summer, receive with the invitation an order to bring an evening and morning dress. He is fond of tufts, trimmings, spangles, top-knots, and embroideries, of grand words and grand titles, of sound and glitter and all the petty glories and glass beads of power. His kinship to the battle of Austerlitz entitles him to dress as a general. He does so.

This man would stain the second plane of history; he defiles the first.

To be despised affects him little: the appearance of respect contents him.

Europe, pointing to Haiti, was laughing at the other continent when she saw this white Souloque make his appearance. There is now in Europe, deep sunk in every mind, even beyond the limits of France, a feeling of profound stupefaction, a feeling of something like a personal indignity; for the interests of Europe, whether she wills or not, are incorporated with those of France, and whatever degrades the one humiliates the other.

Before the 2d of December, it was a common saying among the leaders of the Right with regard to Louis Bonaparte: "He is an idiot." They were mistaken. Certainly that brain of his is muddy, has gaps here and there; but thoughts logically connected and interlinked may, to some extent, be discerned in places. It is a book from which certain pages have been torn out. Louis Bonaparte is a man of one fixed idea, but a fixed idea is not idiocy. He knows what he wants, and marches to his aim. Over justice, over law, over reason, honour, and humanity, if you will, he still marches to his aim.

He is not an idiot. He is a man of other times than ours. He seems absurd and mad because he has no counterpart. Transport him to Spain in the sixteenth century, and Philip II. will recognize him; to England, and Henry VIII. will smile on him; to Italy, and Cæsar Borgia will throw his arms about his neck. Or even confine yourself to placing him outside of European civilization; drop him at Yanina in 1817, Ali Tepelini will tender him his hand.

There are elements of the Middle Ages and the Lower Empire in him. His deeds would seem quite natural to Michael Ducas, to Romanes Diogenes, to Nicephorus Botoniates, to the eunuch Narses, to the vandal Stilicho, to Mahomet II., to Alexander VI., to Ezzelino of Padua, and they seem quite natural to him; only, he forgets or is ignorant that in the times in which we live his actions have to traverse those great currents of human morality loosened by our three centuries of learning and enlightenment and by the French Revolution, and that in the society he belongs to his actions will assume their true form and show forth in all their native hideousness.

His partisans — he has some — are ready to draw a parallel between his uncle the first Bonaparte and him. They say. "One made the 18th of Brumaire, the other has made the

2d of December; one was eager for power, so is the other."
The first Bonaparte wished to restore the Empire of the West,
to make Europe his vassal, to dominate the continent by his
power and dazzle it by his greatness, to sit on a chair of state
and give footstools to kings, to make history say, " Nimrod,
Cyrus, Alexander, Hannibal, Cæsar, Charlemagne, Napoleon,"
to be a master of the world. And he was. For this he made
the 18th of Brumaire. The second Bonaparte wishes to have
horses and mistresses, to be called Monseigneur, and to live
well. For this he has made the 2d of December. Eager for
power both. Yes, the comparison is just. Let us add that,
like the first, he too would be emperor. But what renders the
comparison a little more tranquillizing is the circumstance
that there is perhaps some difference between conquering the
empire and filching it.

Be that as it may, one fact is certain, and cannot be concealed even by the dazzling curtain of glory and misfortune
on which are written, Arcola, Lodi, the Pyramids, Eylau,
Friedland, St. Helena,— one fact, we repeat, is certain, and
it is that the 18th of Brumaire is a crime, the stain of which
on the memory of Napoleon has been magnified by the 2d of
December.

Monsieur Louis Bonaparte readily allows a glimpse of his
socialist leanings to be seen. He feels that he has there an
untilled soil which ambition might work with success. As we
have said, he passed his time in prison in making for himself
a quasi-reputation as a democrat. One fact paints him. When
he published, while in Ham, his book on the " Extinction of
Pauperism,"— a book whose sole apparent aim was to probe
the wound of the misery of the people and point out the means
of curing it,— he sent the work to one of his friends with this
note, which has passed under our eyes: —

"Read this essay on pauperism, and tell me if you think it likely
to do me any good."

The great talent of Monseiur Louis Bonaparte is silence.
Before the 2d of December he had a council of ministers

which, being responsible, imagined it was of some importance. The President presided. He never, or hardly ever, took any part in the discussions. While MM. Odillon Barrot, Passy, Tocqueville, Dufaure or Faucher spoke, *he was engaged in constructing*, as we have been told by one of his ministers, *with thoughtful carefulness courtesans in paper, or dashing off ill-drawn figures on the backs of public documents.*

To pretend to be dead is his great art. He remains mute and motionless, with his eyes averted from the object he pursues, until his hour has come. Then he turns his head and leaps upon his prey. His scheme of policy makes its appearance before you, abruptly, at some unforeseen corner, clutching a pistol in its fist, *ut fur.* Until then, as little motion as possible. For a moment, during the three years that have glided past, he was seen side by side with Changarnier, who also was concocting his own enterprise. " Ibant obscuri," as says Virgil. France was observing these two men with some anxiety. What was there between them? Was one dreaming of Cromwell? Was the other thinking of Monk? Men questioned one another as they watched. In both there was the same attitude of mystery, the same policy of immobility. Bonaparte said not a word; Changarnier made not a gesture, — the one did not stir, the other did not breathe; they seemed playing at who could be most like a statue.

Yet this silence is sometimes broken by Louis Bonaparte. Then he does not speak, he lies. This man lies as other men breathe. He announces that his intentions are honest; beware! he affirms; distrust! he takes an oath; tremble! Machiavelli has begotten children. Louis Bonaparte is one of them.

To blazon forth a flagitious villainy at which the world exclaims, to disavow it with indignation in the name of all that is good and holy, to declare himself an honest man, and then at the very moment every one is reassured and laughing at the possibility of the villainy in question, to execute it,— this is his method. He has carried it into effect for the *coup d'état,* for the decrees of proscription, for the spoliation of the princes of Orleans; he will carry it into effect for the invasion of Switzerland and of Belgium and for all that remains. It is his method; think of it as you please. It serves him, he likes it, it is his own concern. He will have to reckon with history.

You are one of his intimate associates: he lets you see a glimpse of a project which, if not viewed too closely, does not seem immoral, but, rather, insensate and dangerous,— dangerous for himself especially. You raise objections; he listens, he does not answer, sometimes gives up the point for two or three days, then resumes it, and does his will.

In his cabinet at the Elysée there is a drawer in his table, often half open. From it he takes a paper which he reads to a minister; it is a decree. The minister supports or opposes it. If the latter, Louis Bonaparte flings the paper back into the drawer, in which there are many other old papers scribbled with his autocratic dreams, locks the drawer, takes the key, and departs without a word. The minister retires, charmed with the deference shown him. The next morning the decree is in the " Moniteur,"— sometimes with the signature of the minister.

Thanks to this mode of acting, he has always at his service one great force,— the unexpected; and as he never encounters any internal check from what other men call conscience, he pursues his object through everything no matter what, across everything no matter what, as we have said before, and reaches the goal.

He recoils occasionally, not before the moral effect of his acts, but before their material effect.

The decrees expelling eighty-four representatives, published in the " Moniteur " of the 6th of January, shocked public sentiment. Tightly though France was manacled, the universal horror made itself felt. It was not yet far from the 2d of December, and every excitement was attended with peril. Louis Bonaparte understood this well. On the morrow of the 10th, a second decree of proscription was to appear, containing eight hundred names. Louis Bonaparte had the proof brought to him from the office of the " Moniteur; " the list

filled fourteen columns of the official journal. He crumpled
the proof, threw it into the fire, and the decree did not appear.
The proscriptions continued without decrees.

He needs assistants and co-operators in his enterprises; he
requires what he himself calls " men." Diogenes searched for
them with a lantern; he seeks them out with a bank-note in
his hand. He finds them. Certain aspects of human nature
result in the production of an entire species of sorry creatures.
Of these he is the natural centre. They cluster around him
necessarily, according to that mysterious law of gravitation
which rules the moral being not less than the cosmic atom.
For undertaking, executing, and completing the " act of the
2d of December," he required men; he had them. To-day
they encircle him; these men form his court and retinue; they
blend their radiance with his. In some epochs of history there
are constellations of great men; in other epochs there are constellations of caitiffs.

Still, let us not confound the epoch, the minute of Louis
Bonaparte, with the nineteenth century; the toadstool sprouts
up at the foot of the oak, but it is not the oak.

Monsieur Louis Bonaparte has succeeded. From this forth
he has on his side money, the Bank, the Bourse, the stock-
market, the counting-house, and all those who pass so easily
from one shore to the other when they have only to stride
over shame. He has made a dupe of M. Changarnier, a
mouthful of M. Thiers, an accomplice of M. de Montalembert, a robber's cave of power, and treats the budget as a
farm to be worked for his profit. A medal, called the medal
of the 2d of December, is being struck at the Mint, in honour
of the manner in which he keeps his oaths. The frigate
" Constitution " has changed her name; she is now the " Elysée." He may, when he chooses, get himself anointed by M.
Sibour, and barter his bedstead in the Elysée for a couch in
the Tuileries. Meanwhile, for seven months he has been making a parade of his greatness, has harangued, triumphed, presided at banquets, given balls, danced, reigned and strutted to
his heart's content. He has blossomed out in all his ugliness

in a box at the Opera. He has had himself called Prince President, and has distributed flags to the army and crosses of honour to the commissaries of police. When the question arose of selecting a symbol, he stood aside and allowed the eagle to be chosen; such modesty have sparrow-hawks.

CHAPTER VII

THE PANEGYRICS CONTINUE

HE has succeeded. As a consequence he does not want for apotheoses. Of panegyrists he has a larger number than Trajan. And yet one thing strikes me; it is this: among all the qualities for which he has won recognition since the 2d of December, among all the eulogies addressed to him, there is not one word that goes beyond this, ability, coolness, daring, adroitness, an affair planned and conducted with admirable skill, a time well selected, a secret well kept, measures well taken, false keys well made. When these things are said everything is said, except some phrases on " clemency; " and yet no one lauded the magnanimity of Mandrin, who sometimes did not take all his victim's money, or of Jean the Flayer, who sometimes did not slay travellers!

The Senate the while it endows Monsieur Bonaparte with twelve millions, and four millions for keeping his palaces in repair, and is itself endowed in turn by Monsieur Bonaparte with one million, congratulates Monsieur Bonaparte on having " saved society," pretty much as one of the characters in a certain comedy congratulates another on having " saved the cash-box."

As to myself, I have yet to find among the plaudits of which Monsieur Bonaparte is the object, a single commendation bestowed by his apologists which would not do equally well for Cartouche and Poulailler after a good stroke of luck.

For the sake of the French language and the name of Napoleon, I sometimes blush at the thinly veiled crudeness of the terms in which the magistracy and the clergy compliment this man for feloniously appropriating power, laying violent hands on the Constitution, and running away from his oath in the night.

After the successful accomplishment of the robberies and burglaries that make up the sum total of his policy, he has resumed his true name; since then every one has recognized the fact that he was a Monseigneur. But M. Fortoul,[1] to his honour be it said, was the first to perceive it.

When the man is measured and found so little, and his success is measured and found so enormous, it is impossible for the mind not to experience some surprise. We ask ourselves: How has he done it? We analyze the adventure and the adventurer, and, laying aside the advantage he derives from his name, and certain facts which aided him in scaling the ramparts, we can discover nothing at the bottom of the man and of his actions but these,— craft and money.

Craft. We have already commented on this remarkable element of Louis Bonaparte's character, but it is worth while to dwell on it more strongly. On the 27th of November, 1848, he said in his manifesto to his fellow-citizens: —

" I feel under an obligation to make known to you my sentiments and my principles. *There must be nothing equivocal between you and me. I am not an ambitious individual.* Brought up in *free* countries, in the school of misfortune, I *shall ever remain faithful* to the duties your suffrages may impose upon me and to the wishes of the Assembly.

"*I would make it a point of honour to leave to my successor, at the end of four years, power consolidated, liberty intact, and a really accomplished progress.*"

On the 31st of December, 1849, in his first message to the Assembly, he wrote: —

" I intend to prove worthy of the confidence of the nation by maintaining the Constitution *I have sworn to.*"

[1] The first report addressed to Monsieur Bonaparte, and the first in which he is styled *Monseigneur,* is signed FORTOUL.

On the 12th of November, 1850, in his second annual message to the Assembly, he said: —

" If the Constitution contains vices and dangers, you are all at liberty to expose them to the view of the country; I alone, *bound by my oath,* maintain myself within the strict limits it has marked out for me."

On the 4th of September of the same year he had said at Cannes: —

" At a time when prosperity seems to be reviving on all sides, he would indeed be a criminal who attempted to arrest its progress *by changing that which to-day exists.*"

Some time before this, on the 22d of July, 1849, at the time of the inauguration of the St. Quentin railway, he had gone to Ham.   There he beat his breast as he recalled the memory of Boulogne, and uttered these solemn words: —

" The chosen leader to-day of all France, since I have become the legitimate chief of this great nation, I cannot take any pride in a captivity which had for its cause *an attack against a regular government.*
" When we see how many misfortunes the most just of revolutions bring in their train, it is hard to realize *the audacity of the person who would assume to himself the terrible responsibility of a change.* I do not, therefore, complain of having *expiated here,* by six years of imprisonment, *my temerity against the laws of my country;* and it is with real pleasure that, in the very place where I suffered, I now propose a toast in honour of the men who are determined, whatever may be their convictions, to respect *the institutions of their country.*"

While speaking thus, he had in the bottom of his heart that thought which he gave voice to in this very prison of Ham, and which he afterwards tested the truth of in his own fashion: " Great enterprises rarely succeed at the first attempt." [1]

Towards the middle of November, 1851, F——, a Representative belonging to the party of the Elysée, was dining with Louis Bonaparte.

[1] Fragments Historiques.

" What is the talk in Paris and in the Assembly? " asked
the President.

" Ah, Prince! '

" Well? "

" They are speaking always —"

" About what? "

" The *coup d'état*."

" And does the Assembly believe in it? "

" A little, Prince."

" And you? "

" What! I! Not at all."

Louis Bonaparte at once grasped both the hands of M.
F——, and said with deep emotion: " Thank you, Monsieur
F——. You, at least, do not believe me a scoundrel! "

This took place a fortnight before the 2d of December.
At that very time, nay, at that very moment, as we learn
from the confession of his accomplice Maupas, Mazas was
being made ready.

Money. This is the second force of Monsieur Bonaparte.
We speak only of facts judicially proved by the records of
Strasburg and Boulogne.

At Strasburg, on the 30th of October, 1836, Colonel Vau-
drey, an accomplice of Louis Bonaparte, directed the quarter-
masters of the 4th regiment of artillery " to distribute two
pieces of gold to the cannoneers of each battery."

On the 5th of August, 1840, Monsieur Bonaparte called
around him on " The City of Edinburg " the packet-boat he
had chartered, some sixty poor wretches, his servants, whom
he had cheated into the belief that he was going to Hamburg
on a pleasure excursion. He harangued them from the top
of one of his carriages, fastened to the deck, made known his
project, threw among them the uniforms in which they were
to disguise themselves as soldiers, and handed each a hundred
francs. Then he gave them liquor. A little drunkenness does
not hurt great enterprises.—" I saw," said the witness Hobbs [1]
the bartender, before the Court of Peers, " a large sum of

---

[1] Court of Peers. Depositions of the witnesses, p. 94.

money in the room. The passengers were apparently reading some printed papers. The passengers passed the whole night in eating and drinking. I did nothing but uncork bottles and serve food."

After the bartender, comes the captain. The examining magistrate said to Captain Crow,—

" Did you see the passengers drink? "

CROW: " To excess. I never saw anything like it." [1]

After a landing was effected, they reached the custom-house station of Wimereux. The first step of Monsieur Louis Bonaparte was to offer the lieutenant at this station a pension of twelve hundred francs. The examining magistrate put this question to Louis Bonaparte:

" Did you not offer the commandant of the station a sum of money if he would consent to join you? "

THE PRINCE: " I did do so, but he refused." [2]

They arrived at Boulogne. His *aides-de-camp* — from that time out he has had *aides-de-camp* — carried suspended from their necks tin rollers filled with gold-pieces. Others followed with bags of coin in their hands,[3] and threw money to the fishermen and peasants, at the same time calling on them to shout, *Vive l'Empereur.* " If we get three hundred bawlers, it is all that we need," one of the conspirators had said.[4]

The 42d regiment of light infantry was then quartered at Boulogne. Louis Bonaparte appeared among them. To one soldier, Georges Koehly, he said, " I am Napoleon; you shall have promotion and decorations." To another, Antoine Gendre, he said: " I am the son of Napoleon; come with me to the Hôtel du Nord, where I will order a dinner for you and me." To another, Jean Meyer, he said, " You shall be well paid; " and to Joseph Meny: " You must come to Paris; you shall be well paid." [5]

---

[1] Ibid., pp. 75, 88–94.
[2] Court of Peers. Examination of the accused, p. 13.
[3] Ibid. Depositions of the witnesses, pp. 103, 185.
[4] THE PRESIDENT: " Prisoner Querelles, were not those children who shouted, the *three hundred brawlers* you asked for in a letter? "
[5] Court of Peers. Depositions of witnesses, pp. 143, 155, 156, 158.

An officer accompanied him, holding in his hand a hat filled with five-franc pieces, which he distributed among the curious spectators, saying, " Cry, *Vive l'Empereur.*" [1] Geoffroy, a grenadier, speaks as follows of the attempt to seduce his comrades made by an officer and a sergeant who were in the plot: " The sergeant carried a bottle, and the officer had a drawn sword in his hand." In these two lines we have the whole 2d of December.

But to continue: —

" The day after, on the 17th of June, Major Mésonan, whom I believed to have left, was introduced into my study by my *aide-de-camp.* I said,—

" 'Major, I thought you had left.'

" 'No, General, I have not left. I have a letter to deliver to you.'

" 'A letter! and from whom?'

" 'Read, General.'

" I invited him to be seated, and took the letter; but as I was about to open it, I perceived that it bore the superscription: —

" ' *A. M. le commandant Mésonan.*' I said,—

" 'Why, my dear major, this is for you, not for me.'

" 'Read, General!'

" I opened the letter and read: —

" MY DEAR MAJOR,— It is absolutely necessary that you see the general of whom we spoke, at once. You know he is a man of action, and can be counted on. You know, too, that he is a man I have noted down to be one day a marshal of France. *You will offer him 100,000 francs on my account,* and ask him to name some banker or notary with whom *I may deposit 300,000 francs for him,* in case he should lose his command.

" I stopped, overcome with indignation; I turned the sheet, and saw that the letter was signed LOUIS NAPOLEON. This letter I handed back to the Major, saying that he was engaged in a ridiculous and hopeless undertaking."

Who speaks thus? General Magnan. Where? Before

1 Ibid., p. 142.

the full Court of Peers. In presence of whom? Who is the man on the stool of repentance, the man whom Magnan covers with " ridicule," the man towards whom Magnan turns his " indignant " face? Louis Bonaparte.

Money, and with money debauchery, such was his manner of operating in his three enterprises, at Strasburg, at Boulogne, at Paris. Two failures, one success. Magnan, who resisted at Boulogne, sold himself at Paris. If Louis Bonaparte had been vanquished on the 2d of December, the twenty-five millions of the Bank would have been found on him in the Elysée, just as the five hundred thousand francs of London were found on him in Boulogne.

There has been, then, in France,— we must endeavour to succeed in speaking calmly of these things,— in France, in the land of the sword, the land of the chevaliers, the land of Hoche, Drouot, and Bayard, there has been a day when one man, aided by five or six political sharpers, experts in ambuscades and jobbers in *coups d'état*, there has been a day when a man, leaning back in his gilded cabinet with his feet on the fender and a cigar between his lips, has drawn up a tariff of military honour, has weighed it in his scales as if it were merchandise, as if it were a thing purchasable and salable, has estimated this general at a million, that soldier at a louis, and has said of the French conscience, " It is worth so much."

And this man is the nephew of the Emperor. For that matter, this nephew is not too proud; he knows how to accommodate himself to the requirements of his adventures, and assumes with ease the character which destiny allots him. Set him down in London, and, if he have an interest in pleasing the English Government, he will not shrink from the task; and with that hand which would seize the sceptre of Charlemagne, he will grasp the policeman's club. If I were not Napoleon, I would wish to be Vidocq.

And now a truce to reflection.

This is the man by whom France is governed! Governed, do I say? — possessed in supreme and sovereign sway! And every day, and every morning, by his decrees, by his messages, by all the incredible drivel which he parades in the " Moniteur," this emigrant, who knows not France, teaches France her lesson! and this ruffian tells France he has saved her! And from whom? From herself! Before him, Providence committed only follies; God was waiting for him to reduce everything to order; at last he has come! For thirty-six years there had been in France all sorts of pernicious things,— the tribune, a vociferous thing; the press, an obstreperous thing; thought, an insolent thing, and liberty, the most crying abuse of all. But he came, and for the tribune he has substituted the Senate; for the press, the censorship; for thought, imbecility; and for liberty, the sabre; and by the sabre and the Senate, by imbecility and the censorship, France is saved. Saved, bravo! And from whom, I repeat? From herself. For what was this France of ours, if you please? A horde of marauders and thieves, of anarchists, assassins, and demagogues. She had to be manacled, had this mad woman, France; and it is Monsieur Bonaparte Louis who puts the handcuffs on her. Now she is in a dungeon, on a diet of bread and water, punished, humiliated, garotted, safely cared for. Be not disturbed; Monsieur Bonaparte, a policeman stationed at the Elysée, is answerable for her to Europe. He makes it his business to be so; this wretched France is in the strait-jacket, and if she stirs — Ah, what is this spectacle before our eyes? Is it a dream? Is it a nightmare? On one side a nation, the first of nations, and on the other, a man, the last of men; and this is what this man does to this nation. What! he tramples her under his feet, he laughs in her face, he mocks and taunts her, he disowns, insults, and flouts her? What! he says, " I alone am worthy of consideration "? What! in this land of France where none would dare to slap the face of his fellow, this man can slap the face of the nation? Oh, the abominable shame of it all! Every time that Monsieur Bonaparte spits, every face must be wiped! And this can last! and you tell me it will last! No! no! by every drop of blood in every vein, no! It shall not last! Ah, if this did last, it would be in very truth because there would no longer be a God in heaven, nor a France on earth!

BOOK II

THE GOVERNMENT

CHAPTER I

THE CONSTITUTION

R OLL of drums; attention, bumpkins!

THE PRESIDENT OF THE REPUBLIC.

Whereas, all laws restraining the liberty of the press have been an-nulled, all laws against bill-posting and pamphlet-hawking have been abolished, the right of public meeting has been fully restored, all un-constitutional laws and all measures of martial law have been sup-pressed, every citizen has the right to say what he wishes, using all forms of publication, journal, poster, and electoral meeting; all engage-ments undertaken, notably the oath of the 20th of December, 1848, have been scrupulously observed; all acts have been·thoroughly investigated, all questions elucidated and resolved, and all candidatures publicly con-tested, without the possibility of any one being able to say that the least wrong has been done to the least citizen,— in a word, the fullest liberty being enjoyed by all.

The sovereign people, being interrogated on this question: " Does the French People wish to place itself bound hand and foot at the disposal of M. Louis Bonaparte? " has answered YES by seven million five hundred thousand votes. [*Interruption by the author:* We shall return to the seven million five hundred thousand votes.]

PROMULGATES.

THE CONSTITUTION, OF WHICH THE FOLLOWING IS THE TENOR.

ARTICLE THE FIRST. The Constitution acknowledges, affirms, and guarantees the great principles proclaimed in 1789, which are the basis of the public rights of Frenchmen.

ARTICLE THE SECOND, AND FOLLOWING. The tribune and press, which impede the march of progress, are replaced by the police and censorship, and by the secret debates of the Senate, the Legislative Body, and the Council of State.

ARTICLE THE LAST. The thing called human intelligence is suppressed.

Given at the Palace of the Tuileries on the 14th of January, 1852.

LOUIS NAPOLEON.

Duly examined and sealed with the Great Seal.

The Keeper of the Seals and Minister of Justice,
E. ROUHER.

This Constitution, which resolutely proclaims and affirms the Revolution of 1789 in its principles and in its consequences, and which only abolishes liberty, has evidently been a happy inspiration of Monsieur Bonaparte, suggested by an old playbill of a provincial theatre which it is worth while recalling: —

To-day

GRAND REPRESENTATION

OF

LA DAME BLANCHE.

AN OPERA IN 3 ACTS.

☞ As the music interferred with the progress of the action, its place will be supplied by a lively and piquant dialogue.

CHAPTER II

THE SENATE

THE Council of State, the Legislative Body and the Senate are the lively and piquant dialogue. There is, then a senate? Oh, decidedly. That " great body," that " balancing power," that " supreme moderator " is, in fact, the chief splendour of the Constitution. We must devote our attention to it.

The senate. It is a senate. Of what senate are you speaking? Of that which deliberated as to the sauce with which the Emperor should eat his turbot? Or of the one of which Napoeleon said on the 5th of April, 1814: " A nod was a command for the Senate, and it always did more than it was asked to do "? [1] Or the Senate that wrenched very nearly the same cry from Tiberius: " Ah, the infamous creatures! They are greater slaves than I would have them! " Or the Senate which made Charles XII. say: " Send my boot to Stockholm." " Why, sire? " inquired the minister. " To preside over the Senate."— No, we are not jesting. There are eighty senators this year; next year there will be one hundred and fifty. They have the undivided enjoyment of fourteen articles of the Constitution all to themselves, from article 19 to article 33. They are " guardians of the public liberties; " they are unpaid functionaries according to article 22; therefore they have a salary of from fifteen to thirty thousand francs per annum. Their specialty is to receive this income, and their essential quality, " not to oppose " the promulgation of the laws. They are all " illustrious men." [2] This senate is not " a failure," [3] as was that of the other Napoleon; this is a serious senate. The marshals belong to it, so do the cardinals, so does M. Lebœuf.

" What are you doing in this country? " the Senate is asked. " We are charged with guarding the public liberties." " What are you doing in this town? " asks Pierrot of Harlequin. " I am charged," replies Harlequin, " with the thrashing of the horse of bronze."

" We all know what class feeling is; it will induce the Senate to increase its power by all possible means. It will destroy, if it can, the Legislative Body, and if the opportunity comes in its way, it will make a covenant with the Bourbons."

Who says this? The First Consul. Where? At the Tuileries, in April, 1804.

[1] Thibeaudeau: Histoire du Consulat et de l'Empire.

[2] Toutes les illustrations du pays.— Louis Bonaparte. Appel au peuple, 2d of December, 1851.

[3] The Senate has been a failure. France does not like to see people well paid when the result is that only bad persons are chosen.— *Words of Napoleon:* Mémorial de Sainte-Hélène.

" Without title, without power, and in violation of all principle, it betrayed the country and consummated its ruin. It was the sport of high-placed intriguers. I know of no public body that should have a more ignominious record in history than the Senate."

Who said that? The Emperor. Where? At St. Helena. So there is a senate in the Constitution of the 11th of January. But, to be frank, is not this a fault? Now that sanitary science has made such progress, we have been accustomed to see the public roads better kept than this would argue. Since the senate of the Empire, we really thought that no more senates would be dropped on the highway of constitutions.

CHAPTER III

THE COUNCIL OF STATE AND THE LEGISLATIVE BODY

THERE are also the Council of State and the Legislative Body,— the jovial, salaried, chubby-cheeked Council of State, rosy, fat, fresh, and loud-voiced, with a sword at its side, and protuberant stomach, and gold embroidery on its coat; and the Legislative Body, pale, melancholy, and thin, with only silver embroidery. The Council of State comes and goes, steps out and steps in, regulates, arranges, and decides, confirms and prescribes, and sees Louis Napoleon face to face. The Legislative Body walks on the tips of its toes, turns its hat round in its hands, lays a finger on its lips, has a humble smile, sits down on the corner of a chair, and only speaks when spoken to. Its words being naturally obscene, the journals are prohibited from making the slightest allusion to them. The Legislative Body votes the laws and taxes, and when, in the belief that it needs an explanation or elucidation, a hint or detail of some sort, it presents itself, bare-headed, at the door of the minister for the purpose of obtaining an interview

with that minister, the usher, who conducts it into the antechamber with a roar of laughter, gives it a fillip on the nose.
Such are the rights of the Legislative Body.

It is proper to state that this melancholy situation began in
June, 1852, to force some sighs from the rueful individuals
who form a part of the existing institution. The report of
the commission on the budget will be engraved on the memory
of men as one of the most heart-rending masterpieces of the
elegiac school. These sweet strains will bear repeating.

" Formerly, as you know, the communications necessary in such cases
took place directly between the commissaries and the ministers. To the
latter were addressed the demands for such documents as were indispensable for the examination of the affairs in question. Ministers used
to come of their own accord, accompanied by the heads of their several
departments, and give verbal explanations which often sufficed to fore-
stall all ulterior discussion. And the resolutions which the commissions
on the budget drew up after these conferences were directly submitted
to the chamber.

" To-day we can have no relations with the Government except
through the medium of the Council of State, which, as the confidant
and mouthpiece of its opinions, has alone the right to transmit to the
Legislative Body the documents it has received from the ministers.

" In a word, for written reports as well as for verbal communications the commissaries of the Government take the place of the ministers with whom they must have previously come to an understanding.

" As to the modifications the commission may wish to propose, either in
consequence of the adoption of amendments presented by the Deputies,
or after their own examination of the budget, they have, before you
are called to deliberate on them, to be referred to the Council of State,
and there discussed.

" There — it is impossible to avoid noting the fact — they have no
official interpreters or supporters.

" This mode of procedure appears to spring from the Constitution
itself; and *if we speak of it,* it is *solely* for the purpose of pointing
out to you that it must produce delays in the accomplishment of the
work of the commission on the budget." [1]

It is impossible to exaggerate the tender delicacy of these
reproaches; none could receive with a more chaste modesty
and grace what Monsieur Bonaparte, in his autocratic style,
calls " certain guarantees of tranquillity," [2] and what Moliére,

[1] Report of the Commission of the Budget of the Legislative Body,
June, 1852.
[2] Preâmble de la Constitution.

with the freedom allowed a great author, calls, " Kicks —" [1]

There is, then, in the shop where laws and budgets are manufactured, a master of the house, the Council of State, and a domestic, the Legislative Body. According to the provisions of the Constitution, who appoints the master of the house? Monsieur Bonaparte. Who appoints the domestic? The Nation. This is proper.

CHAPTER IV

THE FINANCES

LET us observe that with all these " wise institutions " and with the safeguard of the *coup d'état*, which, as is known to the world, has restored order, financial security, and public prosperity, the budget, by the confession of M. Gouin himself, is balanced by a deficit of a hundred and twenty-three millions.

As to the commercial progress since the *coup d'état*, the prosperity of every form of property, the resumption of business, to form a correct estimate of them, it is enough to discard words and take figures. With regard to figures, we have one which is official and decisive. During the first half year of 1852 the discounts at the central office of the Bank of France yielded only 589,502 francs 62 centimes, and the branches did not rise higher than 651,108 francs 7 centimes. For this we have the authority of the Bank itself in its half-yearly report.

For that matter, the taxes do not give Monsieur Bonaparte much worry. Some fine morning he wakens, yawns, rubs his eyes, takes a pen and decrees — what? the budget. Achmet III. one day desired to raise the taxes to a figure that pleased his fancy.

[1] A coarse expression. See the " Fourberies de Scapin."

" Invincible lord," said his vizier, " thy subjects cannot be taxed beyond what the law and the Prophet allow."

This same Bonaparte wrote at Ham: —

" If the money levied each year on the great mass of the people is spent in unproductive services, such as the creation *of useless places, the erection of barren monuments, the maintenance of an army in a time of profound peace, more costly than that which conquered at Austerlitz,* taxes in such a case become a crushing burden; they exhaust the country, as they take without returning." [1]

With reference to this word " budget " it occurs to us to make an observation. At the present hour, in 1852, the bishops, the counsellors of the Court of Cassation, the first presidents, and the *procureurs-généraux* have each sixty-nine francs a day; the senators, prefects, and generals of division receive eighty-three francs a day; the presidents of the sections of the Council of State, two hundred and twenty-two francs a day; the ministers, two hundred and fifty-two francs a day; Monseigneur the Prince President is the recipient every day of forty-four thousand four hundred and forty-four francs forty-four centimes, including, as is proper, the sum granted for the maintenance of the royal châteaux. The revolution of the 2d of December was made to crush the Twenty-Five Francs!

CHAPTER V

THE LIBERTY OF THE PRESS

WE have seen what the legislature is, what the administration is, what the budget is.

And now for the judiciary! What was once known as the Court of Cassation is now nothing more than the registration office of the councils of war. A soldier leaves the guard-room

[1] Extinction du Paupérisme, p. 10.

and writes on the margin of the book of the law: " I wish " or " I do not wish." On all sides the corporal orders and the magistrate countersigns. " Come now! tuck up your togas, march, or if not —" And as a result we have these judgments, these arrests, these abominable sentences! What a spectacle is that flock of judges, with drooping head and bended back, driven at the butt-end of a musket to the perpetration of every infamy and every crime!

And the liberty of the press! What shall we say of it? Is it not a mockery to utter that word! That free press, the glory of French intellect, a blaze of light flashing from all points at once and illuminating all questions, ever on watch and ward for the nation's weal,— where is it? What has Monsieur Bonaparte done with it? It is where the tribune is. Twenty journals crushed in Paris, eighty in the departments, a hundred journals suppressed; which means, if we look only to the material side of the question, a multitude of families deprived of bread; which means — attend to this point, *bourgeois* — a hundred houses confiscated, a hundred farms taken from their owners, a hundred dividend-warrants torn out of the public ledger. Do you see what a profound coincidence of principles is here? Liberty suppressed is property destroyed.

For a law regulating the press, we have a decree laid upon her, a *fetfa*, a firman, dated from the Imperial Spur; we have the *régime* of the official warning (*avertissement*). We know what this is. We see it at work every day. Only people like Monsieur Bonaparte could invent the monstrosity. Never has despotism appeared more clumsily insolent and stupid than in this censorship of what may be said to-morrow, which precedes and announces the suppression of a journal, and bastonades before it kills. In this government, atrocity is corrected and tempered by imbecility. Every decree of the press may be summed up in two lines: " I permit you to speak, but I require you to be silent."

Who is reigning, I pray? Is it Tiberius, or is it Schahabaham? And so we have three-fourths of the republican jour-

nalists deported or proscribed, the remainder trailed by mixed
commissions, scattered, wandering, hiding from every eye.
Here and there, in four or five surviving journals, in four or
five journals still independent, but closely watched, with the
club of Maupas wielded above their heads, fifteen or twenty
courageous writers, serious and high-minded men of pure and
generous soul, still write with a chain around the neck and a
ball hanging from the leg; talent between two sentinels, independence gagged, honesty never allowed to get out of sight,
and Vueillot crying, " I am free! "

CHAPTER VI

INNOVATIONS IN MATTERS OF LEGALITY

THE rights which the press enjoys at present are subjec-
tion to the censorship, suspension, and suppression. It
has also the right to be tried. Tried! by whom? By the
courts of justice. What courts of justice? The police-courts.
And what about that good and true institution, the packed
jury? An example of progress: we have outstripped it. The
jury is far in our rear; we have come again to government
judges: " Repression is more quick and efficacious," as Maître
Rouher says; and besides, it is better so. " Call up the prisoners: police-court, sixth chamber; first case, name Roumage,
swindler; second case, name Lamennais, writer." This pro-
duces a good effect and trains the *bourgeois* to couple vaguely,
in his conversation a swindler and a writer. Yes, certainly,
this is an advantage; but from the practical point of view,
from the " pressure " point of view, is the Government quite
sure it has acted wisely? Is it quite sure of the superiority of
the Sixth Chamber to that admirable Assize Court of Paris,
for instance, presided over as it was by such an abject creature
as Partarien-Lafosse, and harangued by Suin the base, and

Mongis the dull? Can it be reasonably hoped that the police justices will be more cowardly and contemptible than even these? Will those justices, well-paid though they be, do their work any better than that squad of jurymen which received its orders from the Ministry as a body of raw recruits does from the corporal, and which returned its verdicts of guilty with a pantomimic energy and with the precision of a charge at double-quick? So truly was this the case that the Prefect of Police, Carlier, remarked with guileless simplicity to a celebrated advocate, M. Desm— " The jury! What an absurd institution! Unless you make it up yourself it never returns a verdict of guilty; and if you make it up, it always returns a verdict of guilty." Let us weep over the honest jury which Carlier made up and Rouher made away with.

This government feels that it is hideous. It wants no portrait, above all no mirror. Like the osprey, it takes refuge in the night; if seen it would die. And yet it wishes to last. It is coy of being spoken of, of passing from mouth to mouth. It has imposed silence on the press of France. We have just seen how. But to silence the press of France is only a partial success. It would silence it in foreign lands. There have been two prosecutions tried in Belgium,— a prosecution of the " Bulletin Français " and a prosecution of " La Nation." The loyal Belgian jury acquitted both. This kind of thing is vexatious. What is to be done? We have it. These Belgian journals can be reached through their pockets. You have subscribers in France; if you " criticise " us you shall not enter. You would like to enter? Please yourself. An effort is made to reach the English journals through their fears. If you " criticise " us — clearly one does not like to be *criticised!* — we will hunt your correspondents out of France. The English press has met the threat with a roar of laughter. But this is not all. There are French writers outside France. They are proscribed,— that is to say, free. What if those demagogues should speak? What if they should write? They are quite capable of it. They must be prevented. How? To gag people at a distance is not easy. Monsieur Bonaparte's arms are not long enough for that. Still, some way must be found. What if we were to prosecute them in whatever places they may happen to reside? Do so; the juries of all free lands will understand that these exiles represent justice and that the Bonapartist government represents iniquity. But friendly governments may be asked to expel those who have been expelled, and to exile those who have been exiled. Do so, the proscribed can go elsewhere. They will always find a corner of some free land where they may speak their thoughts. Is there no way, then, of getting hold of them? Rouher joined forces with Baroche, and together they have patched up a law on crimes committed by Frenchmen abroad, and slipped it in among the " Press offences." The Council of State said Yes and the Legislative Body did not say No. To-day this law exists. If we speak outside France we shall be tried in France; and then imprisonment (at some future period, that is, supposing —), fines, and confiscations. We are content. This book will, then, be tried in France and its author condemned in due form. I expect as much, and confine myself to this warning to all individuals calling themselves magistrates, be they whosoever they may, who, whether garbed in black or garbed in red, shall contrive the thing in question, that when the case falls due and the maximum penalty has been fully and fairly rendered, nothing will equal my disdain for the judgment, except my contempt for the judges. This is my plea.

CHAPTER VII

THE ADHERENTS

BUT who are they who cluster around the new establishment? As we have said already, the heart swells with indignation at the thought of them. Ah, well, we remember — we the victims of proscription for the time — how these

rulers of to-day used to demean themselves when they were
Representatives of the People; how proudly they tramped up
and down the lobbies of the Assembly, with head erect and
self-reliant bearing, and all the air of men who felt they were
their own masters. What dignified and imposing attitudes
they assumed! With what a grand gesture they pressed their
hands to their hearts as they shouted, " Long live the Republic!" And if some " terrorist," some " montagnard," some
" red," happened to allude in the tribune to the *coup d'état*
which was being concocted, and the empire which was planned,
how they would shriek, " You are a calumniator!" How they
shrugged their shoulders at the word *senate!* " The empire
to-day," cried one, " would be dirt and blood; you calumniate
us, we shall never plunge into it!" Another asserted he was
minister of the President solely with the object of devoting
himself to the defence of the Constitution and the laws; another eulogized the tribune as the palladium of the country;
another recalled the oath of Louis Bonaparte and said, " Do
you doubt that he is an honest man?" The two latter even
voted and signed his deposition in the mayoralty of the 10th
Arrondissement on the 2d of December. Another sent a note
on the 4th of December to the writer to congratulate him " on
having dictated the proclamation of the Left outlawing Louis
Bonaparte." And they are all now senators, councillors of
State, ministers, bedizened with lace and gold! Wretches!
before you embroider your sleeves, wash your hands!

M. Q.-B. goes in search of M. O.-B. and says to him:
" Fancy the cool impudence of this Bonaparte! He has dared
to offer me the position of master of requests!"

" You refused?"

" Of course."

On the next day he has the offer of the place of councillor
of State, worth twenty-five thousand francs a year; the offended master of requests becomes a softened and grateful
councillor of State. M. Q.-B. accepts.

One class of men has been unanimous in rallying to the new
order,— the fools. They form the sound portion of the Leg-

islative Body. It is to them that the " head of the State "
addresses such claptrap as follows:

" The first trial of the Constitution, altogether French in its origin,
must have convinced you that we possessed the conditions of a strong
and free government. You exercise a real control, discussion is free,
and the vote on the revenue decisive. There is in France a government animated by good faith and the love of justice, which is based
on the people, the source of all power; on the army, the source of all
force; on religion, the source of all righteousness. Receive the assurance of my sentiments."

We know these worthy dupes well. Their leaders were skil-
ful manipulators, and succeeded in inspiring them with terror,
— the surest way of conducting them into whatever path was
desirable. These same leaders, having discovered that the old
scare-crows, *jacobin, sansculotte,* were decidedly out of date,
furbished up anew the word *demagogue.* Accustomed as they
were to all sorts of intrigues, they made good use of " the
Mountain; " they flourished this terrible and magnificent memory with great skill. With some few letters of the alphabet,
arranged in syllables and properly accented,—" demagogism,"
" montagnards," " anarchists," " communists," " reds,"—
they threw an awful glare in front of the eyes of idiots. They
had found a way of perverting the brains of their simple colleagues, and inlaying them as it were with a kind of dictionary, in which every one of the expressions in use among the
orators and writers of democracy is found at once with its
appropriate translation. " Humanity " read " ferocity; "
" universal happiness " read " chaos; " " republic " read
" terrorism; " " socialism " read " pillage; " " fraternity "
read " massacre; " " gospel " read " death to the rich." So
when an orator of the Left said, for example, " We wish for
the suppression of war and the abolition of the penalty of
death," a crowd of unhappy creatures among the Right heard
distinctly these words: " We wish to ravage everything with
fire and sword," and shook their fists furiously at the speaker.
After discourses dealing solely with liberty, universal peace,
happiness by the agency of labour, concord, and progress,
Representatives belonging to the category mentioned at the

head of this paragraph would rise up quite pale; they were
not quite certain that they were not already guillotined, and
went in search of their hats to make sure they had still their
heads. These poor scared creatures did not haggle about their
adhesion to the 2d of December. It was for them especially
that the saying was invented, " Louis Napoleon has saved
society."

And then there were all those eternal prefects, and those
eternal mayors; and those eternal *capitouls*, and those eternal
aldermen, and those eternal adorers of the rising sun or the
lighted lamp, who the day after a success besiege the con-
queror, the triumpher, the master,— his Majesty Napoleon the
Great, his Majesty Louis XVIII., his Majesty Alexander I.,
his Majesty Charles X., his Majesty Louis Philippe, Citizen
Lamartine, Citizen Cavaignac, Monseigneur the Prince President,— kneeling, smiling, joyous, bearing the keys of their
cities on dishes, and the keys of their consciences on their faces.
But the fools are of ancient date; the fools have always made
part of all institutions, and are almost an institution in themselves. And as to the prefects and the *capitouls*, as to these
adorers of every to-morrow, insolent in their good fortune and
their vapidness, they too have been seen in all times. Let us
do this justice to the *régime* of December,— it has not only
partisans of the kind alluded to, it has adherents and creatures that belong to itself only; it has produced notabilities
of quite a novel species. Nations never know how rich they
are in the product of rascaldom. It is only from such com-
motions and disarrangements as this that they are enabled to
form any idea on the subject. Then people stand amazed at
the sight of what springs from the dust; it becomes a glorious
object of their contemplation. So-and-so, who was shod and
clad and famished to a degree to make all the curs in Europe
bark at his heels, rises up an ambassador. This other one, to
whom Bicêtre and La Roquette were not unknown, awakes a
general and grand eagle of the Legion of Honour. Every
adventurer dons an official costume, rests his head on a pillow
stuffed with bank-notes, takes a sheet of white paper and

writes thereon, " End of my adventures."
" You know So-and-so, don't you? "
" Yes."
" He is in the galleys? "
" No, he is a minister."

CHAPTER VIII

MENS AGITAT MOLEM

A T the centre is the man,— the man as we have described
him, the man of Punic faith, the man of baleful destiny, who to arrive at power attacks civilization, who seeks
elsewhere than among the true people a sort of ravenous popularity, speculating on the savage instincts that still remain in
the peasant and the soldier, trying to succeed by the agency
of the coarsest selfishness and of the basest passions, by in-
flaming the appetites of the sensual and stimulating the envy
of the covetous; a man with some of the attributes of Marat,
except that what in Marat was great in Louis Bonaparte is
little; the man who kills, transports, exiles, expels, proscribes,
and robs; the man of languid gesture and glassy eye, who
moves amid the horrible things he does with a vacant air like
some untoward somnambulist.

It has been said of Louis Bonaparte, whether in praise or
blame I cannot tell, for such strange people have strange flat-
terers: " He is a dictator, a despot,— nothing more." He is
so in our opinion, and he is something else besides.

The dictator was a magistrate. He is styled by Livy [1] and
by Cicero [2] *prætor maximus;* by Seneca, [3] *magister populi,*
and his decrees were regarded, says Livy [4] as coming immediately from heaven: " Pro numine observatum." In those

[1] Lib. vii. ch. 331.   [2] De Republica, Lib. i. ch. 40.
[3] Ep. 108.   [4] Lib. iii. ch. 5.

ages of imperfect civilization, the inflexibility of the laws did not foresee every contingency that might arise, and the dictator's function was to provide for the safety of the people in sudden emergencies. He was the product of this text: *Salus populi suprema lex esto.* Twenty-four axes were borne before him,— signs that in him resided the prerogative of life and death. He was outside the law and above the law, but he could not touch the law. The dictatorship was a veil behind which the law remained in its integrity. It took hold of him again on his retirement. He was created for a very short period,— six months; " semestris dictatura," says Livy.[1] Ordinarily, the dictator abdicated before the end of his term, as if this enormous power, although freely consented to by the people, weighed on him like a remorse. Cincinnatus resigned at the end of eight days. The dictator was prohibited from disposing of the public moneys without the warrant of the Senate, and from going outside of Italy. He could not ride on horseback without the permission of the people. He might be a plebeian; Marcus Rutilus, and Publius Philo were dictators. A dictator was created for different objects,— to establish festivals on the holy days, to drive a sacred nail into the wall of the Temple of Jupiter, and, once, to name the senate. Republican Rome submitted to eighty-eight dictators. This intermittent institution lasted one hundred and fifty-three years, from the year of Rome 552 to the year 711. It began with Servilius Geminus, and, after passing through Sulla, reached Cæsar. With Cæsar it expired. The dictatorship came into being to be repudiated by Cincinnatus and espoused by Cæsar. Cæsar was dictator during five years, from 706 to 711. This magistracy was dangerous and in the end devoured liberty.

Is Monsieur Bonaparte a dictator? We see no impropriety in answering yes. *Prætor maximus,*— commander-in-chief? The flag salutes him. *Magister populi,*— master of the people? Ask the cannon levelled on the public squares. *Pro numine observatum,*— considered a god? Inquire of M. Troplong. He has named the Senate, he has instituted holy days;

---

[1] Lib. vi. ch. 1.

he has provided for the " safety of society ; " he has driven a sacred nail into the wall of the Pantheon, and on this nail has hung his *coup d'état*. He even makes and unmakes laws at his good pleasure, rides without asking permission, and as to the six months, he takes a little longer time. Cæsar took five years ; he takes double that. It is quite proper. Julius Cæsar five, Monsieur Louis Bonaparte ten ; the proportion is observed.

From the dictator we pass to the despot. It is another qualification almost accepted by Monsieur Bonaparte. We must be allowed to use to some extent the language of the Lower Empire. It will be in harmony with the subject.

The Despotes came next to the Basileus. Among his other attributes he was general of the infantry and cavalry,— *magister utriusque exercitus*. It was the Emperor Alexis, surnamed the Angel, who created the dignity of despotes. The Despotes was less than the Emperor, but greater than the Sebastocrator or Augustus, and than the Cæsar.

It is plain that the condition of things is pretty much the same. If it be admitted, and there is no reason surely why it should not, that Magnan is a Cæsar and Maupas an Augustus, it is clear that Monsieur Bonaparte is a Despotes.

Despot, dictator ; granted. Still, all this lordly magnificence, all this triumph of power does not hinder the occurrence of little incidents in Paris like the following, which innocent townsfolk, who were witnesses of the fact, relate to you with pensive unconsciousness. Two men are walking in the street, chatting about their own affairs, their business, etc. One of them speaks of some sharper or other of whom he has good reason to complain. " He is a wretch ! " he exclaims ; " he is a swindler, a paltry knave ! " An agent of the police hears these last words : " Sir," he says, " you are talking about the President ; I arrest you."

Now, will Monsieur Bonaparte be emperor or will he not? A fine question ! He is master, he is cadi, mufti, bey, dey, sultan, great khan, grand lama, grand mogul, grand dragon, cousin of the sun, commander of the faithful, shah, czar, sophi, and caliph. Paris is no longer Paris; it is Bagdad, with a Giafar named Persigny and a Scheherezade who risks having her neck cut every morning, and is styled "Le Constitutionnel." Monsieur Bonaparte can do all that he pleases with goods and chattels, with families and with individuals. If French citizens wish to know the depth of the "government" into which they have fallen, they have only to address each other a few questions. "Why, judge, he will tear off your robe and send you to prison!" "Well, what next?" "Why, Senate, Council of State, Legislature, he will take a shovel and tumble you all into a heap in a corner." "And then?" "You are a land-owner, he will confiscate your summer house and your winter house, with all the yards, courts, stables, gardens, and appurtenances thereunto belonging." "And then?" "Father, he will take your daughter; brother, he will take your sister; *bourgeois,* he will take your wife by main force and with a high hand." "And then?" "He does not like your face. O traveller! he will blow your brains out with his pistol and return home." "And then?" And if every one of these things were done, what would be the result? Nothing. "Monseigneur the Prince President took his usual drive in the Champs Elysées on yesterday in a barouche drawn by four horses, accompanied by a single *aide-de-camp.*" This is what the journals would say.

He has effaced the words *Liberty, Equality, Fraternity* from the walls. He has acted with reason. Ah, Frenchmen! you are neither free (the strait-waistcoat is there), nor equal (the man of war is supreme), nor brothers (civil war smoulders under this peace which rests on a state of siege).

Emperor? Why not? He has a Maury answering to the name of Sibour; a Fontanes or Faciuntasinos, if you like it better, who is called Fortoul; he has a Laplace who is styled Leverrier, but who has not made the *Mécanique Céleste.* Esménards and Lance de Lancivals will not be hard to find. His Pius VII. is at Rome in the soutane of Pius IX. He has shown himself in the green uniform at Strasburg; the eagle was seen at Boulogne. Did he not wear his grey greatcoat in

Ham? Cassock or greatcoat, it is all the same to him.
Madame de Staël is seen leaving his palace; she has written
" Lelia." He will smile graciously upon her until he thinks
the time has come to send her into exile. Would he like to
wed an archduchess? Wait a little; he shall have her. *Tu,
felix Austria, nube.* His Murat is called Saint Arnaud, his
Talleyrand is named Morny, his Duke of Enghien is styled
Right.

Look at the matter as closely as you like, and tell me what
does he lack? Nothing, or scarcely anything; hardly Austerlitz and Marengo.

Make up your mind to it, he is emperor *in petto;* one of
these fine days he will be emperor in broad daylight. To do
so only requires the trifling formality of having his oath consecrated, crowned, and ratified in Notre Dame. Then everything will be glorious; look out for a spectacle of imperial
splendour. Look out for freaks of fortune. Look out for
surprises, for wonders,— wonders that paralyze the senses,—
for the strangest union of discordant words, for jarring
sounds coupled with the most fearless intrepidity; look out for
Prince Troplong, for Duke Maupas, for Duke Mimerel, for
Marquis Lebœuf, for Baron Baroche. In line, courtiers; hats
off, senators; the stable opens; My Lord the Horse is Consul.
See that they have the oats of his Highness Incitatus gilded.

All this will be swallowed; the public throat will be distended
to portentous proportions, and every enormity will slip easily
through it. The gullets that once felt a difficulty in the
deglutition of flies can now gulp down whales without em-
barrassment.

For ourselves the empire exists at the present moment, and
without waiting for the truism of the *senatus-consultum* and
the comedy of the *plebiscitum,* we send out the following bulletin for the information of Europe:

The treason of the 2d of December has been brought to
bed of the Empire.

The mother and child are not doing well.

CHAPTER IX

OMNIPOTENCE

PASSING over for a moment this man's 2d of December, passing over his origin, let us see what is his political capacity. Do you wish to judge him during the eight months he has reigned? Place his power on one side and his deeds on the other. What can he do? Everything. What has he done? Nothing. With such authority as his, a man of genius would in eight months have changed the face of France, perhaps of Europe. He would not have, most assuredly, effaced the crime of his origin, but he might have covered it up. By the successful promotion of the material well-being of the people he might possibly succeed in hiding his moral abasement. Given a dictator of genuine sagacity, and, we must confess, the thing was not even difficult. A certain number of social problems, elaborately prepared during these last years by several robust intellects, seemed ripe for actual and relative solution; and such solution would redound to the great advantage and contentment of the nation. Louis Bonaparte does not seem to have even suspected this. He has not approached or caught a glimpse of a single one of these problems. He has not been able to discover in the Elysée an old remnant of his socialistic meditations in Ham. To his first crime he has added several new ones, and in this he has been consistent. These crimes excepted, he has effected nothing. Limitless power and no initiative. He has seized France by the throat and knows not what to do with her. In truth, one is tempted to pity this eunuch struggling in the arms of omnipotence.

Surely, this dictator exerts himself,— we must do him this justice; he is not quiet for a moment. He feels solitude and darkness around him, and he is appalled. Those who are afraid sing during the night; he fidgets. He turns everything topsy-turvy, meddles with everything, runs wild after every scheme. Not being able to create, he decrees; it would seem as if he were seeking to dupe his own incapacity. It is perpetual motion; but alas! the wheels turns in a vacuum. Conversion of government stock? What profit has resulted from it up to the present hour? A saving of eighteen millions. Granted; the fund-holders lose these eighteen millions which the President and Senate pocket. The gain for France, nothing. But there is the *crédit foncier?* No capital is coming into it. Railways? They are decreed; then the decrees are repealed. It is the same with all these things as it is with the workingmen's towns,— Louis Bonaparte subscribes, but does not pay. As to the budget, that budget controlled by the blind in the Council of State and voted by the dumb in the Legislative Body, an abyss yawns beneath it. The only real and effective economy possible would bear upon the army. Two hundred thousand soldiers left in their homes would mean two hundred millions saved. Attempt, then, to meddle with the army! It is true the soldier, who would become a freeman, might applaud; but what about the officer? And at bottom it is not the soldier, it is the officer, who requires to be petted. Besides, Paris and Lyons have to be watched, and all the other cities as well; and then, when we are emperor, we must have a little war now and then in Europe. You see the gulf!

If from financial questions we pass to political institutions, oh, then we find something to dazzle the neo-Bonapartists; then we find creations! And, good God! what creations! A constitution after the Ravrio style, adorned with carvings of palm-leaves and swans' necks, brought with old arm-chairs in the furniture wagons to the Elysée; the *sénat-conservateur*, new-gilt and trimmed; the Council of State of 1806 smartened and tricked-out with some furbished trappings; the old Legislative Body refitted, repaired, and repainted, with a Lainé the less and a Morny the more! with a bureau of public opinion for the liberty of the press, and for individual liberty the ministry of police.

All these " institutions "— we have passed them in review — are simply the old drawing-room furniture of the Empire. Beat and dust them, take off the cobwebs, daub them with splotches of French blood, and you have the establishment of 1852. This *bric-à-brac* governs France. These are your creations! But where is common-sense, where is reason, where is truth? There is not a single sound feature in contemporary opinion that is not wounded, not a real conquest of the century that is not hurled to the earth and dashed to pieces. All sorts of extravagance are now possible. Since the 2d of December we see a mediocre man broke loose, riding at full gallop through the absurd.

These men, the malefactor and his accomplices, have immense power,— power unrivalled, unlimited, absolute, and sufficient, we repeat, to change the face of Europe. This power they use to minister to their pleasures. To amuse and enrich themselves,— such is their " socialism." They have stopped the budget on the highway; the coffers are opened; they stuff their wallets and have money for the taking. All salaries have been doubled or tripled; we have already given the figures. Three ministers — Turgot (there is a Turgot in this business), Persigny, and Maupas — have each a million of secret-service money; the Senate a million; the Council of State half a million; the officers of the 2d of December millions; the soldiers of the 2d of December medals, that is to say, millions. M. Murat wants millions, and shall have them. A minister is about to marry,— quick, half a million! Monsieur Bonaparte, *quia nominor Poleo*, has twelve millions plus four millions,— sixteen millions. Millions! The name of this *régime* is Million.

Monsieur Bonaparte has three hundred blood horses, the fruits and vegetables of the national châteaux, and parks and gardens once belonging to kings. He is surfeited with good things: he said the other day, " All my carriages," just as Charles V. might say, " All my Spains," or Peter the Great, " All my Russias." There is always a Gamache wedding-feast at the Elysée; the spits are turning night and day be-

fore the bonfires.   Six hundred and fifty pounds of meat
are consumed every day,— so we are informed by the bulletins, the bulletins of the New Empire.   The Elysée will soon
have its hundred and forty-nine kitchens, like the castle of
Schoenbrunn; drinking, eating, laughing, and banqueting are
the order of the day,— a banquet at the residence of every
minister, a banquet at the Military School, a banquet at the
Hôtel de Ville, a banquet at the Tuileries, a monster *fête* on
the 10th of May, a still more monstrous one on the 15th of
August; a wallowing in all sorts of profusion and intoxication.

And the man of the people, the poor day-labourer, without work, shoeless, and in rags, to whom summer brings no
bread and winter no wood, whose aged mother is expiring on a
rotten heap of straw, whose young daughter is forced to prostitute herself at the corner of the street in order to live, whose
little children shiver with hunger, fever, and cold in the ken-
nels of the Faubourg Saint Marceau, in the garrets of Rouen,
in the cellars of Lille,— do they think of him.   What becomes
of him?   What do they do for him?   Die, dog!

CHAPTER X

THE TWO PROFILES OF MONSIEUR BONAPARTE

IT is a singular circumstance that these people actually wish
to be respected; a general is venerable, a minister is
sacred.   The Countess d'Andl—, a young woman of Brussels,
was in Paris in 1852; she chanced one day to be in a salon of
the Faubourg Saint-Honoré.   M. de P—— enters.   Madame
d'Andl— is leaving, and passes in front of him; she happens
to shrug her shoulders, probably thinking of something quite
remote from the present scene.   The next day Madame
d'Andl— is warned that henceforth she must abstain from

every mark of approval or disapproval when she sees a minister, under pain of expulsion from France, like a mere Representative of the People.

Under this government of the corporal and constitution of the countersign, everything marches in military fashion. The French people must learn from the order of the day how they are to sleep, rise, and dress, in what toilet they may represent themselves in open court. They are prohibited from making mediocre verses, from wearing the beard; the arrangement of a shirt-frill and the white cravat are laws of State. Regulation, discipline, passive obedience, down-cast eyes, silence in the ranks,— such is the yoke under which bends at the present moment the nation of initiative and liberty, great revolutionary France. The reformer will never stay his hand until France is so like a barracks that the generals can say, " So far, so well! " and the bishops can say, " It is sufficient! "

Are you fond of the soldier? Well, you have him everywhere. The Municipal Council of Toulouse gave in its resignation; the prefect, Chapuis-Montlaville, puts a colonel in the place of the mayor, a colonel in the place of the first assistant, and a colonel in the place of the second assistant.[1] The men of war take the wall. " The soldiers," says Mably, " believing that they took the place of the citizens who had once made consuls, dictators, censors, and tribunes, linked with the government of the emperors a kind of military democracy."

Have you a shako on your skull? Do as you please. A young man returning from a ball is crossing the Rue Richelieu in front of the gate of the Bibliothèque; the sentinel takes aim and kills him; the next day the journals say, " The young man is dead," and that is all. Timour-Beg granted his companions in arms and their descendants up to the seventh generation the right of impunity in case of any crime whatever, unless the delinquent committed the crime nine times. The sentinel of the Rue Richelieu has still eight crimes to commit before he is brought to trial by a council of war. It is nice to be a soldier, but not quite so nice to be a frozen. At the

---

[1] These three colonels are M. M. Cailhasson, Dubarry, and Policarpe.

same time this miserable army is being dishonoured. On the 3d of December, the commissaries who arrested their representatives and their generals were decorated; it is true the army received for its share two louis a head. Oh, shame on all sides! Money for the soldiers, and crosses for the spies!

The Jesuit and the corporal sum up this entire *régime*. Every political expedient of Monsieur Bonaparte is made up of two hypocrisies,— a swashbuckler hypocrisy directed towards the soldiers, and a catholic hypocrisy directed towards the clergy. When it is not Fracasse, it is Basile. Sometimes it is both together. By this method he easily succeeds in charming equally Montalembert, who does not believe in France, and Saint Arnaud, who does not believe in God.

Does the dictator smell the incense; does he smell the tobacco? Find out. He smells the tobacco and the incense. O France! what a government! The soutane covers the spurs. The *Coup d'Etat* goes to Mass, cudgels the cockneys, reads its breviary, cuddles Catin, tells its beads, empties the pitchers, and goes to its Easter duty. The *Coup d'Etat* affirms that we have returned to the age of the Jacqueries; this may be doubtful, but it is clear enough that it is leading us back to the time of the crusades. Cæsar has taken the cross for the Pope. *Diex el volt.* The Elysée has the Templer's faith, and his thirst as well.

To enjoy life to the utmost; to devour the budget; to believe nothing, and turn everything to account; to compromise at the same time two sacred things, military honour and religious faith; to stain the altar with blood, and the flag with the holy-water sprinkler; to render the soldier ridiculous and the priest just a little savage; to mingle the Church and the Nation, the Catholic conscience and the patriotic conscience, in the gigantic political swindle which he calls his power,— such is the method of Bonaparte the Little.

All his deeds, the most enormous as well as the most puerile, the most hideous as well as the most farcical, are marked by this twofold characteristic. For example, the national celebrations worry him. With the 24th of February and the 4th of May there are memories connected, troublesome or dangerous as the case may be, which return obstinately on the appointed day. An anniversary is a vexatious thing; let us suppress anniversaries. It is done. Ah, but we must keep one *fête*, one only,—ours. Nothing could be better. But with one *fête*, a single solitary *fête*, how can two parties be satisfied,— the soldier party and the priest party? The soldier party is Voltairian. Where Canrobert will smile, Riancey will frown. How, then, can it be done? You are about to see. Such a trifle is not likely to embarrass a first-class juggler. One fine morning the " Moniteur " declares that henceforth there shall be but one national festival, the 15th of August. Therewith a semi-official commentary, the two masks of the dictator, sets about speaking through its two mouths. " The 15th of August," says Mouth-Ratapoil, " Day of Saint Napoleon! " " The 15th of August," says Mouth-Tartuffe, " Feast of the Blessed Virgin! " On one side, the 2d of December puffs out its cheeks, roughens its voice, draws its mighty sabre, and shouts, " *Sacre-bleu!* You old growlers, let us celebrate Napoleon the Great! " on the other, it lowers its eyes, makes the sign of the cross, and mumbles, " My dear brethren, let us adore the Sacred Heart of Mary! "

The present government,— a hand bathed in blood steeping a finger in the holy-water font!

CHAPTER XI

CAPITULATION

B UT people say to us: " Are you not going a little too far? Are you not unjust? Allow him something. Has he not to some extent carried socialistic measures into effect? And then we are told of the *crédit foncier*, the railways, abatement of rents, etc.

We have already estimated these measures at their full value; but even admitting that there was something of " socialism " in all this, you would be very simple to attribute any credit for it to Monsieur Bonaparte. It is not he that marches on the path of socialism; it is the time.

A man is swimming against a rapid current; he struggles with unheard-of efforts, he buffets the waves with hand and forehead, with shoulder and knee. You say he will ascend. You look a moment after; he has descended. He is much lower in the river than he was when he started. Without knowing and without suspecting, at every effort he makes he is losing ground. He imagines he is going up, and he is going down always. He believes he is advancing, and he is receding. You are right as to *crédit foncier;* you are quite right as to abatement of rent. · Monsieur Bonaparte has issued several of those decrees which you are good enough to qualify as socialistic, and he will issue more of them yet.   M. Changarnier would have done so, if he, instead of Monsieur Bonaparte, had triumphed.   Henry V. would do so if he returned to-morrow.   The Emperor of Austria is doing so in Galicia, and the Emperor Nicholas in Lithuania.   And now, finally, what does all this prove?   That this current, whose name is Revolution, is stronger than this swimmer, whose name is Despotism.

But what is this socialism of Monsieur Bonaparte?   Real socialism?   I deny it.   Hatred of the *bourgeoisie*, granted; socialism, no.   The Ministry of Agriculture and of Commerce had, if any, a socialistic feature; he abolishes it.   What does he give in compensation?   The Ministry of Police.   Another socialistic ministry is the Minister of Public Instruction. It is in danger.   One of these mornings it will be suppressed. The starting-point of socialism is education, is gratuitous and primary instruction, is light.   To take the children and make men of them, to take the men and make citizens of them,— intelligent, honest, useful, and happy citizens,— is the essential thing.   Intellectual progress in the front, moral progress in the front; material progress afterward.   The two first, from their very nature, lead inevitably to the last. Well, what is Monsieur Bonaparte doing? He is persecuting and stifling education on all sides. There is a pariah in this France of ours of to-day; it is the schoolmaster.

Have you ever reflected on what a schoolmaster is? Have you ever reflected on that magistracy in which the tyrants of other days found a refuge, as criminals did an asylum in the temple? Have you ever bethought yourself of what the man is who teaches children? You enter a wheelwright's; he is manufacturing wheels and shafts; you say, " This is a useful man." You enter a weaver's; he is manufacturing cloth; you say, " This is a valuable man." You enter a blacksmith's; he is manufacturing spades and hammers and ploughshares; you say, " This is a necessary man." You greet with respect these worthy workmen. You enter the schoolmaster's; let your greeting be more respectful still. Do you know what he is doing? He is manufacturing minds. He is the wheelwright, the weaver, the blacksmith of that work in which he is God's helper,— the Future.

Well, to-day, thanks to the predominance of the priest party, as it is not desirable that the schoolmaster should work for this future, as it is desirable that this future be made up of darkness and brutality and not of intelligence and light, would you know in what fashion this great and humble magistrate, the schoolmaster, is made to execute his functions? The schoolmaster serves Mass, rings the bell at vespers, arranges the chairs, sings at the music-desk, renews the flowers before the Sacred Heart, polishes the altar candlesticks, dusts the tabernacle, folds the copes and chasubles, keeps the linen of the sacristy in order, puts oil in the lamps, beats the cushions of the confessionals, sweeps the church and sometimes the presbytery; what time is left him, he may, on condition he pronounce not these words of the Evil One,— Country, Republic, Liberty,— employ in teaching the little children to spell A B C; that is, if he feels so inclined.

Monsieur Bonaparte strikes at the same time education at the top and at the bottom,— at the bottom to please the curés, at the top to please the bishops. At the very moment he is trying to close the village school, he mutilates the Collége de France. With one kick he upsets the chairs of Michelet and Quinet. One fine morning he declares by a decree that Greek and Latin letters are suspect, and shuts out from the intellect, as far as lies in his power, all communion with the old poets and historians of Athens and of Rome, scenting a vague odour of demagogism in Æschylus and Tacitus. With a single stroke of his pen, for example, he has placed physicians beyond the borders of literary instruction, which has made Dr. Serres exclaim: "We are actually dispensed by decree from the obligation of knowing how to read and write!"

New taxes, sumptuary taxes, vestiary taxes; *nemo audeat comedere præter duo fercula cum potagio;* a tax on the living, a tax on the dead, a tax on successions, a tax on carriages, a tax on paper. "Bravo!" howls the beadle party, "fewer books!" a tax on the dogs, the collars shall pay; a tax on the senators, the coats-of-arms shall pay. "We'll see now who is going to be popular," cries Monsieur Bonaparte, rubbing his hands. "Why, we have a socialist emperor!" roar the trusty ones in the faubourgs. "He is a Catholic emperor," murmur the sanctimonious ones in the sacristies. How lucky he would be if he could pass here for Constantine and there for Babeuf! Watchwords are repeated, testimonies of devotion are uttered aloud, enthusiasm runs wild in all quarters. The Ecole Militaire designs his monogram with bayonets and pistol-barrels; the Abbé Gaume and Cardinal Gousset applaud; his bust is crowned with flowers in the Market; Nanterre dedicates to him her prize maidens of virtue (*rosières*); social order is decidedly saved; property, religion, and the family breathe again, and the police raise him a statue.

Of bronze?

For shame! that did well enough for the uncle.

Of marble?

Tu es Pietri, et super hanc pietram ædificabo effigiem meam.[1]

---

[1] We read in a Bonapartist correspondence: "The commission named

What he attacks, what he pursues, what they all pursue in his company, what they all rage about, what they all would crush, burn, suppress, destroy, annihilate, is it that poor obscure man who is called the primary instructor, is it that sheet of paper called a journal, is it that bundle of leaves called a book, is it that engine of wood and iron called a press? No, it is thou, Thought; it is thou, Human Reason; it is thou, Nineteenth Century; it is thou, Providence; it is thou, God!

We who battle with them are "the eternal enemies of order;" we are — they have not yet discovered that this word is threadbare — demagogues.

In the language of the Duke of Alba, to believe in the sanctity of the human conscience; to withstand the Inquisition; to brave the stake for one's faith; to draw the sword for one's country; to defend one's creed, city, home, and family; to uphold one's God, — was only worthy of a rabble of beggars, was, in fact, named *la gueuserie*. In the language of Louis Bonaparte, to struggle for liberty, justice, and right; to wage war in the cause of humanity and progress, of France and civilization; to desire the abolition of war and of the penalty of death; to be zealous for the brotherhood of man; to believe in the obligation of an oath; to take up arms for the Constitution of one's country and defend its laws,— this is named demagogism.

Those who were beggars (*gueux*) in the sixteenth century are demagogues in the nineteenth. Well, if it be assumed that the dictionary of the Academy no longer exists, that it is night at full noon, that a cat is no longer called a

by the employés of the Prefecture of Police has come to the conclusion that bronze was not worthy to reproduce the image of the Prince; it will be cut in marble, and placed on a marble pedestal, the beauty and magnificence of which will be increased by the following inscription, inlaid in the stone: 'Souvenir of the oath of fidelity to the Prince President, taken by the employés of the Prefecture of Police, the 20th of May, 1852, in presence of M. Pietri, Prefect of Police.' The subscriptions of the employés, whose zeal it was found necessary to moderate, will be apportioned thus: Chief of division, 10 fr.; chief of bureau, 6 fr.; employés at 1800 fr., 3 fr.; at 1500 fr., 2 fr. 50 c.; at 1200 fr., 2 fr. It is calculated that this subscription will reach more than 6,000 francs."

cat, and Baroche is no longer called a knave, that justice is a chimera, history a dream, the Prince of Orange one of the beggars, and the Duke of Alba one of the righteous; if it be granted that Louis Bonaparte is identical with Napoleon the Great, that those who have violated the Constitution are its saviours and those who defended it are brigands,— in a word, that human honesty is dead,— then I admire this government.   It is getting on well; it is a model of its kind.   It suppresses, represses, and oppresses; it exiles, slaughters, exterminates, and even " pardons; " its authority is represented by cannon-shot, and its " clemency " by blows with the flat of a sabre.

" 'T is easy talking," some incorrigible worthies of the ex-party of order exclaim.   " Lash yourself into a fury of indignation, mock, flout, stigmatize; it is little we care.   Stability forever!   Whatever you may, say, we have, on the whole, a solid government."

Solid! well, we have already called attention to this solidity.

Solid! yes, I admire this solidity.

If it snowed journals in France for even two days, on the morning of the third not a man would know the spot over which Monsieur Louis Bonaparte passed.

For all this, the man is a weight on the entire age; he disfigures the nineteenth century, and there will perhaps be two or three years in that century marked by some indescribably ignoble trace of the presence of Louis Bonaparte there.   This man, sad to say, is now the question of all men.

At certain epochs in history the entire human race turns its eyes, from every point of the earth, towards one mysterious spot whence the destiny of mankind would seem to be about to issue.   There have been hours when the eyes of the world were directed to the Vatican,— a Gregory VII. or a Leo X. had there his chair; other hours when it has contemplated the Louvre,— a Philip Augustus, a Louis IX., a Francis I., or a Henry IV. was there; San Justo,— Charles V. was dreaming of it; Windsor, Elizabeth the Great ruled in it; Versailles, — Louis XIV., encircled with stars, irradiated it; the Kremlin,— there you caught a glimpse of Peter the Great; Potsdam,— Frederick II. shut himself up in it along with Voltaire. To-day, bow down thy head. O History, the universe has its eyes fixed on the Elysée!

That gate not unlike a street doorway at the extremity of the Faubourg Saint Honoré flanked by two sentry-boxes painted to look like tents,— that gate is regarded by the civilized world to-day with a sort of profound anxiety. Ah, what is that place from which has never issued an idea that was not a snare, an action that was not a crime? What is that place where all that is shameless dwells with all that is hypocritical? What is that place where bishops elbow Jeanne Poisson on the stairs, and, as it was a hundred years ago, salute her to the ground; where Samuel Bernard laughs in a corner with Laubardemont; where Escobar enters leaning on the arm of Gusman d'Alfariche; where, as the horrible report runs, in a thicket of the garden, men whom it is not desirable to try are, they say, dispatched with bayonets; where a man was heard to tell a woman who interceded and wept, that as he overlooked her love intrigues, she must overlook his hatreds! What is that place where the orgy of 1852 troubles and dishonours the morning of 1815; where Cæsarion, with folded arms or hands behind his back, walks beneath the very trees in the very alleys yet haunted by the indignant shade of Cæsar?

This place is the stain of Paris; this place is the defilement of the age; this gate, from which issue all kinds of joyous sounds,— flourish of trumpets, music, laughter, clinking of glasses,— this gate, saluted in the day-time by the passing battalions, illuminated at night, thrown wide open with insolent confidence, is an ever-present public affront. The centre of the shame of the world is there.

Ah, of what is France dreaming? Certainly this nation needs to be awakened; she needs to be taken by the arm and aroused and spoken to. The country should be traversed through and through, the villages entered, the barracks entered; the soldier spoken to, who no longer knows what he is doing; the labourer spoken to, who has an engraving of the

Emperor in his cottage, and because of that engraving votes whatever he is asked.   We must remove the radiant phantom they have before their eyes.   The whole situation is an immense delusion.   We must dispel this delusion; sound its every depth; disabuse the people, and, above all, the people of the country districts; stir up their consciences and their emotions; show them the empty houses, the open graves, and make them lay their finger on the horrors of this *régime*.   They are good and honest; they will understand.   Yes, peasant, there are two,— the great and the little, the illustrious and the infamous, Napoleon and Naboleon! [1]

Let us give a summary of this government.   Who is in the Elysée and Tuileries?   Crime.   Who sits in the Luxembourg?   Baseness.   Who sits in the Palais Bourbon?   Imbecility.   Who sits in the Palais d'Orsay?   Corruption.   Who sits in the Palace of Justice?   Prevarication.   And who is in the prisons, in the forts, in the cells, in the dungeons, in the hulks, at Lambessa, at Cayenne, in exile?   Law, honour, intelligence, liberty, Right.

Proscribed victims, of what do you complain?   Yours is the better part.

---

[1] *Nabot,*— a dwarf, a shrimp. (Always employed to express contempt.)— Tr.

BOOK III

THE CRIME

B UT this government, this horrible government, at once hypocritical and stupid; this government which makes you hesitate between a shout of laughter and a sob of agony; this constitution-gibbet from which our liberties are suspended; this big universal suffrage and this little universal suffrage, the first naming the President, the second naming the legislators,— the little saying to the big: " Monseigneur, accept these millions," the big saying to the little: " Receive the assurance of my sentiments; " this Senate, this Council of State,— whence have all those things issued? My God! have we come to this, that it is necessary to recall it again?

Whence has this government issued? See there! It is still running, it is still smoking. It is blood.

The dead are far away; the dead are dead. Ah, have we reached a point where men already no longer think of this? It is frightful to think so; it is frightful to say so.

Because men eat and drink; because coach-building is prosperous; because you, navvy, find work in the Bois de Boulogne; because you, mason, get your forty sous a day in the Louvre; because you, banker, have made a profit out of the metallurgic industries in Vienne or the shares of Hope and Company; because titles of nobility are restored; because people can call each other Monsieur le Comte or Madame la Duchesse; because processions march on Corpus Christi; because amusement and laughter are the order of the day; because the walls of Paris are placarded with announcements of

5   65

celebrations and theatres,— because of all this must the dead bodies that lie underneath be forgotten?

Because you have been to the ball of the Ecole Militaire; because you have returned with dazzed eyes and weary head and torn garment and faded bouquet; because you have thrown yourself on your bed, and slept, dreaming of some handsome officer,— are you no longer to remember that there, under the grass, in a gloomy ditch, in a deep hollow, in the inexorable shadow of death, is a crowd of human beings, still, icy-cold, terrible, a multitude of human beings already become formless, whom the worms are devouring, who are mouldering into dust and beginning to form one with the earth, and who once existed, wrought, and thought, and loved, who had a right to live and have been killed?   Ah, if this is no longer remembered, let us recall it to those who forget! Awake, ye who sleep!   The dead are about to defile before your eyes.

Extract from an unpublished work entitled "The Crime of the 2d of December"

This book will soon be published.   It will form a complete narrative of the infamous event of 1851.   A large part is already written; the author is at this moment gathering materials for the remainder.

He believes it proper to enter now into some details on the subject of this work which he has imposed on himself as a duty.   The author renders himself this justice,— that in writing this narrative, the austere occupation of his exile, he has unceasingly before his mind the high responsibility of the historian.

When this work appears, it will certainly raise numerous and violent protests; the author expects as much.   You cannot cut into the living flesh of a contemporary crime with impunity, and especially at a time when that crime is all-powerful.   However that may be, however more or less interested these protests may be, that the reader may be enabled to estimate their value in advance, the author thinks it his duty to explain here in what fashion, and with what scrupulous regard for truth this history will be written, or, to speak more correctly, this official report of the Crime will be drawn up.

This story of the 2d of December will contain, besides the general facts of which none are ignorant, a very large number of facts hitherto unknown, which are now brought to light for the first time. Several of these facts the author has seen, touched, and witnessed; of them he may say, *Quæque ipse vidi et quorum pars fui.* The members of the republican Left, whose conduct has been so fearless, have seen them as well as he, and their testimony will not be wanting. For what remains, the author has made a real judicial inquest; he has, so to speak, constituted himself the Examining Magistrate of history. Every actor of the drama, every combatant, every victim, every witness, has come to depose before him; for all doubtful facts he has compared statements, and when necessary confronted one deponent with another. In general, historians address themselves to dead facts; they touch them in the tomb with their judicial wands, make them rise, and question them. He has addressed himself to living facts.

All the details of the 2d of December have in this way passed under his eyes; he has registered and weighed them all,— none has escaped him. History may complete but cannot weaken this narrative. He has done the office of the magistrates who failed in their duty. When direct and verbal testimony was not within his reach, he has sent what may be truly called commissions of inquiry to the places, where this was necessary. He drew up regular lists of questions with regard to such and such a fact, and these questions have been minutely answered.

He has, he repeats, submitted the 2d of December to a long and severe inquisition. He has carried the torch as far and as forward as he could. He has, thanks to this inquiry, nearly two hundred files of documents; and this book will be their result. There is not a fact of this narrative behind which, when the work is published, the author cannot place a name. It will be easily understood why he abstains from doing so, it will also be understood why he substitutes sometimes for proper names, and even for certain indications of localities, designations as little transparent as possible, in presence of the proscriptions pending. He does not desire to furnish Monsieur Bonaparte with a supplementary list.

Certainly the author is no more " impartial " in this story of the 2d of December than in the work he is actually publishing. People are in the habit of calling an historian impartial when they wish to praise him. Impartiality is a singular sort of virtue, and Tacitus was without it. Woe be to the writer who would remain impartial in presence of the bleeding wounds of Liberty! Before the deed of December, 1851, the author feels all his human nature rise in revolt; he does not conceal this, and every reader of his work must perceive it. But in him the passion for truth equals the passion for right. The indignant man does not lie. This history of the 2d of December, then, will be, he declares now while quoting from it, written with the most absolute regard for fact.

We have deemed it useful to detach a chapter [1] from that work, and publish it here. This chapter will, we think, strike every mind as throwing a new light on the " success " of Monsieur Bonaparte. Thanks to the reservations of the official historiographers of the 2d of December, it is not sufficiently known how near the *coup d'état* was to its fall, and none know fully by what means it was saved. Let us place this special fact before the eyes of the reader.

I

DAY OF THE 4TH OF DECEMBER. THE COUP D'ÉTAT AT BAY

THE resistance had assumed unexpected proportions. The combat had become threatening; it was no longer a combat, it was a battle, and was waged in all directions. In the Elysée

[1] The author has wished to reserve, for Napoleon the Little solely, the following chapter, which forms an integral part of this work. He

and in the ministerial palaces men were growing pale. They had asked for barricades; they had them.

The entire centre of Paris was becoming covered with redoubts got up at a moment's notice.   The barricaded quarters formed an immense trapezium between the Public Markets and the Rue Rambuteau on one side and the boulevards on the other, and bounded on the east by the Rue du Temple and on the west by the Rue Montmartre.   This vast network of streets, intersected on all sides by redoubts and intrenchments was wearing a more and more terrible aspect every hour, and was becoming a kind of fortress.   The combatants of the barricades extended their advanced guards to the very quays. Beyond the trapezium we have referred to, barricades were erected even in the Faubourg Saint Martin and the environs of the Canal.   The quarter of the schools, where the Committee of Resistance had sent Representative De Flotte, was more eager for revolt than on the evening before; the suburbs were taking fire, and the people of Batignolles were beating the call to arms.   Madier de Montjau was stirring up Belleville, and three enormous barricades were constructed at Chapelle-Saint-Denis.   In the business streets the merchants were giving up their guns, and the women making lint. "Things are getting on! Paris is on the move!" cried B—— as he entered the Committee of Resistance,[1] radiant with joy.   We received news at every moment; all the permanent committees of the various quarters were putting themselves in communication with us.   The members of the Com-

has therefore rewritten for "The History of a Crime" the narrative of the "Day of the 4th of December," with new facts, and from another point of view.

[1] A Committee of Resistance, charged with the centralization of the action and management of the struggle, had been named on the evening of the 2d of December by the members of the Left, who met and organized as an Assembly at the house of Representative Lafon, No. 2, Quai Jemappes. This committee, which had to change its place of meeting twenty-seven times in four days, and which, sitting to some extent night and day, never ceased for a single moment to act during the variable emergencies of the *coup d'état,* was composed of Representatives Carnot, De Flotte, Jules Favre, Madier de Montjau, Michel de Bourges, Schœlcher, and Victor Hugo.

mittee were deliberating and issuing orders and instructions
with regard to the different scenes of action. Victory seemed
certain. There was a moment of enthusiasm and of joy in
which these men, placed between life and death, embraced
each other. " Now," exclaimed Jules Favre, " let but a regi-.
ment turn or a legion declare itself and Louis Bonaparte is
a lost man ! " "To-morrow the Republic will be at the Hôtel
de Ville," said Michel de Bourges. The excitement and agitation was general; in the most peaceful quarters proclamations
were torn down and orderlies dismounted. At Rue Beau-
bourg, while a barricade was being constructed, the women
at the windows cried out, " Courage ! " The ferment even
reached the Faubourg Saint Germain. At the hotel of the
Rue Jérusalem,— that centre of the huge spider's web the
police stretches over Paris,— at that spot was fear and trembling; the anxiety there was deep; a victorious republic did
not look impossible. In the courts, offices, and lobbies, clerks
and policemen were beginning to speak of Caussidière with
tender emotion.

If we are to believe what has leaked out from that den,
Prefect Maupas, so ardent on the evening before and so ac-
tive in his hateful mission, was beginning to recoil and to
weaken. He seemed to lend a terrified ear to the roar of the
rising tide of insurrection, the sacred and legitimate insurrection of Right; he stammered, he faltered, and :..c word of
command died away on his lips. " This little young fellow
has the colic," said ex-Prefect Carlier on leaving him. In his
trepidation, Maupas clung to Morny. The electric telegraph
was the medium of a perpetual dialogue between the Per-
fecture of Police and the Ministry of the Interior. Every
disturbing rumour, every sign of panic and confusion, came
one after another from the prefect to the minister. Morny,
less alarmed, and at least a man of wit, received all these shocks
in his cabinet. The story goes that at the first he said,
" Maupas is sick," and to the question " What am I to do? "
replied by telegraph, " Go to bed! " To the second he an-

swered also, " Go to bed!" To the third, losing patience, he answered, " Go to bed, you ——!"

The zeal of the police agents slackened; they were beginning to think of changing sides. An intrepid man sent by the Committee of Resistance to raise the Faubourg Saint Marceau was arrested in the Rue des Fosses-Saint-Victor, his pockets full of proclamations and decrees of the Left. Conducted by the soldiers towards the Prefecture of Police, he expected to be shot. When his guards were passing the Morgue on the Quai Saint-Michel, a roar of musketry was heard from the Cité; the police officer leading the squad, said to the soldiers; " Go back to your post, I will take charge of the prisoner." The soldiers out of sight, he cut the cords tying the wrists of the prisoner, and said to him: " Get off! I am saving your life. Remember it was I who set you at liberty! Look me well in the face, so that you can recognize me."

The principal military accomplices were holding a council. The question under discussion was whether it was necessary for Louis Bonaparte to quit at once the Faubourg Saint Honoré and repair to the Palace of the Luxembourg or to the Invalides,— two strategic points more easy to defend from a sudden attack than the Elysée. Some were for the Invalides, others for the Luxembourg. There was an altercation on the subject between two generals.

It was at this moment the ex-King of Westphalia, Jerome Bonaparte, seeing the *coup d'état* stagger, and taking thought of the morrow, wrote to his nephew this significant letter:—

MY DEAR NEPHEW,— French blood has run; stop its further effusion by an appeal to the people. Your sentiments are badly understood. The second proclamation, in which you speak of the *plebiscitum*, is badly received by the people, who do not regard it as the restoration of universal suffrage. Liberty is without a guaranty if an Assembly does not form an element in the Constitution of the country. The army has the upper hand. Now is the time to complete a material victory by a moral victory; and what a government cannot do when it is beaten, it ought to do when it is victorious. After destroying the old parties, work for the renovation of the people; proclaim that universal suffrage, sincerely acting in harmony with the greatest liberty, will name the President and the Constituent Assembly, in order to save and restore the Republic.

I write to you in the name of my brother, and as one who shares his horror of civil war. Trust to my old experience, and remember that France, Europe, and posterity will be called on to judge your future conduct.

Your affectionate uncle,

JEROME BONAPARTE.

Two Representatives, Fabvier and Crestin, happening to meet in the Place de la Madeleine, General Fabvier pointed out to his colleagues four pieces of ordnance on gun-carriages which were leaving the boulevard and galloping in the direction of the Elysée. " It is possible that the Elysée is already on the defensive? " observed the General. And Crestin, directing his attention to the façade of the Palace of the Assembly, beyond the Place de la Révolution, answered: " To-morrow, General, we shall be there." From certain mansard-roofs overlooking the stables of the Elysée, three travelling carriages had been noticed in the yard since morning, put to and loaded, with postilions in saddle, and ready for starting.

The impulse had indeed been given, and the outburst of anger and hatred had become universal. The *coup d'état* seemed lost; one shock more, and Louis Bonaparte was ruined. Let the day end as it had begun, and all was over. The *coup d'état* was in despair. The hour for some supreme resolution had come. What was it going to do? It had to strike hard; it had to strike a blow that would be unforeseen,— a blow that would be horrible. It was reduced to this situation,— to perish, or to save itself by an atrocious deed.

Louis Bonaparte had not left the Elysée. He stayed in a cabinet on the ground-floor, adjoining that splendid gilded salon, where, in 1815, he, then a child, was present at the second abdication of Napoleon. He was there, alone; orders had been given to allow no one to come near him. From time to time the door half opened, and the grey head of General Roguet, his *aide-de-camp*, appeared. No one except General Roguet had permission to open this door and

enter. The news brought by the General had become more
and more alarming, and frequently ended with the words " It
does not get on," or, " It is getting on badly." When he
finished, Louis Napoleon, leaning on a table, seated, with his
feet on the fender, before a big fire, turned his head half
round on the back of his arm-chair, and without apparent
emotion, invariably replied in his coldest and most phlegmatic
tones: " Let my orders be executed!" The last time General Roguet entered with his usual bad news, it was near one
o'clock. (He has himself since related these details as re-
flecting honour on the impassiveness of his master.) He informed the Prince that the barricades in the central streets
were holding out successfully, and others were multiplying;
that on the boulevards cries of " Down with the dictator! "—
he did not dare to say of " Down with Soulouque! "—
and hisses were heard in every direction as the troops marched
by; that in front of the Galerie Jouffroy an adjutant-major
had been pursued by the crowd, and at the corner of the Café
Cardinal a staff captain was torn from his horse.

Louis Bonaparte half rose from his arm-chair, and fixing
his eyes on the General, said calmly: " Well! let Saint Arnaud
be told to execute my orders."

" What are those orders? "

" You shall see."

Here we collect our thoughts, and the narrator lays down
the pen with a kind of hesitation and anguish. We are
approaching the horrible catastrophe of that lugubrious day
of the 4th,— the monstrous deed from which has sprung, all
bathed in blood, the success of the *coup d'état*. We are going
to unveil the most sinister of the premeditations of Louis
Bonaparte; we are going to recount, disclose, and lay open
that which all the historiographers of the 2d of December
have concealed, which General Magnan has carefully omitted
in his report, which in Paris itself, where these things have
been seen, one hardly dare whisper in his neighbour's ear.
We are entering into the horrible.

The 2d of December is a crime which the night covers,—

a coffin, closed and dumb, through the chinks of which flow streams of blood. We are going to open this coffin.

II

EARLY in the morning,— and here the premeditation is placed beyond question, let us lay special stress on this point, — early in the morning strange placards had been pasted on all the street corners. These placards we have transcribed; the reader can recall them. For sixty years the thunder of cannon has been heard in revolutionary Paris on certain days, and menaced power has sometimes had recourse to desperate expedients, but nothing had yet been seen like unto this. These placards announced that all assemblies, of what nature soever, would be dispersed by force, *without a summons to disperse.* In Paris, the central city of civilization, it was difficult to believe that a man would push his crime to its utmost limit; and the public saw in these proclamations only an act of intimidation, hideous, indeed, and savage, but almost ludicrous. They were mistaken. These placards contained in the germ the plan of Louis Bonaparte. These placards were serious things. And now a word on the future theatre of the unexampled deed prepared and perpetrated by the Man of December.

From the Madeleine to the Faubourg Poissonnière the boulevard was free; from the Gymnase Theatre to that of Porte Saint Martin it was barricaded, as were the Rue de Bondy, the Rue Meslay, the Rue de la Lune, and all the streets bordering or debouching on Porte Saint Denis and Porte Saint Martin. Beyond Porte Saint Martin the boulevard became once more free as far as the Bastille, close by a barricade roughly constructed on a level with the Château d'Eau. Between Porte Saint Denis and Porte Saint Martin, seven or eight redoubts intersected the causeway at certain distances. A square of four barricades enclosed the Porte Saint Martin.

One of these four barricades, facing the Madeleine and

intended to meet the first shock of the troops, was erected on the highest point of the boulevard. Its left rested on the corner of the Rue de la Lune, and its right on the Rue Mazagran. Four omnibuses, five furniture-vans, the fittings of the office of the inspector of cabs, the columns torn down from the public water-closets, the benches on the boulevard, and the iron hand-rail of the sidewalk wrenched off at a single effort by the stout arms of the crowd, entered into the composition of this pile, which yet scarcely sufficed to stop up the boulevard, very wide at this particular spot. The barricade, then, did not even reach from one curbstone of the boulevard to the other, and there was an extensive space vacant towards the Rue Mazagran. At this spot a house was in course of construction. A fashionably dressed young man, on noticing this gap, mounted the scaffolding, and alone, without any hurry, without even dropping the cigar in his mouth, cut all the ropes. Persons in the neighbouring windows laughed and applauded. A moment after, the scaffolding fell with a great noise, in a single piece, and its downfall allowed the barricade to be completed.

While this redoubt was being finished, a score of men entered the Gymnase by the actor's door, and left it, a few moments after, with some guns and a drum found in the store-room. These formed a portion of what, in the language of the theatre, is called the "properties." One of the men took the drum and set about beating the roll-call. The others, with some of the pillars and furniture-vans laid on their sides, with window-blinds and shutters unhooked from their hinges and with old stage-scenery, erected a little barricade on a level with the Bonne Nouvelle station, as an outpost, or rather small demi-lune to guard the Poissonnière and Montmartre boulevards and the Rue Hauteville. The troops had evacuated the guard-house in the morning, and the flag belonging to this guard-house was taken and planted on the barricade. This is the flag since declared by the journals of the *coup d'état* to have been the " red flag."

At this advanced post fifteen men took their stand. They

had guns, but few or no cartridges. The great barricade in their rear, which covered the Porte Saint Denis, was held by a hundred combatants, among whom were seen two women and an old man with white hairs supporting himself by a cane with his left hand and holding a gun in his right. One of the women bore a sabre in a cross-belt. She had cut three of her fingers in helping to wrench off the hand-rail, and showed her wounds to the crowd, shouting, "Vive la République!" The other woman having ascended the top of the barricade and leaned against the flagstaff, read in a loud voice the appeal to arms of the Representatives of the Left. She was escorted by two men in blouses, who presented arms. The people clapped their hands.

All this took place between noon and one o'clock. The number of people on this side of the barricade was immense, and covered both the footpaths of the boulevard. In some places they were silent, in others they cried: "Down with Soulouque! Down with the traitor!"

Gloomy processions passed through this multitude at intervals, consisting of lines of litters borne by hospital nurses and soldiers. Men walked in front holding long staves from which hung blue placards, on which were written in large letters the words: "Service des hopitaux militaires." On the curtains of the litters might be read: "The wounded. Ambulances." The weather was dark and rainy.

At this time there was a crowd at the Bourse, and bill-posters were pasting on all the walls dispatches announcing the adhesion of the departments to the *coup d'état*. The stockbrokers, while buying for a rise, were laughing and shrugging their shoulders at these placards. Suddenly a well-known speculator and admirer of the *coup d'état* for the two last days rushes in, pale as death, gasping like one fleeing from some danger, and says: "They are sweeping the boulevards with grape-shot!"

And now for what was happening.

III

A LITTLE after one o'clock, a quarter of an hour after the last order given by Louis Bonaparte to General Roguet, the boulevards throughout their entire length from the Madeleine were suddenly covered with infantry and cavalry. The Carrelet division, almost at its full complement, composed of the five brigades of Cotte, Bourgon, Canrobert, Dulac, and Reybell, and presenting an effective force of 16,410 men, had taken position and formed in echelons from the Rue de la Paix to the Faubourg Poissonnière. Each brigade had its battery with it. On the Boulevard Poissonnière alone eleven pieces of ordnance were counted. Two of these were placed back to back, and pointed, one at the entrance of the Rue Montmartre, the other at that of the Faubourg Montmartre, for no reason that any one could see, as neither showed signs of any barricade. The people whom curiosity brought to the sidewalks and windows were astounded at this jumble of gun-carriages, sabres, and bayonets.

"The troops were laughing and chatting," says one witness; another witness says, "Most of them, with the butt-ends of their muskets resting on the ground, were supporting themselves on the barrels, and seemed to be in a half-staggering condition from fatigue or from something else." One of those old officers who have made it their study to sound the very depths of the soldier's soul, General L——, said, while passing the Café Frascati: "They are drunk."

Symptoms of this were becoming apparent. At a moment when the crowd was shouting to the soldiery: "Vive la République! Down with Louis Bonaparte!" an officer was heard to whisper: "We shall have some pig-sticking soon."

A battalion of infantry was debouching by the Rue-Richelieu. In front of the Café Cardinal it was received with a unanimous cry of, "Vive la République!" A writer who was there, the editor of a conservative journal, added, "Down with Soulouque!" The staff-officer who was lead-

ing the detachment dealt him a sword-cut, which was evaded
by the writer, and lopped off one of the small trees on the
boulevard.

As the 1st Lancers, commanded by Colonel Rochefort,
reached the Rue Taitbout, a numerous crowd was spreading
over the boulevard. It consisted of the inhabitants of the
quarter, merchants, artists, journalists, and some women
holding their children by the hand. When the regiment was
passing, all — men, women, and children — cried out: " Vive
la constitution! vive la loi! vive la République! " Colonel
Rochefort — he is the man who took the chair at the banquet given by the 1st Lancers to the 7th at the Ecole Militaire, and who at that banquet uttered this toast: " To
Prince Napoleon, to the Chief of the State: he is the per-
sonification of that order which we are the defenders of," —
Colonel Rochefort, we say, at this cry, which was perfectly
legal, spurred his horse through the middle of the crowd
and over the chairs on the sidewalk; the Lancers dashed
after him, and men, women, and children were sabred. " A
good number of them were killed," says an apologist of
the *coup d'état*, adding: " It was the affair of a moment." [1]

About two o'clock, howitzers were levelled at the extremity
of the Poissonnière boulevard, a hundred and fifty paces from
the little demi-lune barricade of the Bonne Nouvelle station.
While placing these pieces in battery, the train-soldiers,
though little in the habit of making unskilful manœuvres,
broke the pole of an ammunition wagon. " You can well
see that they are full! " exclaimed a man of the people.

At half-past two — we must follow step by step and minute by minute the details of this hideous drama — firing
began in front of the barricade, languidly, and, as it seemed,
at random. The military leaders appeared to have their
minds fixed on something else besides a combat. We shall
know what they were thinking of.

The first shot, badly aimed, passed above all the barricades. The projectile killed a young lad in the Château

[1] Le Capitaine Mauduit: Revolution militaire du 2 Décembre, p. 217.

d'Eau who was drawing water from the fountain. The shops were shut, and nearly all the windows as well. One casement, however, remained open in the upper story of a house at the corner of the Rue du Sentier.

Influenced by curiosity, more and more people came flocking into the boulevard, thronging on the sidewalk on the south especially. It was a crowd, and nothing more,— men, women, children, and greybeards, on whom the barricade, which was hardly attacked or defended, produced all the effect of a sham battle.

This barricade remained a spectacle until it became a pretext.

IV

For about a quarter of an hour there was some poor firing on the part of the soldiers, replied to in a way, by the barricade, but not one wounded on either side, when suddenly as if by an electric impulse an extraordinary and terrible movement was made, first by the infantry, then by the cavalry. In a moment the soldiery wheeled completely round.

The historiographers of the *coup d'état* have related that a shot fired at the soldiers came from an open window at the corner of the Rue du Sentier. Others have said from the top of the house at the corner of the Rue Notre-Dame-de-Recouvrance and the Rue Poissonnière. Others again say it was a pistol-shot fired from the roof of the high house at the corner of the Rue Mazagran. The shot is disputed; but what there can be no dispute about is, that for firing this problematic pistol-shot, which may, after all, have been nothing else than the noise made by a door shut to with violence, a dentist living in the neighbourhood was executed. After all, did any one hear either gun-shot or pistol-shot fired from one of the houses on the boulevard? Is the story true? Is it false? It is denied by a crowd of witnesses. If the shot was fired, another question remains to be cleared up. Was it a cause, or was it a signal?

Be this as it may, on a sudden, as we have just said, cavalry, infantry, and artillery faced about and confronted the multitude massed on the sidewalks, and without warning, without any one being able to guess why, without motive, without a summons to disperse, (*sans sommation*) as the infamous placards of the morning had announced, from the Gymnase to the Chinese Baths,— that is to say, along the whole length of the richest, the most animated and joyous boulevard in Paris, a butchery was begun.

The soldiery commenced to shoot down the people with their muskets close to the people's breasts. Who shall describe the horrors that ensued! — the cries, the arms raised to heaven, the surprise, the terror, the crowd flying in all directions, a hail of balls raining down on the pavements and rising again to the roofs, the dead bodies scattered in a moment along the causeway, young men falling with the cigar still between their lips, women in velvet robes dropping stone dead, two booksellers slaughtered on the threshold of their shops without knowing in what they had offended, shots fired through the openings in cellars and killing it mattered not whom, the Bazaar riddled with shells and bullets, the Hôtel Sallandrouze bombarded, the Maison d'Or raked with grape-shot, Tortoni carried by assault, hundreds of corpses on the boulevard, the Rue Richelieu a stream of blood!

And here the historian must again be allowed to interrupt his narrative for a while.

In presence of these deeds without a name, I who write these lines proclaim myself the recording officer who registers the crime; I bring the cause before the court. All my function is in this. I cite Louis Bonaparte; I cite Saint Arnaud, Maupas, Morny, Magnan, Carrelet, Canrobert, Reybell, his accomplices; I cite the others whose names will be found elsewhere; I cite the executioners and the murderers, the witnesses and the victims, the red-hot cannon and smoking sabres; the drunkenness of the soldiery, the agony of families, the dying and the dead, the horror, the blood and the tears, before the bar of the civilized world.

The narrator, be he who he may, would not be believed alone. Then let living, bleeding facts speak. Let us listen to the evidence.

V

WE will not print the names of the witnesses, — we have said why,— but the sincere and bitter accent of truth will be easily recognized.

A witness says: —

" I had hardly taken three steps on the sidewalk when the troop which was defiling suddenly halted, wheeled round towards the south, lowered its arms, and fired on the bewildered crowd, by an instantaneous movement. The firing continued without interruption for twenty minutes, the roll of cannon being now and then heard above it.

" At the first fire I threw myself flat on the ground, and crawled like a reptile along the sidewalk up to the first half-open door I met. It was a wine-merchant's warehouse, at No. 180, close to the Bazar de l'Industrie. I was the last to enter. Meanwhile, the fusilade never stopped.

" In this warehouse there were about fifty persons, and among them five or six women, and two or three children. Three unfortunates had entered wounded, two of whom died at the end of a quarter of an hour in horrible suffering; the third was still alive when I left the place at four o'clock, but did not survive his wound, as I learned later.

" To enable you to form an idea of the class of people on whom the soldiers fired, I cannot do better than give the following examples of the persons assembled in this warehouse: —

" Amongst them were some women who had gone out to buy provisions for their dinner; a bailiff's clerk sent on an errand by his master; two or three stock-jobbers; two or three proprietors; and some workmen, most of whom had no blouses. One of these unhappy fugitives made a strong impression on me; he was a man about thirty years old, in a grey overcoat. He was going, in company with his wife, to dine with his family in the Faubourg Montmartre when he was stopped on the boulevard by the passing of the column of troops. At the first volley both he and his wife fell; he rose up and was dragged into the wine-merchant's, but he had no longer his wife on his arm, and his despair was indescribable. He insisted absolutely, in spite of our representations, on having the door opened and running in search of his wife through the grape-shot that was sweeping the street. We had the greatest difficulty in keeping him back for an hour. The next day I learned that his wife had been slain, and her corpse had been recognized. I learned also, a fortnight later, that the unhappy man, having threatened Louis Bonaparte with the penalty of *lex talionis,* was arrested and transported to Brest, on his way to Cayenne. Nearly all the citizens assembled in the warehouse held monarchical opinions; and I met only two,— an ex-compositor of " La Réforme," named Meunier, and one of his friends,— who avowed themselves republicans. I left the warehouse about four o'clock."

A witness, one of those who believe they heard the shot fired in the Rue Mazagran, adds: —

" That shot was the signal for a simultaneous discharge of musketry on all the houses between the Café du Grand-Balcon and the Porte Saint Denis. It continued at least thirty minutes. Soon the roar of cannon was mingled with that of musketry."

A witness says: —

" At a quarter past three a singular evolution took place. The soldiers fronting the Port Saint Denis suddenly faced about, backing themselves on the houses near the Gymnase, the Maison du Pont-de-Fer and the Hôtel Saint-Phar, and at once kept up a running fire on the persons on the side opposite, between the Rue Saint Denis and the Rue Richelieu. In a few minutes the sidewalks were covered with dead bodies; the houses were riddled with balls, and this paroxysm of fury lasted for three-quarters of an hour."

A witness says: —

" The first cannon shots fired at the Bonne Nouvelle barricade served as a signal for the rest of the soldiery, who fired almost at the same time on everything within reach of their muskets."

A witness says: —

" It is impossible for words to give an idea of the barbarism of such a deed. One must have witnessed it to venture on asserting the truth of an action so utterly meaningless. Thousands of shots were fired by the soldiery— the number is *inappreciable* [1]— on inoffensive persons, without any reason whatever. It was desired to produce a strong impression; this explains everything."

A witness says: —

" When the agitation on the boulevard was at its height, the Line, followed by the artillery and cavalry, arrived. A soldier was seen to fire a shot from the middle of the troops, and it was easy to observe that it was fired in the air, as the smoke rose perpendicularly; therefore it was the signal for firing *sans sommation* and charging the

---

[1] The witness means " incalculable." We did not wish to change anything in the text.

people with the bayonet. This is significant, and shows that the soldiery wished to have a semblance of reason for beginning the massacre
that followed."

A witness relates : —

"The cannon loaded with grape-shot tore away the fronts of the
houses between the Magasins de Prophète and the Rue Montmartre.
A cannon-ball must also have been fired from the Bonne Nouvelle
boulevard into the Maison Billecocq, for it was struck on the corner
near Aubusson; and the ball, after piercing the wall, penetrated the
interior."

Another witness, one of those who deny the shot in the
Rue Mazagran, says : —

"It has been tried to extenuate this fusilade and these assassinations
by pretending that the troops were fired on from the windows of some
houses. Not only does the official report of General Magnan seem
to give the lie to this rumour, but I assert strongly that the discharges
were instantaneous from the Port Saint Denis to the Port Saint Martin,
and, until the general discharge, there was not a single shot fired,
either from the windows or by the soldiery, between the Faubourg
Saint Denis and the Boulevard des Italiens."

Another, who did not hear the shot either, says : —

"The troops defiled in front of Tortoni's, where I had been for
about twenty minutes, when before a report of any shot reached us,
they moved forward, the cavalry at a gallop, the infantry in double-
quick time. Suddenly we saw in the direction of the Boulevard Poissonnière a sheet of fire which increased and spread rapidly. I can
guarantee that no explosion preceded the fusilade then begun, and that
not a single shot was fired from the houses between the Café Frascati
and the place where I was standing. At last we saw the soldiers in
front of us lower their guns in a threatening fashion. We took refuge
under a gateway on the Rue Taitbout. At that very moment the balls
were passing over us and around us. A woman was killed within ten
paces of me when I was hiding under the gateway. There was, I
swear it, neither insurgents nor barricade there; there were *hunters
and game on the run,* that was all."

This image of " hunters and game " seems to have been
in the mind of every one who beheld this thing of horror.
We find it in the testimony of another witness :—

"I saw the mobilized gendarmes — and I know it was the same in
the rest of the neighbourhood — holding their guns and themselves in

the attitude of a hunter *on the lookout for the starting of the game;* that is to say, with the gun near the shoulder, ready to aim and shoot. " The utmost attention was given to the wounded who fell in the Rue Montmartre, near the city gates. At certain distances a door would open, a hand would be stretched out, and the dead or dying for whom the balls were still disputing, dragged in."

In the testimony of another witness we meet the same image: —

" The soldiers in ambush at the corners of the streets were watching for citizens to cross over, as *hunters watch for game;* and when they saw them in the street, fired at them *as they would at a target.* Several citizens were killed in this manner in Rue de Sentier, Rue Rougemont, and Rue du Faubourg Poissonnière.

"'Begone!' the officers would say to the unoffending citizens who asked their protection; and at this word they started off quickly and confidently. It was but a watchword, and it meant *death;* a few paces on, and they fell on their backs."

Says another witness: —

" At the moment the firing began on the boulevards, a bookseller near the carpet warehouse was hurrying to close his doors and shutters, when some fugitives who tried to enter were suspected by the soldiery or gendarmes, I don't know which, of having fired on them. The soldiers made their way into the bookseller's house; he was led out in front of his door, and his wife and daughter had barely time to fling themselves between him and the soldiers when he fell dead. His wife had her thigh broken, and the daughter was saved by the busk of her corset. The wife, I have been told, has since gone mad."

Another witness: —

" The soldiers rushed into the two bookstores between the house of the Prophète and that of M. Sallandrouze. The murders they committed have been verified. The two booksellers were butchered on the sidewalk, the other prisoners in the warehouses."

We will finish with these three extracts, which cannot be written down without a shudder. Says a witness: —

" During the first quarter of an hour of this horrible deed there was a moment of inaction, and some citizens who were lying wounded made an attempt to rise. Among those stretched in front of the Prophète two succeeded in getting up. One of them fled down the Rue du Sentier, from which he was separated only by a few yards. He escaped with the loss of his hat, which was pierced by balls. The second could only rise on his knees, and with clasped hands he begged the soldiers to give him quarter; but he was shot down on the instant. The next morning a spot might be seen near the perron of the Prophète, not more than a few yards wide, which was struck by over a hundred bullets.

"At the entrance to the Rue Montmartre, near the fountain, there were sixty corpses spread over a length of sixty paces, men and women, young girls and children. All these unfortunate victims had been stationed on the side of the boulevard opposite the gendarmes and soldiery, and were the first victims of their fire. They fled at the first report, but had hardly taken some steps forward when they fell, never to rise again. A young man who took refuge in a gateway and was trying to shelter himself under a wall projecting in the direction of the boulevards, *was used as a target* by the soldiers. After some ten minutes' clumsy firing, he was hit in spite of all his efforts to make himself as small as possible, and he too sank down never to rise again."

Another: —

"The mirrors and windows of the Maison Pont-du-Fer were broken. A man who happened to be in the courtyard fell dead from fright. The cellars were filled with women, but they could not escape. The soldiers fired into the shops and down the opening of the cellars. Such was the condition of things between Tortoni and the Gymnase. It lasted more than an hour."

VI

LET us have done with these extracts now; let us close this mournful indictment. The evidence is sufficient. The horror of the deed is patent. A hundred other testimonies are before our eyes; they repeat the same facts almost in the same terms. From this forth it is certain, it is proved beyond doubt and beyond question, it is as clear as the noonday sun, that on the Friday of the 4th of December, 1851, the inoffensive inhabitants of Paris, the inhabitants who took no part in the combat, were mowed down by grape-shot *sans sommation,* and massacred for the simple purpose of intimidation, and that the mysterious phrase of Monsieur Bonaparte is capable of bearing no other meaning than this.

The execution lasted until nightfall. For more than an hour the boulevard was the scene of something like an orgy of musketry and artillery. During cannonading and platoon firing, the soldiers interchanged shots at random, and

at certain moments killed one another.   The battery of the
6th regiment of artillery, which formed a part of the Canrobert brigade, was dismounted; the horses, rearing amid
the bullets, smashed the gun-carriages in front, and the
wheels and shafts of others; and of the whole battery there
was but one piece left fit for action.   An entire squadron
of the 1st Lancers was obliged to take refuge in an out-
house on the Rue Saint Fiacre.   The next day, the lance
pennants were found to be pierced with seventy holes made
by bullets.   Fury had seized on the soldiery.   At the corner of the Rue Rougemont, a general, in the midst of the
smoke, was seen attempting to restrain them by violent ges-
ticulations; an assistant surgeon-major of the 27th narrowly
escaped death at the hands of the soldiers whom he was
trying to hold back.   A sergeant said to an officer who
seized his arm: " Lieutenant, you are a traitor."   The soldiers no longer knew what they were doing; they seemed
maddened by the crime they were forced to commit.   There
comes a time when the very abomination of the wickedness
you are doing compels you to do it with redoubled energy.
Blood is a sort of horrible wine; massacre intoxicates.

It looked as if some unconscious hand was hurling death
from the depths of a cloud.   The soldiers were but pro-
jectiles.

Two pieces of ordnance were pointed at the façade of the
Sallandrouze warehouse from the causeway of the boulevard,
and poured several discharges into the building, firing care-
lessly, at random, within a few yards of it.   This house,
once a palace, noted for its almost historic perron, was split
asunder by the balls as if by iron wedges, and was cracked
and shattered from top to bottom; the soldiers became more
indefatigable in the work of destruction than ever.   After
every discharge a crash made itself heard.   Suddenly an artillery officer galloped up and cried, " Stop! stop!"   The
house leaned forward; another ball fired and it would have
fallen on the cannon and the cannoneers.

The cannoneers were so drunk that several of them, no

longer knowing what they were doing, let themselves be killed by the recoil of the guns. The balls came at the same time from the Porte Saint-Denis, the Boulevard Poissonnière, and the Boulevard Montmartre; the artillery-men, when they heard them whistling by their ears, threw themselves flat upon their horses, the train-soldiers took refuge under the gun-carriages or behind the ammunition wagons; soldiers were seen to drop their *kepis* and fly along the Rue Notre-Dame-de-Recouvrance, in a state of utter bewilderment; some troopers lost their heads and fired their carbines in the air; others leaped to the ground, and sheltered themselves behind the flanks of their horses. Three or four horses broke loose and ran here and there, dazed with terror.

There were two horrible pastimes combined with the massacre. The tirailleurs of Vincennes had taken a position on one of the barricades which they carried at the point of the bayonet, and from there engaged in target practice on the pedestrians at a distance. Such hideous dialogues as the following were heard in the neighbouring houses: " I bet I'll bring that one down." " I bet you wont." " I bet I shall." And the shot was fired. When the man fell, a roar of laughter told of the success. If a woman was passing, the officers cried: " Fire at the woman! Always fire at the women! "

This was one of the watchwords; on the Boulevard Montmarte, where bayonets were much used, a young staff-captain shouted: " Prod the women! " A woman with a loaf under her arm thought she might be able to cross the Rue Saint-Fiacre safely. A tirailleur killed her.

On the Rue Jean-Jacques-Rousseau the soldiers did not go to such extremes; a woman cried: " Vive la République! " she was only whipped by them. But let us return to the boulevard.

A bailiff was aimed at as he was walking along, and hit in the forehead. He fell on his hands and knees, crying " Spare me! " He received thirteen more balls in the body. He is alive to-day. By such a chance as was never heard of, no wound was mortal. The ball in the forehead had ploughed along the skin and travelled round the skull without breaking it. An old man of eighty, found skulking in some hole or other, was led in front of the perron of the Prophète and shot. He fell. " He won't get a bump on the head," said a soldier. The old man had fallen on a heap of corpses. Two young men of Islay, who had been a month married to two sisters, were crossing the boulevard after their day's work. They saw some soldiers taking aim at them. They fell on their knees and cried, " We have married two sisters! " They were slain. A cocoa peddler named Robert, residing at No. 97 Faubourg Poissonnière, was flying down the Rue Montmartre, with his cocoa barrel on his back. He was slain.[1] A saddler's apprentice, a child of thirteen years, was passing in front of the Café Vachette; muskets were levelled at him. He uttered piercing cries; he shook a bridle which he held in his hands saying, "I am going on an errand." He was slain. Three balls were lodged in his breast. All along the boulevard might be heard the howls and spasmodic starts of the wounded; the soldiers were pinking them with their bayonets, but went no further. They denied their victims even the indulgence of finishing them off.

Thieves availed themselves of the occasion for plying their trade. A cashier whose office was in the Rue de la Banque, left it at two o'clock, went to the Rue Bergère, collected an account, returned with the money, and was killed on the boulevard. When his dead body was lifted he had no longer on him his ring or watch or the money he was carrying back with him.

The soldiers, under the pretext that shots had been fired at them, entered ten or twelve houses at random and bayoneted every one they could discover. All the houses on the boulevard

---

[1] We are able to name the witness who saw the deed. He has been proscribed. His name is Versigny, a Representative of the People. He says: " I saw also at the top of the Rue du Croissant, a lemonade-seller with his tin apparatus on his back fall dead against a shop-front. He alone, although his only weapon was his little bell, had the honour of being fired at by a whole platoon." The same witness adds: " The soldiers swept streets with musketry, in which there had not been a single bit of pavement uprooted or a single combatant seen."

have cast-iron pipes through which the dirty water is emptied into the gutters outside. The soldiers, without knowing why, contracted a feeling of distrust or hatred for one of such houses, closed from top to bottom; dull and gloomy, like all the houses of the boulevard, and seeming to be uninhabited, the silence was so profound. They knocked at the door; it was opened, and they entered. A moment after, a red and smoking stream was seen to flow from the mouth of the cast-iron pipe. It was blood.

A captain, with the eyes starting out of his head, shouted to the soldiers: " No quarter! " A major yelled, " Enter the houses and kill every one! " Sergeants were heard to exclaim, " Punch the brutes [*bédouins*]! Give it to the brutes! " " In the time of the uncle," relates a witness, " the soldiers used to call the bourgeois *pékins;* now we are *bédouins.* When the soldiers were massacring the people, it was to the cry of ' Pitch into the bédouins! ' "

At the Frascati Club, where several of the *habitués,* among others an old general, were assembled, the roar of cannon and musketry was commented on. They could not believe that balls were being fired. " It is only powder," they said to one another. They laughed and joked: " How well the thing has been staged! Truly a first-class performer is this Bonaparte of ours! " They fancied they were at the Cirque. Suddenly some soldiers entered in a fury and wanted to kill every one of them. They never suspected the danger they were running, and continued to laugh. One of those present said to us: " We believed this was a part of the buffoonery! " However, when the soldiers became more menacing, they began to understand at last. " Let us kill every man of them! " cried a soldier. A lieutenant who recognized the old general prevented a butchery. Nevertheless, a sergeant could not keep from using obscene language towards his superior, and saying, " You leave us alone! This is our business, and not yours."

The soldiers killed for the mere sake of killing. A witness says: " In the courtyards of some houses they shot the very dogs and horses."

In the house that, with Frascati, forms the angle of the Rue Richelieu, the soldiers had quietly arranged to shoot even the women and children. The latter were set in front of a platoon for this purpose, when a colonel arrived on the scene. He put off the murder, placed these poor trembling creatures in the gallery of the Panoramas, locked the gate, and saved them. A distinguished writer, M. Lireux, who had escaped when first fired on, was taken prisoner and handed about from guard-room to guard-room, expecting to be shot every moment. He was saved by a miracle. The celebrated artist Sax, who happened to be in the music warerooms of Brandus, was about to be shot when a general recognized him. People were killed at random in every direction.

The first person slain in this butchery — history has also preserved the name of the first person killed at the Massacre of St. Bartholomew — was named Theodore Debaëcque, and resided in the house at the corner of the Rue du Sentier, where the carnage began.

VII

THE moment the carnage was over,— it had begun in broad daylight, and ended in the darkness of the night,— the dead bodies were carried away. They were in such heaps that more than three hundred were counted in front of a single shop,— the shop of Barbedienne. Every square of earth cut round the trees of the boulevard was a reservoir of blood. " The dead," says a witness, " were piled up on top of one another,— old men, children, blouses and broadcloth, heads, arms, and legs, jumbled together in indescribable confusion."

Another witness thus paints a group of three: " Two were turned over on the back ; a third, having got himself entangled between their legs, had fallen on top of them." Single corpses were rare, and therefore more noticed than the others. A young man, well dressed, was seated, leaning against a wall, his legs wide apart, his arms half folded, and a malacca cane in his hand; he seemed to be staring at something. He was dead. A little farther on the balls had pinned to the shop-front a youth in velveteen trousers, holding some proof-sheets in his hand. The wind tossed these bloody leaves on which the fingers of the dead boy had contracted. A poor old man, with white hairs, lay stretched in the middle of the causeway, with his umbrella beside him. His elbow almost touched the body of a young man in varnished boots and yellow gloves; his eye-glass had not dropped from his eye. A few paces farther on lay a woman of the people, with her head on the sidewalk and her feet on the pavement; she had been flying with her child in her arms. Mother and child were both dead, but the mother still held the child.

Ah, you will tell me, Monsieur Bonaparte, that you are very sorry, but that the calamity was unavoidable; that in presence of Paris on the point of revolution you had to decide on some course or other, and that you were driven to a stand; and that, as to the *coup d'état*, you had debts, your *aides-de-camp* had debts, your lackeys had debts; that you took all the responsibility; that, confound it! what is the use of being a prince if a man cannot now and then squander a few millions over and above? that a little amusement and enjoyment is indispensable; that it was the Assembly's fault not to understand this and want to condemn you to two paltry millions per annum, and, worse still, force you to quit office at the end of four years and comply with constitutional obligations; that, after all, it was impossible for you to leave the Elysée and enter Clichy; that you had recourse without success to the little expedients provided for by Article 405; that scandals were approaching, the demagogic press was babbling, the affair of the gold ingots was making a noise; that you owed some respect to the name of Napoleon; and that, egad! rather than be one of the vulgar swindlers of the code, you preferred to be one of the great assassins of history!

So, instead of soiling you, this blood has washed you. Very well!

I continue.

VIII

WHEN all was ended, Paris came to have a look; the people flocked in crowds to these terrible spots. They were allowed to do so. It was the object of the assassin that they should do so. Louis Bonaparte did not perpetrate this thing with the view of hiding it.

The south side of the boulevard was covered with papers and torn cartridges; the sidewalk on the north disappeared under the plaster detached from the fronts of the houses by the balls, and was as white as if it had been snowing; pools of blood made wide blackish stains on this snow. The foot escaped a corpse only to strike against fragments of glass, plaster or stone; some houses were so shattered by grape-shot and bullets that they appeared ready to fall, among others the Maison Sallandrouze, of which we have spoken, and the mourning warehouse at the corner of the Faubourg Montmartre. " The Maison Billecocq," says a witness, " is still propped up by strong wooden stays to-day, and the façade will be in part rebuilt. There are gaps in several places in the carpet warehouse." Another witness says, " All the houses from the Cercle des Etrangers to the Rue Poissonnière were literally riddled with balls, especially on the right side of the boulevard. One of the large mirrors of the Petite Jeannette warehouse had certainly more than three hundred for its share. There was not a window intact. You breathed an atmosphere of saltpetre. Thirty-seven corpses were piled up in the Cité Bergère, and the passers-by might count them through the grating. A woman was stopped by something at the corner of the Rue Richelieu. She looked. Suddenly she felt that her feet were wet. ' Why,' she exclaimed, ' it has rained, then? ' ' No, madame,' some one replied, ' it is not water.' Her feet were in a pool of blood." In the Rue Grange Batelière, three bodies were seen in a corner, entirely naked.

During the massacre the barricades on the boulevard were carried by the Bourgon brigade. The dead bodies of the defenders of the barricade of Porte Saint Denis, of which we spoke at the beginning of this narrative, were heaped up in front of the door of the Maison Jouvin. " But " says a witness, " it was nothing compared with the heaps that covered the boulevard."

Two steps from the Théâtre des Variétés, the crowd came to a pause before a cap filled with blood and brains hanging from the branch of a tree. A witness says: " A short distance beyond the Variétés I came upon a corpse with the face resting on the earth. I tried to raise it, assisted by some others. The soldiers drove us back. A little farther there were two bodies, a man and a woman, then one by itself, a workman," (We abridge his story). " From the Rue Montmartre to the Rue du Sentier, *one literally walked in blood;* it covered the sidewalk in certain places, and was nearly an inch deep. Without exaggeration or hyperbole, you had to be very cautious to avoid putting your feet in it. I counted thirty-three corpses. This spectacle was more than I could bear, and big tears coursed down my cheeks. I asked permission to cross the causeway in order to return home; it was ' *graciously granted.*' "

A witness says: " The aspect of the boulevard was horrible. *We literally walked in blood.* We reckoned eighteen corpses in a length of twenty-five paces."

A witness who is a merchant in the Rue du Sentier says: " I crossed the Boulevard du Temple; when I reached my house I found there was an inch of blood on my trousers."

Representative Versigny relates: " We perceived in the distance, reaching nearly to the Porte Saint Denis, the immense camp-fires of the troops. With the exception of an odd lamp here and there, these afforded the only means of finding one's way in this frightful carnage. The combat of the daytime was a mere nothing in comparison with these corpses and this silence. R—— and I were paralyzed. A citizen happened to pass; hearing one of my passionate outbursts, he approached and took me by the hand, saying: ' You are a republican; I was what is called a friend of order, a reactionary; but he who would not execrate this hideous carnage must be abandoned of God and man. France is dishonoured!' and he left, sobbing."

A witness of high character, M. de Cherville, a legitimist, who allows the use of his name, declares: " In the evening I wished to begin again these gloomy investigations. In the Rue Peletier I met MM. Bouillon and Gervais (de Caen); we went some steps together, and I slipped. I caught hold of M. Bouillon and looked at my feet; I had stepped into a wide puddle of blood. Then M. Bouillon told me that he had seen in the morning, while at his window, the druggist whose shop he pointed out to me, busy shutting his door. A woman fell, and the druggist ran out to raise her. At that very moment a soldier, ten yards from him, took aim and shot him in the head. M. Bouillon, indignant and forgetful of his own danger, shouted to those who were passing by: ' You will all testify as to what has just taken place? ' "

About eleven in the evening, when the bivouacs were lighted up everywhere, Monsieur Bonaparte was pleased to allow the soldiers to amuse themselves. The boulevard was the scene of something like a night festival. They laughed and danced as they flung the débris of the barricades into the fire; then, as at Strasburg and Boulogne, came the distribution of money. Let us listen to what a witness relates: " I saw a staff-officer give two hundred francs to the leader of a detachment of twenty men, saying: ' The Prince has charged me to hand you this money for distribution among your brave soldiers. He will not limit himself to this evidence of his satisfaction.' Each soldier received ten francs."

On the evening of Austerlitz, the Emperor said, " Soldiers I am satisfied with you! "

Another adds: " The soldiers, with cigars between their lips, jeered the passers-by and rattled the money they had in their pockets."

Another says: " The officers broke rouleaux of louis with as much indifference as they would sticks of chocolate."

The sentinels allowed women only to pass; if a man presented himself, they shouted to him, " Be off! " Tables were set in the bivouacs, at which officers and soldiers drank. The flames from the wood-fires were reflected on all these merry faces. The corks and white caps of the champagne bottles swam on the red streams of blood. One bivouac called and replied to another with loud cries and obscene pleasantries. They exchanged salutes: " Vive les gendarmes! " " Vive les lanciers! " And all together added: " Vive Louis Napoléon! " The clinking of glasses and noise of broken bottles made themselves heard. Here and there, in the shadow, women prowled among the corpses, with a taper of yellow wax or a lantern in their hands, gazing into those pallid faces one after the other and searching for a son or a husband or a father.

IX

LET us get rid at once of these frightful details.

On the morrow of the 5th, in the cemetery of Montmartre, a horrible thing was seen.

A vast space, vacant until that day, was " utilized " for the provisional interment of some of the massacred. They were buried with their heads above the ground, in order that their families might recognize them; most had their feet also exposed, with a little earth on their breasts. The curious came there in crowds, pushing, jostling one another, and wandered amid the graves; sometimes the ground would sink when trodden on,— it was really the stomach of a corpse. On turning round and looking, you saw boots and sabots or women's dress shoes rising from the earth; opposite was the head which on account of your pressure on the body had made a movement.

An illustrious witness, the great sculptor David, to-day proscribed and wandering in foreign lands, says: " I saw about forty dead bodies in the cemetery of Montmartre with their clothes still on them; they were placed side by side. A few shovelfuls of earth covered them up to the head, which was left exposed so that their friends might recognize them. The feet were half uncovered. It was a horrible thing to see people walking on top of these corpses. There were there some noble young faces bearing the impress of lofty courage; in the middle was a poor woman, a baker's servant, who was killed while carrying bread to her master's customers, and beside her a lovely young girl who sold flowers on the boulevard. Those who were searching for the missing were compelled to trample on the bodies in order to examine the faces nearer. I heard a man of the people say with an expression of horror: ' It's like walking on a spring-board.' "

The crowd continued to flock to the various places where the bodies of the victims were deposited,— notably to the Cité Bergère,— until the number of sightseers became so large and troublesome that a placard was posted at the entrance to the Cité Bergère with these words in large letters: " There are dead bodies here no longer." The three naked corpses of the Rue Grange-Batelière were not carried away until evening.

It is evident then, and we urge this point earnestly, that at first the *coup d'état* made not the slightest pretence at concealment of its crime. It did so because it saw its profit in doing so. It was later on that it became bashful. But on the first day it made, on the contrary, a parade of its iniquity. Atrocity was not enough; it needed cynicism. To massacre was but the means; to terrify was the aim.

X

WAS this aim reached? Yes.

From the 4th of December the public effervescence subsided immediately. A dull stupor froze the blood of Paris. The indignation that raised its voice in presence of the *coup d'état* was suddenly dumb in presence of the butchery. Nothing resembling this had ever occurred in history before. Men felt they were dealing with some monstrous individuality heretofore unknown.

Crassus crushed the gladiators; Herod massacred the Innocents; Charles IX. exterminated the Huguenots; Peter of Russia the Strelitz, Mehemet-Ali the Mamelukes, Mahmoud the Janissaries; Danton massacred the prisoners. Louis Bonaparte had just invented a new kind of massacre,— the massacre of the pedestrians in the streets.

This massacre ended the struggle. There are times when that which should inflame nations strikes them with dismay. The people of Paris felt that the foot of a bandit was on its neck. It no longer struggled. That very evening Mathieu (de la Drôme) entered the place where the Committee of Resistance was sitting and said to us: " We are no longer in Paris, we are no longer under the Republic; we are in Naples, and under King Bomba."

From this moment, whatever were the efforts of the Committee, the Representatives and their courageous auxiliaries, there was resistance at only a few points,— as for instance, at that barricade of the Petit Carreau where Denis Dussoubs, the brother of the Representative, fell with such heroism; and that resistance bore less resemblance to a conflict than to the last convulsions of despair. All was ended.

On the morning of the 5th the victorious troops paraded the city. A general was seen to point his naked sword at the people and cry, " There is your republic! "

Thus an infamous butchery, a massacre of the people in the streets, entered as an element of the supremest importance into the " measure " of the 2d of December. For its elaboration a traitor was needed; for its success a murderer.

This was the method by which the *coup d'état* conquered France and vanquished Paris. Yes, Paris! It is at Paris — we must repeat it again to ourselves — that this thing occurred.

Great God! the Cossacks entered Paris with uplifted lance, singing their wild songs, Moscow had been burned; the Prussians entered Paris, Berlin had been taken; the Austrians entered Paris, we had bombarded Vienna; the English entered Paris, the camp of Boulogne had menaced London. They arrived at our barriers, did these men of all nations, with drums beating, trumpets sounding, flags flying, with naked swords, and cannon rolling and matches lighted, flushed with victory, enemies, conquerors, avengers, shrieking wrathfully

in front of the domes of Paris the names of their capitals,—
London, Berlin, Vienna, Moscow! And then! No sooner did
they set a foot on the threshold of that city, no sooner did the
hoofs of their horses ring on the pavements of our streets,
than all,— Austrians, English, Prussians, and Russians,—
when they had penetrated Paris, saw dimly in those walls, in
those edifices, in that people, something awe-inspiring, pre-
destined, and august; all felt a sacred terror of the sacred
city; all understood that there, before them, was the city not
of a people, but the city of mankind; all lowered the uplifted
sword! Yes, to massacre the Parisians, to treat Paris as a
fortress carried by assault, to sack one of its quarters, to
violate the second Eternal City, to assassinate civilization in
its sanctuary, to mow down old men, women, and children with
grape-shot in that grand arena, that fatherland of the Universe, to do what Wellington had forbidden to his half-naked
Highlanders, what Schwartzenberg interdicted to his Croats,
what Blücher did not permit to his Landwehr, what Platow'
did not dare to let his Cossacks do,— all this hast thou done;
and thy instruments were French soldiers, wretch!

BOOK IV

THE OTHER CRIMES

CHAPTER I

SINISTER QUESTIONS

WHAT is the sum total of the dead?
Knowing the hour is at hand when History will raise her voice, and imagining that a Charles IX. can palliate a St. Bartholomew, Louis Bonaparte has published what he calls an " official return of the dead," as a voucher. In this *alphabetic list* [1] we find such notices recorded as follows: —

" Adde, bookseller, 17 Boulevard Poissonnière, killed in his house.
" Boursier, child seven and a half years old, killed Rue Tiquetonne.
" Belval, cabinet-maker, 10 Rue de la Lune, killed in his house.
" Coquard, proprietor at Vire (Calvados), killed, Boulevard Montmartre.
" Debaëcque, merchant, 45 Rue du Sentier, killed in his house.
" De Couvercelle, florist, 257 Rue Saint Denis, killed in his house.
" Labilte, jeweller, 63 Boulevard Saint Martin, killed in his house.
" Grellier, charwoman, 209 Faubourg Saint Martin, killed on the Boulevard Montmartre.
" Guillard, shop-woman, 77 Faubourg Saint Denis, killed on the Boulevard Saint Denis.
" Garnier, confidential waiting-woman, 6 Boulevard Bonne Nouvelle, killed on the Boulevard Saint Denis.
" Ledaust, charwoman, Passage du Caire, in the Morgue.

[1] The employé who has drawn up this list is, we know, an able and exact statistician, and he has, we do not doubt, drawn it up in good faith. He has verified what he was permitted to see and examine; but as to what was concealed from him, he was, of course, helpless. This field remains open to conjecture.

" Françoise Noël, waistcoat-maker, 20 Rue des Fosses-Montmartre, died in the Charité.

" Count Poninski, fundholder, 32 Rue de la Paix, killed on the Boulevard Montmartre.

" Raboisson, seamstress, died in the Maison Nationiale de Santé.

" The woman Vidal, 97 Rue du Temple, died in the Hôtel Dieu.

" The woman Seguin, embroiderer, 240 Rue Saint Martin, died in the Hospice Beaujon.

" Seniac, shop-girl, 196 Rue du Temple, died in the Hospice Beaujon.

" Thirion de Montauban, proprietor, Rue de Lancry, killed at his door," etc.

Let us abridge. Louis Bonaparte, in this document, confesses to *a hundred and ninety-one* assassinations.

Having recorded this inventory for what it is, we ask what is the total? What is the real number of the victims? How many corpses has the *coup d'état* of December scattered along its path? Who can tell? Who knows,— who shall ever know? As we have seen before, a witness deposes: " In that place I reckoned thirty-three bodies; " another, who was somewhere else on the boulevard, says: " We counted eighteen corpses in a length of twenty or twenty-five yards." Another, stationed at a different point, says: " There were more than sixty corpses within a length of sixty yards." The writer, who was so long threatened with death, has himself said to us: " I saw with my own eyes more than eight hundred corpses along the boulevard." Now just try to compute the number of skulls and breasts shattered and riddled by grape-shot required " literally " to cover the boulevards with blood for considerably over a quarter of a mile. Do as the women did, do as the sisters, daughters, and despairing mothers did,— take a torch and go out into the night, grope along the ground, grope along the pavement, grope along the wall, pick up the dead bodies, question the spectres, and then reckon if you can.

The number of victims! We can only conjecture it. It is a question reserved for history; and that question we solemnly bind ourselves, as far as in us lies, to examine and to fathom later.

On the first day Louis Bonaparte made a public display of his massacre. We have said why. It was useful to him to do so. Having gained by this course of action all the advantage he desired, he then concealed it. Orders were given to the Elysian gazettes to be silent, to Magnan to omit, to the historiographers to ignore. The dead were buried after midnight, without torches, without funeral procession, without chant, without priest, by stealth. Families were forbidden to weep too loudly.

And the massacre of the boulevard was not the only one; there were others,— summary fusilades, unpublished executions.

One of the witnesses whom we have interrogated asked the major of the mobilized gendarmerie, which distinguished itself in these slaughters: " Now, what was the real number? Was it four hundred? " The man shrugged his shoulders. " Was it six? " He shook his head. " Was it eight? " " Put it at twelve hundred," returned the officer, " and you will not be still near the mark."

At the present moment, no one knows exactly what the 2d of December is, what it has done, what it has dared, whom it has killed, entombed, and buried. Since the morning of the crime the printing-houses have been placed under seal, and free speech has been suppressed by Louis Bonaparte, the man of silence and of night. On the 2d, the 3d, the 4th, the 5th, and afterward, Truth was taken by the throat and strangled at the moment she was about to speak. She has not been able even to utter a cry. He has sought to enshroud his ambuscade in thicker darkness, and he has in part succeeded. Whatever be the efforts of history, the 2d of December will for a long time still, perhaps, be plunged in a species of awful twilight. This crime is composed of audacity and of shadow. On one side it parades cynically in the broad daylight; on the other, it steals away and vanishes in the fog; a malignant and hideous shape, a front of brass, hiding under its mantle monstrosities that are unknown.

What we get a glimpse of is enough for our purpose. On one particular side of the 2d of December all is darkness, but we see graves dimly in that darkness.

Under that greatest of crimes we have a confused perception of a crowd of others. Providence wills that this be so; it makes treasons dependent on necessities. Ah, you perjure yourself! Ah, you violate your oath, and bridle right and justice. So far so good! But now take a cord, for you shall be forced to strangle; take a dagger, for you shall be forced to stab; take a bludgeon, for you shall be forced to crush; take darkness and night, for you shall be forced to hide. One crime calls for another. Horror is full of logic. You cannot stop; you cannot halt in the middle of a footrace. Go on! First this; very well. Now that, and now that other. Go on! go on always! The law is like the veil of the temple; when it is rent, it is rent from top to bottom.

Yes, we repeat, in what is styled " the act of the 2d of December " you find crime throughout the whole depth; perjury on the surface, assassination at the bottom; partial murders, wholesale slaughters, volleys of grape-shot in broad daylight, nocturnal fusilades,— from every part of the *coup d'état* arises a vapour of blood.

Look into the common graves of the cemeteries, search under the pavements of the streets, under the slopes of the Champs de Mars, under the trees of the public gardens, search the bed of the Seine. There are few revelations. It is easily understood why. Bonaparte has had the monstrous art of binding to himself a multitude of unhappy men in the official class by a frightful universal complicity, the nature of which words are powerless to reveal. The stamped papers of the magistrates, the inkstands of the recording-clerks, the cartridge-boxes of the soldiers, the prayers of the priests, are his accomplices. He has flung his crime around him as if it were a net, and in it he has caught prefects, mayors, judges, officers, and soldiers. This complicity gravitates from the general to the corporal, and soars again from the corporal to the president. The police-agent feels as much compromised as the minister. The gendarme, the muzzle of whose pistol has touched the ear of some unfortunate, and whose uniform has been daubed with brains, knows that he is as guilty as the colonel. Atrocious men on high have given orders which have been executed by ferocious men below. Ferocity keeps the secret of atrocity. Hence this hideous silence.

Between this ferocity and this atrocity there was even a rivalry and a struggle; what escaped the one was laid hold of by the other. The future will not believe in these marvels of inhuman rage. A workman was passing over the Pont-du-Change, when he was stopped by some mobilized gendarmes. They smelled his hands. "Gunpowder," said a gendarme. The workman was shot. Four balls passed through his body. "Throw him into the water!" shouts a sergeant. The gendarmes took him by the head and feet and flung him over the bridge. The man, thus shot and drowned, floated down the stream. Yet he was not dead. The icy chill of the river revived him. He was incapable of making a movement; his blood spurted into the water through four holes, but his blouse held him up, and he came ashore under the arch of a bridge. There he was discovered by some wharf porters, picked up, and carried to the hospital. He was cured, and when cured, he left. The next day he was arrested and brought before a court-martial. Death had refused him, Louis Bonaparte has recaptured him. The man is to-day at Lambessa.

What the Champ de Mars, in particular, has seen, the awful nocturnal massacres that dismayed and dishonoured it, history cannot record as yet. Thanks to Louis Bonaparte, that august arena of the Federation may henceforth be called Haceldama. One of the miserable soldiers whom the Man of December transformed into executioners relates with horror and in a whisper that in a single night the number shot down was not less than eight hundred.

Louis Bonaparte has hastily dug a trench and flung his crime into it. A few shovelfuls of earth and the holy-water sprinkler of a priest, and there was nothing more to be said. Now the imperial carnival is dancing above it.

Is this, then, all? Is this, then, ended? Does God allow and accept such entombments as these? Do not believe it. Some day, under the feet of Bonaparte, that trench shall open suddenly, and we shall see rise up one after another between the marble flagging of the Elysée or of the Tuileries every corpse with its wound,— the young man shot through the heart, the old man shaking his white head pierced by a ball, the sabred mother holding her slaughtered babe in her arms,— all standing livid and terrible, and fixing on their assassin their blood-shot eyes.

Waiting for that day, history begins your trial now, Louis Bonaparte. It throws aside your official list of the dead and your vouchers. History says that they lie and that you lie.

You have placed a bandage on the eyes of France and a gag in her mouth. Why? To accomplish loyal deeds? No, to commit crimes. He who is afraid of the light is doing evil.

You have fusiladed the people on the Champs de Mars, at the Prefecture, at the Palace of Justice, on the squares, on the quays,— everywhere.

You say, No; I say, Yes.

Considering what you are, to us belongs the right to conjecture, the right to suspect, the right to accuse. And when you deny, to us belongs the right to believe. Your disavowal adds force to our averment.

Your 2d of December is pointed at by the public conscience. No one thinks of it without a secret shudder. What have you been doing in that background of shadow?

Your days are hideous, your nights are under suspicion. Ah, man of darkness that you are!

Let us return to the massacre on the boulevard, to the words, " Let my orders be executed! " and to the events of the 4th.

On the evening of that day Louis Bonaparte must have drawn a parallel between himself and Charles X., who refused to burn Paris, and Louis Philippe, who refused to shed the blood of the people; and he must have done himself the justice of thinking that he was a great statesman. Some days after this, General Th——, formerly a member of the household of one of the sons of Louis Philippe, came to the Elysée. As soon as Louis Bonaparte saw him in the distance, drawing in his own mind the comparison we have just indicated, he cried out to the general, with an air of triumph: " Well? "

Monsieur Louis Bonaparte is truly the very person who said to a man who had been his minister, from whom we have the story: " If I had been Charles X., and if, in the days of July, I had taken Lafitte, Benjamin Constant, and Lafayette, I would have had them shot like dogs."

On the evening of the 4th of December Louis Bonaparte would have been torn from the Elysée, and the law would have triumphed, if he had been one of those men who hesitate before a massacre. Happily for him, he was not troubled by any such squeamish delicacy. What do a few dead bodies, more or less, matter? Forward! kill! kill at random, sabre, fusilade, cannonade, crush, mangle, strike terror into this hateful city of Paris! The *coup d'état* was tottering to its fall; this grand murder restored it. The felony of Louis Bonaparte all but ruined him; his ferocity saved him. If he had been only a Faliero, his destruction was inevitable; luckily, he was a Cæsar Borgia. He jumped with his crime into a river of blood. A less guilty man might have been drowned; he swam across safely. This is what is styled his success. To-day he is on the other shore, trying to wipe and dry himself, streaming with that blood which he takes for the purple, and claiming the empire.

CHAPTER II

CONTINUATION OF THE CRIMES

A ND there stands the malefactor!
   And would none applaud thee, O Truth, if before the eyes of Europe, the eyes of the world, in presence of the people, in the face of God, appealing to honour, to violated faith, to religion, to the sanctity of human life, the magnanimity of all souls, wives, sisters, mothers, to civilization and liberty, to the Republic and to France,— if before his lackeys, his Sen-

ate, his Council of State, his priests, and his police, thou, who dost represent the people, for the people is reality; thou, who dost represent intelligence, for intelligence is light; thou, who dost represent humanity, for humanity is reason,— if in the name of the people in bondage, in the name of intelligence proscribed, in the name of humanity, outraged, in presence of that heap of slaves who cannot or dare not say a word, — thou shouldst slap this brigand of order on the face?

Ah, let others search for moderate words. I am frank and harsh; I am without pity for that pitiless man, and I glory in this implacability.

Let us continue.

To what we have just related, add all the other crimes to which we shall have more than one opportunity of reverting, and which, if God spares us our life, we shall relate in detail. Add the incarcerations *en masse* accompanied by every circumstance of ferocity, the prisons overflowing,[1] the sequestration of the goods of the proscribed in ten departments,[2] notably in

[1] The " Bulletin des lois " publishes the following decree, dated the 27th of March: —

" *Whereas* the law of the 10th of May, 1838, which classes the ordinary expenses of the departmental prisons among those to be inscribed on the departmental budgets; *whereas* such is not the character of the expenses occasioned by the arrests which have taken place in consequence of the events of December; *whereas* the acts because of which these arrests have been multiplied are connected with a *plot against the safety of the State*, the repression of which concerned society at large, and because it is therefore just that the public treasury should be responsible for the excess of expenditure resulting from the *extraordinary increase* of prisoners,—

" Decrees: An extraordinary credit of 250,000 francs is opened at the Ministry of the Interior, on the funds of receipt and expenditure, to be applied to the payment of the expenses resulting from the arrests made in consequence of December."

[2] *Digne, Jan. 5,* 1852. The colonel commanding the state of siege in the Department of the Lower Alps, decrees: At ten days' notice, the goods of those charged with crime who have taken flight shall be sequestrated and administered by the director of the domains of the Department of the Lower Alps, in conformity with civil and military laws, etc.— FRIRION.

We might quote ten other decrees issued by the commandants of the state of siege of a similar character. The first of these malefactors who committed this crime of confiscation and who gave the example of this

the Nièvre, in the Allier, and in the Lower Alps; add the confiscation of the property of the Orleans family, a morsel of it
being thrown to the clergy (Schinderhannes always took the
part of the curé); add the Mixed Commissions, and the so-
called Commission of Clemency; [3] the councils of war in con-
spiracy with the examining magistrates and multiplying abom-
inations, exiles hurried off in batches, three thousand two hundred banished or deported from one department alone, the
Herault; add that frightful proscription, worthy of comparison with the most tragic desolations of history, which, for a
mere leaning, for an opinion, for an honest dissent from this
government, for a word becoming a freeman spoken even before the 2d of December, takes, seizes, apprehends and drags
the labourer from his field, the artisan from his trade, the
proprietor from his house, the doctor from his patients, the
notary from his study, the councillor-general from the people
of his department, the judge from his tribunal, the husband
from his wife, the brother from his brother, the father from
his children. No one escapes. A man in rags, with a long
beard, entered one morning my chamber in Brussels. " I am
here at last," said he; " I travelled the whole way on foot; I
have eaten nothing for the last two days." He was given
some bread. When he had eaten I said to him:

" Where do you come from? "

" From Limoges."

" Why are you here? "

" I do not know. I have been hunted from my home."

kind of decree is named Eynard. He is a general. On the 18th of December he placed the property of a certain number of citizens of Moulins
under sequestration; " because," he said cynically, " *the examination begun* leaves no doubt as to the part they have taken *in the insurrection*
and pillage of the Department of the Allier."

[3] The number of condemnations which have been confirmed (there is
question here of transportations for the most part) up to the date of
the reports is given below: —

By M. Canrobert	3,876
By M. Espinasse	3,625
By M. Quentin-Bauchard	1,634
Total	9,135

" What are you? "

" I am a sabot-maker."

Add Africa, add Guiana, add the atrocities of Canrobert, the atrocities of Bertrand, the atrocities of Espinasse, the atrocities of Martimprey; the cargoes of women sent out by General Guyon; Representative Miot dragged from casemate to casemate; hovels, each containing a hundred and fifty human beings, under the sun of the tropics, promiscuously living amid filth and vermin, and where all these innocent creatures, all these patriots, all these honest people are dying, far from those dear to them, in fever, in misery, wringing their hands in horror and despair. Add all those unfortunates surrendered to the gendarmes, tied two by two, packed in the orlops of the " Magellan," the " Canada," or the " Duguesclin," flung out at Lambessa, flung out at Cayenne with felons, without an idea of what their offence was, without being able to guess what they had done. For instance, Alphonse Lambert of the Indre, torn dying from his bed; Patureau Franccœur, a vine-grower, deported because some people in his village wanted to make him a president of the Republic; Vallette, a carpenter at Châteauroux, deported for having six months before the 2d of December, refused to erect the guillotine on the day a criminal was to be executed.

Add the hunt after men in the villages, the battue of Viroy in the mountains of Lure, the battue of Pellion in the woods of Clamecy with fifteen hundred men; order restored in Crest, — of the two thousand insurgents three hundred being killed; the movable columns everywhere, every one rising in defence of the law sabred and shot down. Charles Sauvan shouts " Vive la République " in Marseilles; a grenadier of the 54th fires on him; the bullet enters the loins and comes out through the belly. Another — Vincent, of Bourges — is deputy mayor of his commune; he protests as magistrate against the *coup d'état;* he is tracked to his village; he flies, and is pursued; one trooper cuts off two of his fingers with a sabre-stroke, another cleaves his skull; he falls; he is transported to the fort of Ivry before his wound is healed; he is an old man of seventy-six.

Add facts like those which follow. In the Cher, Representative Viguier is arrested. Arrested, why? Because he is a Representative, because he is inviolable, because the suffrage of the people has made him sacred. Viguier is thrown into prison. One day he is permitted to go out *for an hour* to regulate some matters that imperiously demand his presence. Before leaving, two gendarmes, named Pierre Guéret and Dubernelle (the latter a non-commissioned officer) take hold of Viguier; the non-commissioned officer joins his two hands so that the palms touch, and binds the wrists tightly with a chain; the end of the chain was hanging; the officer passed it forcibly and repeatedly between the two hands of Viguier at the risk of breaking his wrists by the pressure. The hands of the prisoner became blue and swollen.

" You are, then, applying the torture to me," said Viguier, tranquilly.

" Hide your hands," replied the gendarme, with a grin, " if you are ashamed of them."

" Wretch! " returned Viguier. " It is thou, not I, whom this chain dishonours! "

And Viguier crossed the streets of Bourges in this fashion, where he has lived for thirty years, between two gendarmes, raising his hands and showing his chains. Representative Viguier is seventy years old.

Add the summary fusilades in twenty departments. " Every one resisting," writes Saint Arnaud, the Minister of War, " should be shot in the name of society acting in lawful defence." [1] " Six days have sufficed *to crush* the insurrection,"

---

[1] We give this odious dispatch as it is in the " Moniteur ": —

"All armed insurrection has ceased in Paris owing to a vigorous repression. The same energy will have the same effect everywhere.

" Bands engaging in pillage, violation, and arson are thereby placed outside the law. With them there can be no parley or summons to disperse. They must be attacked and dispersed.

" All who resist must be SHOT, in the name of society acting in lawful defence."

announces General Levaillant, commanding the state of siege in the department of the Var. " I have made some good captures," writes Viroy from Saint Etienne. " I have had eight individuals shot on the spot; I am tracking the leaders in the woods." At Bordeaux, General Bourjoly orders the chiefs of the movable columns " to have all persons taken with arms in their hands shot at once." At Forcalquier it is better still; the proclamation of the state of siege runs thus : —

" The town of Forcalquier is in state of siege. The citizens who have not taken part in the events of the day, but who withhold arms, are summoned to surrender them under penalty of being shot."

The movable column of Pézenas reaches Servian; a man tries to escape from a house surrounded; he is killed by a shot. At Entrain, eighty prisoners are made; one is escaping by swimming; he is fired on; the ball hits him, and he disappears under the water. The rest are shot down.

To these execrable deeds add these other infamous deeds. At Brioude, in the Upper Loire, a man and woman were thrown into prison for ploughing the field of a proscribed. At Loriol, in the Drôme, a field-keeper named Astier, was condemned to twenty years of hard labour for giving asylum to fugitives.

Add (and the pen trembles in writing this) the penalty of death restored, the political guillotine raised once more, and these horrible sentences, in virtue of which citizens are condemned to death on the scaffold by the janissary judges of the councils of war; at Clamecy, Milletot, Jouannin, Guillemot, Sabatier, and Four; at Lyons, Courty, Romegal, Bressieux, Fauritz, Julien, Roustain, and Garain, first assistant of the mayor of Cliouscat; at Montpellier, seventeen for the affair of Bédarrieux,— Mercadier, Delpech, Denis, André, Barthez, Triadou, Pierre Carrière, Galzy, Calas (known as the Cowherd), Gardy, Jacques Payès, Michel Hercule, Mar, Vène Frié, Malaterre, Beaumont, Pradal (the six last, fortunately for themselves, in a state of contumacy) ; and at Montpellier four others,— Choumac, Vidal, Cadelard, and Pagés. What is the crime of these men? Their crime is yours, if you are a good citizen; it is mine also who write these lines,— it is obedience to Article X. of the Constitution; it is armed resistance to the outrage of Louis Bonaparte. The council " decrees that the execution take place *in the ordinary form* on one of the public squares of Beziers " for the last four, and for the seventeen others " on one of the public squares of Bédarrieux." The " Moniteur " so announces. It is true the " Moniteur " announces at the same time that the last ball of the Tuileries was arranged by three hundred stewards according to the rigorous etiquette prescribed by the ceremonial of the old imperial house! Unless a universal cry of horror arrest this man in time, all these heads shall fall.

At the very hour we are writing this, the following incident has just occurred at Belley: —

A workman named Charlet, from Bugez, near Belley, ardently supported the candidature of Louis Bonaparte on the 10th of December, 1848. He distributed voting papers, hawked pamphlets, propagated his opinions, and supported his favourite in every way. The election was for him a triumph; he placed his hopes in Louis Napoleon and took quite seriously the socialist writings of the man of Ham and his " humanitarian " and republican programmes. There were on the 10th of December many such honest dupes; to-day they are the most indignant of men. When Louis Bonaparte was in power, when they saw the man at his work, their illusions vanished. Charlet, being a man of intelligence, was one of those whose republican probity rose in revolt; and gradually, as Louis Bonaparte sank lower in presence of the reaction, Charlet separated from him; he thus passed from the most trustful adhesion to the most loyal and vehement opposition. It is the history of many other noble hearts.

On the 2d of December Charlet did not hesitate. Brought face to face with that infamous act of Louis Bonaparte in which all the other outrages met, Charlet felt the law stir within him; he told himself it was his duty to be so much the more severe as he was one of those whose confidence had been most betrayed. He clearly understood that there was now but

one duty for the citizen,— an imperative duty, and one insep-
arable from right,— to defend the Republic, to defend the
Constitution, and to resist by all means the man whom the
Left, and his own crime still more than the Left, had just out-
lawed.   The refugees in Switzerland passed the frontier in
arms, crossed the Rhone near Anglefort, and entered into the
department of the Ain.   Charlet joined them.   At Seyssel the
little band met the custom-house officers.   The custom-house
officers, voluntary or misled accomplices of the *coup d'état*,
opposed their passage.   An engagement resulted; an officer
was slain, and Charlet was taken prisoner.

The *coup d'état* brought Charlet before a council of war.
He was charged with the death of the officer, which after all
was but an incident of the fight.   In any case, Charlet was a
stranger to this death.   The custom-house officer fell pierced
by a ball, and Charlet's sole weapon was a sharpened file.
Charlet refused to acknowledge the competency of the group
of men who pretended to try him.   He said to them: " You are
not judges; where is the law?   It is on my side."   He refused
to answer.   They questioned him on the circumstances attend-
ant on the officer's death.   With a word he could have cleared
up the whole matter.   But to condescend to an explanation
would have been in a certain measure to accept this tribunal.
He would not do so; he kept silence.   These men condemned
him to death " according to the ordinary forms of criminal
executions."

After the sentence was announced, he appeared to be forgotten; days, weeks, months, glided past.   Everybody connected with the prison said to Charlet: " You are saved."   On
the 29th of June, at break of day, the town of Belley saw a
doleful thing.   The scaffold had sprung up from the earth
during the night, and rose in the midst of the public square.
The inhabitants approached one another with pallid faces, and
the question ran from lip to lip,—

" Have you seen what is in the square? "

" Yes."

" For whom? "

It was for Charlet.

The sentence of death had been reported to Monsieur Bonaparte; it had long slept in the Elysée. People there had other things to think of; but one fine morning, after seven months, when no one was thinking either of the engagement of Seyssel, or of the killed officer, or of Charlet, Monsieur Bonaparte, having need probably of putting something between the *fête* of the 10th of May and the *fête* of the 15th of August, signed the order of execution.

On the 29th of June, then, hardly a few days ago, Charlet was drawn from his prison. He was told he was going to die. He continued calm. A man who is at one with justice does not fear death, for he feels that in him are two things,— the body which may be killed, and justice, whose arms are not bound and whose head does not fall under the knife. They wished to persuade Charlet to ride in the cart. " No," he said to the gendarmes, " I will go on foot; I can walk. I am not afraid." There was a great crowd on his passage. Everybody in the town knew him and loved him; his friends sought his eyes. Charlet, with his arms tied behind his back, saluted those on his right and left by a movement of the head. " Adieu, Jacques! adieu, Pierre! " he would say with a smile. " Adieu, Charlet! " they answered, and all wept. The gendarmerie and soldiers of the Line surrounded the scaffold. He mounted it with a slow and firm step. When the crowd saw him standing on the scaffold, there was a protracted groan; the women uttered cries, the men clinched their fists. When they were tying him on the plank he looked up at the knife and said, " When I think I have been a Bonapartist! " then raising his eyes to heaven, he cried, " Vive la République! " A moment afterwards his head fell.

There was mourning in Belley and in all the villages of the Ain. " How did he die? " people asked. " Bravely! " " God be praised! "

It is in this fashion that a man has just been slain. Thought gives way and plunges into horror in presence of so monstrous a deed. This crime added to the other crimes completes them and seals them with a sort of sinister seal. It is more than the complement, it is the crowning. We feel that now Monsieur Bonaparte must be content. To shoot during the night, in darkness, in solitude, on the Champ de Mars, under the arches of the bridges, behind a deserted wall, unknown persons, mere shadows; to shoot them at random, with such carelessness that their numbers are not even guessed at; to have persons whose names are buried in oblivion slain by his myrmidons who are equally nameless,— and to have all this go on in the dusk, in mystery and shadow, is on the whole not very satisfactory to one's self-love. The person who does these things in this manner looks as if he were trying to hide, and, in good truth, he does hide. This is a rather commonplace proceeding. Scrupulous people have the right to say to you: " You see well that you are afraid; you would not dare to do those things in public; you recoil before your own actions." To a certain degree these people seem to think soundly. To massacre people in the night is a violation of all laws, human and divine, but it is not sufficiently insolent. The individual accomplishing this does not feel triumphant after it is done. Something better is possible.

The broad daylight, the public square, the legal scaffold, the regular apparatus of society's vengeance on the lawbreaker,— ah, to deliver the innocent to this, to slay them in this manner, is quite another thing! This is what I like to hear about! To commit a murder in full noon in the beautiful centre of the town, by means of a machine called a " tribunal " or " council of war," by means of another machine slowly built by a carpenter, fitted up, jointed, screwed, and greased at your leisure; to say, " It shall be at such an hour; " to bring two baskets, and say, " This will be for the body, and this for the head; " when the hour has come, to lead the victim to the spot, tied with cords and supported by a priest; to proceed to this murder with calmness, see that a proper report is drawn up by a clerk, that gendarmes with naked swords encompass the murder so that the people standing there may shudder and no longer know what they are looking at, and doubt whether these men in uniform are a brigade of gendarmerie or a band of brigands, and ask themselves as they gaze on the man who lets the knife fall, whether he is the executioner and not rather an assassin! — to do all this is truly something that shows boldness and firmness; it is a parody of the legal fact altogether, shameless, and very enticing, and well worth the trouble of being executed; it is a large and splendid slap on the face of justice; it is just the thing!

Then to do this seven months after the struggle, coldly, uselessly, as an omission atoned for, as a duty accomplished, is horrible, is perfect; there is an air of one's being in his right about it that completely disconcerts consciences, and makes honest folk shudder.

There is here a terrible comparison that sums up the whole situation. We have here two men,— a workman and a prince. The prince commits a crime,— he enters the Tuileries; the workman does his duty,— he mounts the scaffold. And who erects the scaffold for the workman? It is the prince.

Yes, this man who if he had been vanquished in December would have escaped the penalty of death only because of the omnipotence of progress and by an extension (most undoubtedly too generous in this case) of the principle of the inviolability of human life,— this man, this Louis Bonaparte, this prince who carries the methods of the Poulmanns and Soufflards into politics,— it is this man who rebuilds the scaffold! And he does not tremble! he does not grow pale! he does not feel that it is a fatal ladder,— that you may raise it up, but that once risen you are no longer at liberty to throw it down, and that he who erects it for others finds later that he has erected it for himself: it recognizes him and says, " Thou hast placed me here; I have waited for thee." No, this man does not reason; he has needs, caprices, and they must be gratified; he has the hankerings of the dictator. Omnipotence would be insipid if it could not be seasoned in this fashion. " Well, then, cut me off the head of Charlet and the heads of others! " Monsieur Bonaparte is Prince President of the French Republic; Monsieur Bonaparte has sixteen millions a year, (forty-four thousand francs a day), twenty-four cooks for his personal service, and as many *aides-de-camp;* he has his hunting and fishing rights over the forests of Laigne, Ours-camp, and Carlemont; the ponds of Saclay and Saint-Quentin, and the woods of Champagne and Barbeau; he has the Tuileries, the Louvre, the Elysée, Rambouillet, Saint-Cloud, Versailles, Compiègne; he has his imperial box at all the plays, *fête* and banquet and music every day; he has the smile of M. Sibour and the arm of Mylady the Marchioness of Douglas to enter the ball-room. All this, however, did not content him; the guillotine was a further necessity for him. Among his baskets of champagne he desired to find some of those red baskets as well.

Oh, let us hide our faces with both our hands! This man, this hideous butcher of right and justice, had still the leather apron over his belly, had his hands in the smoking bowels of the Constitution and his feet in the blood of all the slaughtered laws, when you, judges, magistrates, men of law, men of right — But I stop here; I shall find you later on, with your black robes and your red robes, your robes the colour of ink and your robes the colour of blood; and I shall find also your chiefs, whom I have chastised already and intend still further to chastise,— those juridical bullies of the ambuscade, those prostitutes, Baroche, Suin, Royer, Mongis, Rouher, Troplong,— deserters of the laws; all those names which no longer express aught except the quantity of contempt possible to man!

And if he has not sawed his victims between two planks like Christiern II.; if he has not buried people alive like Ludovico the Moor; if he has not built the walls of his palace with living men and stones like Timur-Beg, who was born, they say, with his hands closed and full of blood; if he has not opened the womb of pregnant women like Cæsar, Duke of Valentinois; if he has not strappadoed women by their breasts, *testibusque viros,* like Ferdinand of Toledo; if he has not broken men alive on the wheel, burned them alive, boiled them

alive, flayed them alive, crucified, empaled, and quartered them,— if he has not done all this, do not blame him, it is not his fault; it is because the age is obstinately opposed to such courses. He has done all that was humanly or inhumanly possible. Given the nineteenth century,— a century of softness, a century of decadence, as say the Absolutists and Papists,— and Louis Bonaparte has equalled his contemporaries Haynau, Radetzky, Filangeri, Schwartzenberg, and Ferdinand of Naples, and has even surpassed them. A rare merit of his is that the scene took place in France, which was for him a difficulty the more. Let us do him this justice: in the time in which we live, Ludovico Sforza, the Valentinois, the Duke of Alba, Timur, and Christiern II. would not have done more than Louis Bonaparte; in their age he would have done all they did; in ours, the very moment they attempted to construct and rear their gibbets, their wheels, their wooden horses, their strappado-cranes, their living towers, their crosses and their stakes, they would be stopped as well as he, in spite of themselves and without their knowledge, by the secret and invincible resistance of their moral environment, by the invisible force of progress accomplished, by the formidable and mysterious refusal of a whole century rising north, south, east, and west around tyrants, and saying to them,—
" No! "

CHAPTER III

WHAT 1852 WOULD HAVE BEEN

BUT supposing this 2d of December had not occurred, " necessary " as it was, according to the accomplices and their dupes subsequently, what would have taken place in France? Great heavens! this simply.

Let us go some steps backward and recall briefly the situation as it was before the *coup d'état*. The party of the past,

under the name of order, resisted the Republic,— in other
words, resisted the future.   Oppose it or not, consent to it
or not, leaving all illusion aside, the Republic is the future,
far or near,— the inevitable future of nations.

How shall this Republic be established?   It can be established in two ways,— by strife or by progress.   The democrats would have it by progress; their adversaries, the men of
the past, would seem to wish to have it by strife.

As we have just recalled, the men of the past resist.   They
resist obstinately; they strike the tree with their axes, and
fancy they can arrest the course of the ascending sap.   They
are lavish of their strength, their childishness, and their rage.

Let no bitter word be flung at our old adversaries, fallen
the same day as ourselves, and many fallen with honour, let
us confine ourselves to the statement that the majority of the
Legislative Assembly of France from the first days of its installation, from the month of May, 1849, had entered on this
strife.

This policy of resistance is a fatal policy.   This wrestling
of man with God is necessarily vain; but null as to result, it
is fruitful in catastrophes.   What ought to be shall be, what
ought to flow must flow, what ought to fall must fall, what
ought to be born must be born, what ought to grow must
grow; but place an obstacle in the way of these natural laws,
trouble arises, disorder begins.   And the sad thing is that this
disorder has been called order.

Tie up a vein, you become sick; dam a river, you have an
inundation; bar the future, you have revolutions.   Preserve
with obstinate determination in your midst, as if it were alive,
the part which is dead, and you produce a sort of moral
cholera.   Corruption spreads around; it is in the air,— you
breathe it.   Entire classes of society, functionaries, for example, fall into rottenness.   Keep the dead bodies in your
houses, and a plague will burst forth.

From a kind of fatality this policy blinds those who practise
it.   Those men calling themselves statesmen cannot understand
that they, with their own hands, with great toil and with the

sweat of their brows, have themselves produced those terrible
events which they lament, and that those catastrophes which
overwhelm them have been constructed by them. What would
be said of the peasant who made a weir from one bank to the
other of a river in front of his cabin, and who, when the river,
having become a torrent, casts down his dike, overflows its
banks, and carries away his roof, should say, " Wicked river ! "
The statesmen of the past, those grand constructors of dikes
across currents, spend their time in crying, " Wicked people ! "
Take away Polignac and the ordinances of July,— that is to
say, the dike,— and Charles X. would have died in the Tuileries. Reform the electoral law in 1847,— that is to say again,
take away the dike,— and Louis Philippe would have died on
the throne.

Do I mean to say that the Republic would not have come?
No. The Republic, we repeat, is the future. It would have
come, but step by step, progress by progress, conquest by conquest,— as a river that flows, and not as a deluge that dev-
astates; it would have come at its hour, when everything had
been made ready to receive it; it would have come, not certainly with more vitality, for now it is indestructible, but with
more tranquillity, without a possible reaction, without princes
waylaying it, without a *coup d'état* behind it.

The policy of resistance to the movement of humanity ex-
cels — let us insist on this point — in creating artificial cata-
clysms. Thus it succeeded in making of the year 1852 a
formidable eventuality, and this always by the same method,—
by means of a dike. A train is going to pass over yonder
railway in an hour: throw a beam across the rails; when the
train reaches that point it will be crushed to pieces; you will
have Fampoux. Take away the beam before the arrival of
the train: the travellers are carried through without even suspecting that there was any danger there. This beam is the
law of the 31st of May. The leaders of the majority of the
Assembly had flung it across 1852, crying, " It is there ! society will be crushed ! " The Left said to them: " Take away
the beam ! take away the beam ! let universal suffrage pass

over freely!" This is the whole history of the law of the 31st of May. There are things which a child might understand, and which the "statesmen" do not understand.

Now to answer the question we proposed a moment ago: "But for the 2d of December, what would have taken place in 1852?" Suppress the law of the 31st of May; take from the people its dike; take from Bonaparte his lever, his arm, his pretext; let universal suffrage alone; take the beam from the rails,— do you know what would have happened in 1852?

Nothing. Some elections. A few calm Sundays on which the people would have come to vote; yesterday toilers, to-day electors, to-morrow toilers, always sovereign.

But the retort comes: "Yes, elections! You speak of them at your ease. But what about the 'Red Chamber' that would spring out of these elections?" Was it not proclaimed that the constituant of 1848 would be a "Red Chamber"? Red Chambers, red ogres,— all these predictions have their value. Those who parade these fantastic apparitions before the sacred inhabitants of the rural districts know perfectly what they are doing, and laugh behind the horrible rag they wave. Under the long scarlet robe of the phantom to which the name "1852" has been given, it is easy to recognize the heavy boots of the *coup d'état*.

CHAPTER IV

THE JACQUERIE

HOWEVER, after the 2d of December,— the crime being finished and done with,— it became necessary that public opinion should be put on the wrong scent. The *coup d'état* at once set about crying, "Stop the Jacquerie!" like the assassin who cried, "Stop thief!"

Let us add that a *Jacquerie* had been promised, and Monsieur Bonaparte could not, without some inconvenience, fail in all his promises at the same time. What was the " red spectre " if not the *Jacquerie?* Some reality must be given to this spectre. It was absolutely necessary. You cannot abruptly break out into a roar of laughter in presence of the whole people and say, " There was nothing the matter! I have the whole time been making you afraid of yourselves."

There has, then, been a *Jacquerie.* The promises of the proclamation have been kept. The set around Louis Bonaparte gave their imaginations full scope; the terrors of the nursery were exhumed, and more than one child on reading a newspaper must have been able to recognize the ogre of our worthy old friend Perrault disguised as a socialist. Implications and inventions became the order of the day. As the press was done away with, the thing became very simple: to lie is easy when you have previously torn out the tongue of the person lied to. The cry was: " Look out, *bourgeois!* Had it not been for us, you would have been ruined. We mowed you down with grape-shot, but it was for your good. Consider, the Lollards were at your gates, the Anabaptists were scaling your walls, the Hussites were knocking against your Venetian blinds, the lean ones were climbing your stairs, the empty bellies had an eye to your dinner. Look out! Have not Mesdames your wives been a trifle violated by them? "

One of the chief editors of " La Patrie " (his name is Froissard) has been given leave to write up the subject:

" I would not dare to write or relate the horrible and unseemly acts they did to the ladies. But among the other licentious and villainous deeds, they killed a knight and put him on a spit, and turned him before the fire and roasted him before his lady and children. After ten or twelve had forced and violated the lady, they tried to make her and the children eat of the knight by force; and then they killed them, and made them die a miserable death.

" These wicked people robbed and burned everything, and killed and forced and violated all dames and maids without pity and without mercy, like mad dogs.

" In like manner people of the same class maintained themselves between Paris and Noyon, and between Paris and Soissons, and Ham and

Vermandois, throughout the entire land of Coucy. The great violators and malefactors were there; but in the county of Valois, in the bishoprics of Laon, of Soisson, and of Noyon, more than a hundred castles and good houses of knights and squires were destroyed: and they killed and robbed whatever they found. But God by his grace brought such remedy to this that much ought we to thank him therefor."

Monseigneur the Prince President has only taken the place of God. It was the least that could be expected.

To-day, after eight months have passed, we know the real meaning of this *Jacquerie;* the facts have at last become clear. Where? How? Before the tribunals of Monsieur Bonaparte himself. The sub-prefects whose wives had been violated had never been married; the curés who had been roasted alive and whose hearts had been eaten by the *Jacques* have written that they are in very fair health; the gendarmes around whose dead bodies they danced came afterward to give their evidence before the councils of war; the public money-boxes which were pillaged have since been found in the hands of Monsieur Bonaparte, who has " saved " them; the famous deficit of five thousand francs at Clamecy has been reduced to two hundred francs expended for loaves of bread. An official publication said on the 8th of December: " The curé, the mayor, and the sub-prefect of Joigny and several gendarmes have been massacred in a cowardly manner." Some one has answered this in a letter given to the public: " Not a drop of blood was shed in Joigny; the life of nobody was threatened." Who is the author of this letter? This same mayor of Joigny *massacred in a cowardly manner!* M. Henri de Lacratelle, from whom an armed band extorted two thousand francs in his château of Cormantin, is astounded up to the present hour, not at the extortion but at the invention. M. de Lamartine, whom another band wished to sack and probably treat *à la lanterne,* and whose château of Saint-Point was burned down, and who had written to demand the protection of the " government," learned of the thing through the journals.

·The following paper was produced before the council of war of the Nièvre, presided over by ex-Colonel Martimprey: —

ORDER OF THE COMMITTEE.

Probity is the virtue of republicans.
Every robber and plunderer shall be shot.
Every withholder of arms, who in twelve hours does not deposit them at the mayoralty, or who does not return them, shall be arrested and detained until further orders.
Every drunken citizen shall be disarmed and imprisoned.
Long live the Social Republic.

THE SOCIAL REVOLUTIONARY COMMITTEE.
CLAMECY, 7th of December, 1851.

What we have just been reading is the proclamation of the *Jacques.* " Death to pillagers! Death to thieves! " such is the cry of these pillagers and thieves. One of these *Jacques* named Gustave Verdun-Lagarde, of Lot-et-Garonne, died in exile at Brussels on the 1st of May, 1852, leaving a hundred thousand francs to his native town to found a school of agriculture. This communistic " sharer " (*partageux*) has shared indeed!

There has not been, then, a *Jacquerie;* and the honest sharpers of the *coup d'état* are the first to acknowledge this among themselves, with an amiable enjoyment of the fact. Yes, it is true there was no *Jacquerie;* but it served their turn.

There was in the departments what there was in Paris,— a legal resistance; the resistance prescribed for citizens by Article 110 of the Constitution, and by that which is above the Constitution, by natural right. There has been legitimate defence (this time the word is in its proper place) against the " saviours; " there has been the struggle of men armed by the law and by the right against the infamous insurrection of power. The Republic, surprised by an ambuscade, and the *coup d'état* have collared each other. That is the whole. Twenty-seven departments arose. The Ain, the Aude, the Cher, the Bouches-du-Rhone, the Côte d'Or, the Upper Garonne, the Lot-et-Garonne, the Loiret, the Marne, the Meurthe, the Nord, the Lower Rhine, the Rhone, and Seine-et-Marne have nobly done their duty; the Lower Alps, the Aveyron, the Drôme, the Gard, the Gers, the Hérault, the Jura, the Nièvre, the Puy-de-Drôme, the Saône-et-Loire, the

Var, and the Vaucluse have acted fearlessly. They succumbed as well as in Paris. The *coup d'état* was as ferocious there as it was at Paris. We have just cast a summary glance over these crimes.

It was this resistance, at once legal, constitutional, and virtuous,— this resistance in which all the heroism was on the side of the citizens, and all the atrocity on the side of power, — it was this resistance which the *coup d'état* has called the *Jacquerie.* But let us repeat, a little of the " red spectre " was useful. This *Jacquerie* had two ends; it served in two ways the policy of the Elysée; it offered a double advantage. On one side it forced an affirmative vote on the question of the plebiscite; to force a vote under the sabre and in face of the spectre; to suppress the intelligent, to frighten the credulous; terror for one, fear for the other, as we shall explain later on,— all the success and all the secret of the vote of the 2d of December lie in this. The other end was to give a pretext for proscriptions. 1852 did not, then, contain in itself any real danger. The law of the 31st of May, killed morally, was dead before the 2d of December. A new Assembly, a new President, the Constitution purely and simply put in practice, and some elections,— nothing more. Take away Monsieur Bonaparte, and you had 1852. But it was necessary for Monsieur Bonaparte to go; that was the difficulty, and from that came the catastrophe.

And so one fine morning this man took the Constitution, the Republic, the law, in France by the throat; he gave the future an assassin-stab in the back; he trampled under his feet right, common-sense, justice, reason, and liberty; he arrested men who were inviolable, he sequestrated men who were innocent, he banished men who were illustrious; he seized the people in the person of its Representatives; he raked the boulevards of Paris; he made his cavalry plunge about in the blood of old men and women; he shot down *sans sommation*, he fusiladed without sentence; he filled Mazas, the Conciergerie, Sainte-Pélagie, Vincennes, the forts, the cells, the casemates, and the dungeons with prisoners and the graveyards with corpses; he put in Saint-Lazare the woman who brought bread to her concealed husband, and sent to the galleys for twenty years the man who gave shelter to an outlaw; he tore all codes and violated all mandates; he caused thousands of the deported to rot in the horrible holds of the prison ships; he sent to Lambessa and Cayenne a hundred and fifty children from twelve to fifteen years old. He, who was more grotesque than Falstaff, has become more terrible than Richard III.; and all this for what? Because, as he says, " there was a plot against his power; " because the year that was closing had a traitorous understanding with the year that was opening, for his overthrow; because Article 45 had a perfidious arrangement with the calendar to thrust him out; because the second Sunday of May would " depose " him; because his oath had the audacity to plot his downfall; because his word of honour conspired against him! The day after his triumph he is reported to have said: " The second Sunday of May is dead." No! it is probity that is dead, it is honour that is dead, it is the name of the Emperor that is dead!

How the man who lies in Saint-Jérôme Chapelle must start, and what despair must be his! For now unpopularity mounts around that great figure, and it is this fatal nephew who has placed the ladder! And now the great memories are all effaced and all the evil ones return. Men dare speak no longer of Jena, of Marengo, of Wagram. Of what do they speak? Of the Duc d'Enghien, of Jaffa, of the 18th Brumaire. The hero is forgotten, and only the despot is visible. Caricature is already beginning to take liberties with the profile of Cæsar. And then what a personage beside him! There are already people who confound the uncle with the nephew, to the joy of the Elysée and the shame of France. The counterfeit passes as the head of the family. Alas! This immense stain could alone sully that immense splendour! Yes, worse than Hudson Lowe! Hudson Lowe was but a jailer; Hudson Lowe was but an executioner. The man who really assassinates Napoleon is Louis Bonaparte. Lowe killed his life; Louis Bonaparte kills his glory.

Ah, the wretch! he takes everything, uses everything, soils and dishonours everything. He selects for his ambuscade the very month, the very day, of Austerlitz. He returns from Satory as if he was returning from Aboukir. He draws out from the 2d of December some bird of night and perches it on the banner of France and says, "Soldiers, behold the eagle!" He borrows from Napoleon his hat, and from Murat his plume. He has his imperial etiquette, his chamberlains, his *aides-de-camp*, his courtiers. Under the empire they were kings; under him they are lackeys. He too has his own policy, his own 13th Vendémiaire, his own 18th Brumaire. He draws a parallel between himself and his uncle. At the Elysée Napoleon the Great has vanished. They say: "Napoleon the uncle? The Man of Destiny is a by-gone Geronte. The perfect one is not the first, but the last. It is evident the first came only to make the bed of the second." Louis Bonaparte, surrounded with valets and prostitutes, fits to the needs of his table and his bed the coronation and anointing, the Legion of Honour, the Boulogne Camp, the Vendôme Column, Lodi, Arcola, Saint-Jean d'Acre, Eylau, Friedland, Champaubert. Ah, Frenchmen! gaze on that hog, covered with mud, rolling on the lion's skin!

BOOK V

PARLIAMENTARISM

CHAPTER I

1789

ONE day sixty-three years ago, the French people, owned by one family for eight hundred years; oppressed by the barons up to Louis XI., and by the parliaments since Louis XI.,— that is to say, to use the sincere expression of a great lord of the eighteenth century, " eaten up first by the wolves, and then by the lice; " penned up in provinces, in castilanies, in bailiwicks, in seneschal jurisdictions; exploited, squeezed, overtasked, overtaxed, flayed, shaved, misused, abused at mercy; fined indefinitely for the good pleasure of its masters; governed, led, driven, overdriven, dragged, tortured; scourged, and branded with a hot iron for an oath; sent to the galleys for a rabbit killed on the king's lands; hanged for stealing five sous; furnishing its millions to Versailles and its skeleton to Montfaucon; loaded down by prohibitions, by ordinances; patents, letters-royal, fiscal edicts, rural edicts, laws, codes, and customs; crushed by gabelles, aids, quit-rents, mortmains, dues, acsises,[1] excises, tithes, tolls, corvées, and bankruptcies; beaten with a stick which was called a sceptre; sweating, suffering, moaning, marching always; crowned indeed, but on its knees; a beast of burden rather than a nation, — this French people on a sudden raised its head, determined

[1] Taxes on necessaries.

to become human, and set about asking an account from the monarchy, an account from Providence, and liquidating its eight centuries of misery.

It was a great effort.

CHAPTER II

MIRABEAU

A VAST hall was chosen, and benches were placed around it; then some planks were taken, and with these planks a sort of platform was erected in the centre of this hall.   When the platform was finished all that at that time was styled the nation,— namely the clergy in their red and violet soutanes, the *noblesse* adorned with their white plumes, with swords at their sides, and the *bourgeoisie* clad in black,— came and sat down on the benches.   Hardly were all seated when an extraordinary figure was seen to mount the platform and draw himself up thereon.

" Who is that monster? " said some.

" Who is that giant? " said others.

This was a singular being, unexpected and unknown, abruptly risen from the darkness, at once frightful and fascinating; a hideous malady made his head seem somewhat like a tiger's; all kinds of ugliness appeared to have been branded on this face, which was also marked by all kinds of vices. Like the *bourgeoisie*, he was clad in black; that is to say, in mourning.   His tawny eye threw its dazzling flashes over the Assembly, with a semblance of reproach and of menace; all observed him with a sort of curiosity mingled with horror. He raised his hand,— there was silence.

Then from that distorted face came sublime words.   It was the voice of the new world speaking through the mouth of the old.   It was '89 standing erect, and questioning, accusing, and denouncing to God and men the fatal dates of the monarchy. It was the past, an august spectacle,— the past bruised by chains, branded on the shoulder, a slave of old, a felon of old; the unhappy past calling with loud cries on the future, the liberating future. Such was this unknown, and this was what he did on that platform. At his words, which at moments became the roar of the thunder, prejudices, fictions, abuses, superstitions, errors, intolerance, ignorance, infamous fiscalities, barbarous penalties, decaying authorities, worm-eaten magistracies, rotten laws,— all that which was destined to perish felt a trembling, and that the crumbling of these things had begun. This formidable apparition has left a name in the memory of men. He should have been called the Revolution; he is called MIRABEAU.

CHAPTER III

THE TRIBUNE

ON the day when that man set his foot on that platform, the platform was transfigured; the French tribune was founded.

The French tribune! A book were needed to tell all that word contains. The French tribune!— it has been for sixty years the open mouth of the human mind,— of the human mind saying all, blending and combining all, fructifying all; the good and the evil, the true and the false, the just and the unjust, the high and the low, the horrible and the beautiful, dream and reality; passion, reason, love, hatred, matter, the ideal. But its sublime and eternal task is that it makes right, or order, to draw day from it, chaos to draw life from it, the Revolution to draw the Republic from it.

What has passed on that tribune, what it has seen, what it has done, what tempests have assailed it, what events it has begotten, what men have shaken it with their clamours, what men have consecrated it by their words, is it possible .to re-count?   After Mirabeau were Vergniaud, Camille Desmoulins, Saint-Just, that austre young man; Danton, that gigantic tribune; Robespierre, that incarnation of the immense and ter-rible year.   There were heard those fierce interruptions: " Ah, indeed! so you will cut off my words to-day? " exclaimed an orator of the Convention.   " Ay," answered a voice, " and your neck to-morrow! "   And those superb apostrophes: " Minister of Justice," said General Foy to an unjust keeper of the seals, " I condemn you on leaving this enclosure to gaze on the statue of L'Hôpital! "   There, as we lately remarked, all was defended,— the bad causes as well as the good; the good only have been won finally.   There, in presence of re-sistances, of denials, of obstacles, those who wished the future as well as those who wished the past lost patience; there it be-fell truth to become violent, and falsehood to become furious; there all extremes surged.   On this tribune the guillotine had its orator,— Marat; and the Inquisition also,— Montalembert. Terrorism in the name of public safety, terrorism in the name of Rome,— poison in these two mouths, anguish in the audi-tory.   When one spoke, you thought you saw the gliding of the knife; when the other spoke, you thought you heard the crackling of the fagots.   There all parties combated,— all with fury, some with glory.   There the royal power violated popular right in the person of Manuel, who became august for history in virtue of this violation.   There appeared, dis-daining the past which yet they served, two melancholy old men,— Royer-Collard, lofty honesty; Châteaubriand, intense genius.   There Thiers (adroitness) wrestled with Guizot (strength).   There men intermingled, came into collision, fought one another, brandished evidence as if it were a sword. There, for more than a quarter of a century, all hatreds, rages, egotisms, impostures, and superstitions howled and hissed and barked and reared and writhed, always shouting the same calumnies, always showing the same clinched fist, spitting since Christ the same saliva, whirling like a tempest cloud around thy face serene, O Truth!

CHAPTER IV

THE ORATORS

ALL this was living, ardent, fruitful, tumultuous, and
great. And when every question had been pleaded, de-
bated, scrutinized, explored, sounded, defended, and attacked,
what issued from the chaos? Ever some spark of flame.
What issued from the cloud? Always light. All the tempest
could do was to shake the ray and turn it to lightning.
There, on that tribune, all questions were proposed, analyzed,
enlightened and almost always resolved,— questions of credit,
questions of labour, questions of circulation, questions of
wages, questions of State, questions of territory, questions
of peace, questions of war. There was pronounced for the
first time that phrase in which was contained an entire new
society,—" The Rights of Man." There was heard ringing
during fifty years the anvil on which the hammers of super-
human forgers forged pure ideas,— ideas, those swords of the
people, those lances of justice, those armours of right. There
all those whose breasts were nurseries of the sacred flame, penetrated on a sudden by sympathetic influences, like live coals
that redden in the wind,— powerful advocates like Ledru-
Rollin and Berryer; great historians, like Guizot; great poets,
like Lamartine,— became immediately and naturally great
orators.

This tribune was a place of strength and virtue. It saw
everything, it inspired everything; and from its strength
and from its virtue emanated, as we would willingly believe,
all devotions, all abnegations, all energies, all intrepid deeds.
As to ourselves, we honour courage everywhere, even in the
ranks of our antagonists. On a certain day the tribune was
enveloped in shadow; it looked as if a chasm was formed
around it. From that shadow a sound like the roar of the
sea burst forth, and suddenly from that livid night a pike ap-

peared, near the marble rim on which the strong hand of Danton was tightly pressed, and on it a severed head. Boissy d'Anglas saluted that head. That day was a day of menace.

But the people do not overthrow the tribune; the tribune belongs to the people, and the people know this. Place a tribune in the centre of the world, and before long in every corner of the earth, the Republic will rise. The tribune shines for the people, and the people are not ignorant that it does so. Sometimes the tribune infuriates the people, who foam with rage, who beat on it with their waves and even cover it, as on the 15th of May, then draw back majestically like the ocean and leave it standing, as the lighthouse. To overthrow tribunes would be madness in the people; but for tyrants it is a profitable task. Once the people rose, irritated and indignant. Some generous error had taken hold of them, some illusion led them astray; they mistook the meaning of a fact, an act, a measure, a law; they had become wrathful; they had lost that superb calm which is the resting-place of force; they flocked to all the public squares with low and menacing murmurs and terrific bounds; they had become a riot, an insurrection, civil war, a revolution perhaps. The tribune was there. A beloved voice arose and said to the people: " Stop, consider, listen, judge!" *Si forte virum quem conspexere, silent,*— this was true in Rome; it is true in Paris. The people became still.

O Tribune! pedestal of strong men! from thee have issued forth eloquence, law, authority, patriotism, devotion, and great thoughts,— those curbs of nations, those muzzles of lions. For sixty years all intellectual natures, every quality of mind, and every species of genius have uttered their thoughts on this the most resounding spot on earth. From the first Constituent Assembly to the last, from the first Legislative Assembly to the last, through the Convention, the Councils, and the Chamber, reckon up the men if you can! It would be an enumeration of Homer. Follow the series. How many figures that contrast, from Danton to Thiers! How many figures that are like, from Barrère to Baroche, from Lafayette to Cavaignac! To the names we have already mentioned,— Mirabeau, Vergniaud, Danton, Saint-Just, Robespierre, Camille Desmoulins, Manuel, Foy, Royer-Collard, Châteaubriand, Thiers, Guizot, Ledru Rollin, Berryer, Lamartine,— add these names also; names belonging to men widely apart and sometimes hostile; scholars, artists, statesmen, warriors, lawyers, democrats, monarchists, liberals, socialists, republicans; all famous, some illustrious, having each his own peculiar halo,— Barnave, Cazalès, Maury, Mounier, Thouret, Chapelier, Pétion, Buzot, Brissot, Sieyès, Condorcet, Chénier, Carnot, Lanjuinais, Pontécoulant, Cambacérès, Talleyrand, Foutanes, Benjamin Constant, Casimir Périer, Chauvelin, Voyer d'Argenson, Lafitte, Dupont (de l'Eure), Camille Jordan, Lainé, Fitz James, Bonald, Villèle, Martignac, Cuvier, Villemain, the two Lameths, the two Davids (the painter in '93, the sculptor in '48), Lamarque, Mauguin, Odillon Barrot, Arago, Garnier-Pagès, Louis Blanc, Marc Dufraisse, Lamennais, Emile de Girardin, Lamoricière, Dufaure, Crémieux, Michel (de Bourges), Jules Favre. What talents, what diversified aptitudes! what services rendered! what a struggle of all realities with all errors! what teeming brains! what an expenditure (and all to the profit of progress) of knowledge, philosophy, passion, conviction, experience, sympathy, eloquence! what a genial warmth spread around! what an immense trail of light! And we do not name all. To use an expression borrowed from ourselves, " We pass over even the best." We have not noticed that valiant legion of young orators which started up among the Left in these last years, — Arnauld (de l'Ariège), Bancel, Chauffour, Pascal Duprat, Esquiros, De Flotte, Farconnet, Victor Hennequin, Madier de Montjau, Morellet, Noël Parfait, Pelletier, Sain, Versigny.

Let us insist on this: Beginning with Mirabeau, there has been in the world, in the fellowship of humanity, in civilization, a culminating point, a central spot, a hearth, a summit. This summit was the French tribune,— that admirable starting-point of the nations marching on, that dazzling pinnacle in peaceful times, that beacon in the obscurity of catastrophes.

From the extremities of the intelligent universe the people fixed their eyes on that height whence the human mind radiated. When some sudden cloud enveloped them they heard from there a great voice, which spoke to them in the shadow,—" Admonet et magna testatur voce per umbras," a voice that suddenly, like that of chanticleer announcing the dawn, like the cry of the eagle calling to the sun, rang out like a clarion of war or a trumpet of doom; and at that sound all those heroic dead nations — Poland, Hungary, Italy — stood erect, terrible, shaking their winding-sheets and seeking swords in their sepulchres! And so, at this voice of France, the glorious sky of the future half opened; the old blinded and frightened despotisms bowed down their heads in the darkness beneath, and mankind saw Liberty appear,— Liberty, the archangel of nations; her feet on the cloud, her brow among the stars, her great wings open in the azure!

CHAPTER V

THE POWER OF SPEECH

THIS tribune was the terror of all tyrannies and of all fanaticisms; it was the hope of all the oppressed under heaven! Whoever planted his foot on this summit felt distinctly the pulsations of the great heart of humanity. There, provided he was a man of good will, his soul swelled within him and radiated beyond him; something universal took hold of him, and filled his spirit as the breath of the breeze fills the sail. As long as he stood on those four planks, he was a stronger and a better man. At that sacred moment he knew he was a living part of the collective life of nations; generous words came to his mouth on behalf of all men; he perceived beyond the Assembly, grouped around his feet, the people, attentive and serious, with finger on lip, listening with all their might; and beyond the people the human race, sad and grave, seated in a circle, and heedful of what they hear.

Such was this grand tribune from whose height a man spoke to the world. From this tribune, ever in ceasless vibration, issued perpetually sonorous surges, immense oscillations of sentiments and ideas which ran from billow to billow and from people to people, to the very limits of the earth, stirring up those thinking waves called souls. Often no one knew why such a law, such an edifice, such an institution was staggering yonder, farther than our frontiers, farther than our seas,— the Papacy beyond the Alps, the throne of the Czar at the extremity of Europe, slavery in America, the penalty of death everywhere. It was because the tribune of France had started. At certain hours a start of this tribune is an earthquake. The tribune of France spoke! all that thinks here below became meditative; the words spoken sank into the darkness, travelled through space, at random, it mattered not where. " It is only wind, it is only noise," said those barren minds whose lifeblood is irony,— and the next day, or three months later, or a year later, something fell or something arose on the surface of the globe. What had caused this? This " noise " that had vanished, this " wind " that had passed. This " wind " this " noise " was the Word,— a sacred force. From the Word of God were all beings created; from the word of man shall spring the fellowship of the nations.

CHAPTER VI

WHAT THE ORATOR IS

ONCE mounted on this tribune, the man there was no longer a man,— he was that mysterious workman seen in the evening twilight marching with great strides along the furrows, and with an imperial gesture launching into space the germs, the seeds, of the future harvest, the riches of the neighbouring summer, bread and life. He goes, comes, returns;

his hand opens and empties, is filled and emptied again.   The gloomy plain stirs; the unknown abyss of creation begins its travail; the suspended dews descend; the bit of wild oat thrills and dreams of the blade of wheat that will succeed it. The sun hidden behind the horizon loves what this man does, and knows its rays will not be lost.   Holy and marvellous work!

The orator is the sower.   He takes from his heart his instincts, his passions, his beliefs, his sufferings, his dreams, his ideas, and throws them in handfuls among men.   Every brain is his furrow.   A word fallen from the tribune always takes root somewhere, and becomes a thing.   You say: " It is nothing, it is a man talking; " and you shrug your shoulders. O short-sighted minds! it is a future germinating; it is a world dawning.

CHAPTER VII

WHAT THE TRIBUNE DID

TWO great problems are suspended over the world: war must disappear, and conquest must continue.   These two necessities of growing civilization would seem to exclude each other.   How satisfy the one without losing the other? What could solve the two problems at once?   What was resolving them?   The tribune.   The tribune is peace, and the tribune is conquest.   As for conquest by the sword, who wants it?   No one.   The nations are the fatherlands of their inhabitants.   Conquest by idea, who wants it?   Every one. The nations are humanity.

Now, two brilliant tribunes were dominating nations,— the English tribune, by doing its own work; the French tribune, by creating ideas.   The French tribune had elaborated since '89 all the principles that form the political Absolute; and it had begun since 1848 to formulate all the principles that

form the social Absolute. Once a principle was drawn from
limbo and born into life, it threw that principle into the world
armed at all points, and said, " Go! " This conquering
principle was opening the campaign, was meeting the custom-
house officers on the frontier and passing in spite of the
watchdogs; was meeting the sentinels at the gates of cities,
and was passing in spite of the countersigns; was taking the
railway train; was mounting the packet-boats; was travers-
ing continents, crossing seas, accosting the travellers on the
highways, sitting at the hearths of families; was gliding
between friend and friend, between brother and brother, between man and woman, between master and slave, between
people and king; and to those who asked, " Who art thou? "
it answered: " I am Truth! " and to those who asked,
" Whence comest thou? " it answered, " I come from France! "
Then he who questioned it stretched forth his hand, and it
was better than a province,— it was an intelligence annexed.
Henceforth between Paris — the metropolis — and this man
isolated in his solitude, and this city lost in the depth of
woods or steppes, and this people bent under the yoke, a current of thought and of love was established. Under the influence of these currents certain nationalities were growing
weak, others were growing strong and rising to their feet.
The savage felt less a savage, the Turk less a Turk, the
Russian less a Russian, the Hungarian more of a Hungarian,
the Italian more of an Italian. Slowly and gradually the
French nation, in the cause of universal progress, was assimi-
lating other nations. Thanks to that admirable French language, composed by Providence with a marvellous balancing
of consonants enough to be pronounced by the peoples of the
north, and vowels enough to be pronounced by the peoples
of the south,— thanks to that language, which is a power
of civilization and humanity, step by step, by the force of its
own radiance, that lofty central tribune of Paris was conquering the nations and making them France. The material frontier of France was as it might be; but there were no
treaties of 1815 for the moral frontier. The moral fron-

tier was falling back unceasingly, and growing wider from day to day; and perhaps before a quarter of a century men would have spoken of the French world as they once did of the Roman world.

This is what the tribune was; this is what it was doing for France. The tribune! that huge water-wheel of ideas, that gigantic apparatus of civilization, perpetually elevating the intellectual level throughout the entire universe, and setting free, in the midst of humanity, an enormous quantity of light!

And this is what Monsieur Bonaparte has suppressed!

CHAPTER VIII

PARLIAMENTARISM

YES, Monsieur Louis Bonaparte has overthrown this tribune. That power created by our great revolutionary childbirths he has broken, mangled, crushed, torn at the point of bayonets, and trodden under the feet of horses. His uncle uttered an aphorism: "The throne is a plank covered with velvet;" he too has uttered his: "The tribune is a plank covered with cloth, on which may be read Liberté, égalité, fraternité." He has flung plank and cloth and liberty, equality and fraternity into the fire of a bivouac. A roar of laughter from his soldiers, a little smoke, and all is over.

Is this true? Is this possible? Has this passed away so? Could such a thing be seen? Good heavens! yes. It is even very simple. To cut off Cicero's head and nail his two hands to the rostrum, all that was required was a brute with a knife, and another brute with nails and hammer.

For France the tribune was three things: a means of exterior initiation; a method of interior government; a glory. Louis Bonaparte has suppressed initiation. France was teaching the nations, and was conquering them through love: what was the use? He has suppressed that mode of government,— his own is superior. He has breathed on the glory, and has extinguished it. Certain breaths have this quality.

Besides, to assault the tribune is a family crime. The first Bonaparte had committed it already; but at least what he brought into France to replace this glory was glory also, not ignominy. Louis Bonaparte has not contented himself with overthrowing the tribune; he has bethought himself of making it ridiculous. This sort of thing is his style. It does not matter so much in one who cannot say two words consecutively, or indulge in a tirade, without a notebook in his hand; who verbally and mentally is a stammerer, and who has his little gibe at Mirabeau! General Ratapoil said to General Foy, " Hold your tongue, babbler! "

" What is this tribune, then? " cries Monsieur Louis Bonaparte; " it is parliamentarism! " What say you to that, " parliamentarism " ? " Oh, parliamentarism pleases me; parliamentarism is a pearl. The Dictionary is enriched indeed! This academician of our *coups d'état* is inventing words. As a matter of fact, there is no use in a person being a barbarian if he does not fling a barbarism round now and then. He too is a " sower; " things like that do germinate in the brains of idiots. The uncle had " the ideologues; " the nephew has " the parliamentarists." Parliamentarism, Messieurs! parliamentarism, Mesdames! That is an answer to everything. But you hazard this timid observation: " It is perhaps a sad thing to have ruined so many families, deported so many families, proscribed so many citizens, filled so many litters, dug so many graves, shed so much blood." " Ha! I see! " returns a coarse voice with a Dutch accent, " you are regretting ' parliamentarism,' then? Get out of this! " Parliamentarism is a godsend. I shall give my vote to Monsieur Bonaparte for the first vacant chair in the Institute! Why so, pray? Why, we must really encourage neology! This man comes forth from the charnel-house, this man comes forth from the Morgue, this man has his

hands reeking with blood like a butcher's, and he scratches
his ears and smiles, and invents vocables like Julie d'An-
gennes. He unites the wit of the Hôtel de Rambouillet with
the odour of Montfaucon. It is fine. We will both vote for
him, shall we not, Monsieur de Montalembert?

<hr />

CHAPTER IX

THE TRIBUNE DESTROYED

THEN " parliamentarism," that is to say, the security of
citizens, the liberty of discussion, the liberty of the
individual, the control of taxation, a clear knowledge of receipts and of expenditures, the safety lock of the public
money-box, the right to know what is done with your money,
the solidity of the public credit, liberty of conscience, liberty
of worship, the support of property, the resource of men
against confiscations and spoliations, the security of each, the
counterpoise of arbitrary power, the dignity of the nation,
the grandeur of France, the rigid morality of free peoples,
the public initiative, movement and life,— is now no more.
All this has been effaced, annihilated; has disappeared! And
this " deliverance " has cost France only some twenty-five millions of francs, divided between twelve or fifteen saviours,
and forty thousand franc's worth of brandy for the brigades! In truth, it is not dear; these gentlemen of the *coup
d'état* have done the thing at a discount.

To-day it is finished, perfected, completed. Grass is growing in the Palais Bourbon. A virgin forest is already sprouting between the Pont de la Concorde and the Place Bourgogne. Through the thickets you can distinguish the box
of a sentry. The Legislative Body pours out its urn among
the reeds and runs to the foot of this sentry-box with a
gentle murmur.

To-day all is over; the great work is accomplished. And what fine results the thing has had! Attend to your own affairs, have a good time, laugh and grow fat; the question for you no longer is to be a great people, to be a powerful people, to be a free nation, to be the luminous centre of the world; France is no longer clear-sighted. This, indeed, is a success! France votes Louis Napoleon, carries Louis Napoleon, fattens Louis Napoleon, contemplates Louis Napoleon, admires Louis Napoleon; and it all stupefies her. The aim of civilization is attained.

To-day there is no more noise or bustle, no more palaver, parliament, or parliamentarism. The Legislative Body — the Senate and the Council of State — are all tongue-tied. No one has any reason to fear that he shall read some fine discourse when he gets out of bed in the morning. It is all up with those who thought, meditated, created, spoke, shone, or beamed among this great people. Be proud, Frenchmen! lift your heads, Frenchmen! You are no longer anything, and this man is everything. He holds in his hands your understanding as a child holds a bird. On whatever day he pleases he will strangle the genius of France. There will then be another noise the less. Meanwhile let us repeat in chorus: " No more parliamentarism! no more tribune! " Instead of all those grand voices that conferred together in order to instruct the world,— one voice being idea; another, fact; another, right; another, justice; another, glory; another, hope; another, science; another, genius, — instead of those voices that educated, charmed, encouraged, consoled, reassured, fertilized,— instead of all those sublime voices, what do we hear in this black night which covers France? The noise of a sounding spur, and a sabre dragging along the pavement.

Alleluia! says M. Sibour. Hosanna! replies M. Parisis.

BOOK VI

THE ABSOLUTION

First Form

THE SEVEN MILLION, FIVE HUNDRED THOUSAND VOTES

CHAPTER I

THE ABSOLUTION

THEY say to us: " Are you not dreaming! All these facts which you call crimes are henceforth ' facts accomplished,' and consequently respectable. All this is accepted, all this is adopted, all this is legitimated, all this is covered, all this is absolved."

" Accepted, adopted, legitimated, covered, absolved! — by what? "

" By a vote."

" What vote? "

" The seven million, five hundred thousand votes."

" Oh, indeed! Yes, there has been a *plebiscite*, and vote, and seven million, five hundred thousand yes's. Let us speak of them."

142

CHAPTER II

THE DILIGENCE

A BRIGAND stops a diligence at the corner of a wood. He is at the head of a determined band. The travellers are more numerous, but they are separated, disunited, penned in compartments, half asleep, surprised in the middle of the night, seized unexpectedly and without arms. The brigand orders them to descend, to utter no cry, to suffer no word to escape their lips, and to lie flat on the ground. Some resist; he blows out their brains. Others obey, and lie on the road dumb, motionless, terrified, jumbled together with the dead, and like the dead themselves. The brigand, while his accomplices have their feet on the backs of the passengers and their pistols at their heads, rummages their pockets, breaks open their trunks and takes all he finds worth his while. The pockets emptied, the trunks pillaged, the *coup d' état* over, he says: —

" Now, in order to make things right with the law, I have written on a paper that you acknowledge that all I have taken belongs to me, and that you surrender it fully and freely. I conclude that this is your opinion. A pen will be placed in your hand, and without saying a word, without making a gesture, without quitting the attitude in which you are [the belly on the ground and the face in the mud], you shall stretch out your right hands and sign this paper. You see the muzzle of my pistol: still you are free."

The travellers stretch out their hands and sign. When this is over the brigand raises his head and says:

" I have seven million, five hundred thousand votes."

CHAPTER III

EXAMINATION OF THE VOTE.   RECALLING PRINCIPLES.
FACTS

MONSIEUR LOUIS BONAPARTE is president of this
diligence.   Let us call attention to certain principles.
That a political ballot be valid three conditions are absolutely necessary: (1) That the vote be free; (2) That the
vote be an enlightened vote; (3) That the figures be genuine.
If one of these conditions be wanting, the balloting is null.
What then if the three conditions are absent at the same
time?   Let us apply these rules.

1. *That the vote be free.*   What the freedom of the vote
on the 20th of December was we have just seen.   We have
given expression to this freedom by a plain and striking representation.   We might dispense ourselves from adding anything further.   Let each one of those who have voted enter
into himself and ask under what moral and material pressure
he deposited his ballot in the box.   We could mention a certain commune of the Yonne where out of five hundred heads
of families four hundred were arrested,— the remainder voting *yes;* a commune of the Loiret where out of six hundred
and thirty-nine heads of families four hundred and ninety-
seven were arrested or expelled,— the hundred and forty-two
who escaped voting *yes.*   And what we say of the Yonne and
Loiret might be said of every one of the departments.   Since
the 2d of December, every city has had its swarm of spies;
every market-town, every village, every hamlet has had its
denouncers.   To vote *no* was prison, exile; was Lambessa.
In the villages of a certain department, we are told by an
ocular witness, " ass-loads of ballots marked *yes* " were
brought to the doors of the mayoralties.   The mayors,
flanked by field-guards, handed them to the peasants, and the
peasants had to vote *yes.*   At Savigny, near Saint-Maur, en-

thusiastic gendarmes declared on the morning of the balloting that he who did not vote would not sleep in his bed that night.   The gendarmerie imprisoned in the jail of Valenciennes M. Parent (*fils*), deputy of the justice of the peace of the canton of Bouchain, for urging the inhabitants of Avesne-le-Sec to vote *no*.   The nephew of Representative Aubry (du Nord), having seen the agents of the prefect distributing ballots marked *yes* in the public square of Lille, went to the same place the next day and distributed ballots marked *no;* he was arrested and locked up in the citadel.   As to the vote of the army, some have voted for a cause they had made their own by their deeds; the rest followed suit.

But let the army speak for itself on the freedom of this vote of the soldiers.   A soldier belonging to the 6th of the Line commanded by Colonel Garderens de Boisse writes as follows : —

" As far as the common soldiers were concerned, the voting was really a roll-call.   The non-commissioned officers, corporals, drummers, and soldiers were mustered into their ranks in presence of the colonel, lieutenant-colonel, major, and officers, and as each man answered 'Present' to the call of the quartermaster, his name was inscribed by the sergeant-major.   The colonel said, rubbing his hands, '*Ma foi,* Messieurs, the thing is getting on capitally!'   While the colonel was speaking, a corporal of the company to which I belonged approached the table where the sergeant-major was, and asked him for his pen in order to inscribe his name himself on the register marked 'No,' which had remained blank.   'What!' cried the colonel, 'you who are to be appointed quartermaster at the first vacancy,— you formally disobey your colonel, and that in presence of your company!   Still, it would not matter so much if what you are now doing was only an act of insubordination; but do you not know, unhappy man, that by your vote you are calling for the destruction of the army, the burning of your father's house, the annihilation of the entire social system?   You are holding out a hand to debauchery!   What! you X ——, whom I intended to promote, you come to-day and say all this to my face?'   As may easily be conjectured, the poor devil allowed himself to be inscribed like all the rest."

Multiply this colonel by six hundred thousand, and you have the pressure exerciesd by functionaries of all classes, military, political, civil, administrative, ecclesiastic, judicial, excise, municipal, educational, commercial, and consular, in every part of France, on soldier, bourgeois, and peasant. Add, as we have already pointed out, the so-called communistic *Jacquerie* and the real Bonapartist terrorism, the government overbearing the weak by its spectres and the reluctant by its absolute authority, and striking terror with both at the same time. A special volume would be needed to relate, expose, and thoroughly examine the innumerable details of this enormous extortion of signatures called the vote of the 20th of December.

The vote of the 20th of December has demolished the honour, the initiative, the intelligence, and the moral life of the nation. France has been, in relation to this vote, like a flock of sheep going to the slaughter-house. Let us pass on.

2. *That the vote be a enlightened vote.* The following is an elementary principle: where there is no liberty of the press, there is no vote. Liberty of the press is the condition *sine qua non* of universal suffrage. A radical nullity of every ballot exists in the absence of the liberty of the press. The liberty of the press draws after it as necessary corollaries the liberty of meeting, the liberty of hawking pamphlets, tracts, etc.,— all the liberties which right, primal and pre-existence, has engendered as agents of enlightenment before a vote is given. Can we imagine a blind pilot at the helm? Can we imagine a judge with his ears stuffed, and his eyes knocked out? Liberty, therefore,— liberty to enlighten one's self by every possible means, by inquiry, by the press, by speech, by discussion,— is the express guarantee, the essential condition of universal suffrage. For a thing to be done validly, it must be done knowingly. Where there is no light there is no validity. These are axioms. Outside these axioms everything is null and void.

Now, let us consider. Has M. Bonaparte in his ballot of the 20th of December obeyed these axioms? Has he fulfilled these conditions of free press, free meetings, free tribune, freedom to post placards and hawk pamphlets, free inquiry? The answer is a roar of laughter even in the Elysée.

So you are yourselves forced to acknowledge the way in which " universal suffrage " has been dealt with!

What! I know nothing of what has taken place. People have been killed, butchered, fusiladed, assassinated, and I am kept in ignorance! Men have been sequestrated, tortured, expelled, exiled, deported, and I have had hardly a glimpse of the outrage! My mayor and curé say to me: " These folk they are leading away tied with cords are ticket-of-leave men!" I am a peasant; I cultivate a bit of land down in one of the provinces; you suppress the newspaper, you stifle revelations, you prevent the truth from reaching me, and you make me vote! Make me vote; how? In the depth of night! groping in the dark! What! you spring abruptly from the shadow with a sabre in your hand, and you say to me, " Vote!" And you call this a ballot! Oh, yes! a ballot " free and spontaneous," say the sheets of the *coup d'état.* Every sort of knavery has been at work in this vote. A village mayor, a sort of sapling Escobar, sprouting in the open field, said to his peasants: " If you vote *yes,* you vote for the Republic; if you vote *no,* you vote against the Republic." The peasants voted *yes.*

And now let us throw a light on another side of this turpitude named " the *plebiscite* of the 20th of December." How has the question been put? Has there been a choice possible? Has the door been opened to every party (and it was the least that might be expected from a man of the *coup d'état* in a ballot so strange as this, where everything was called in question) through which the principle it rested on could find an entrance? Have the Legitimists been allowed to turn towards their exiled prince and the ancient honour of the *fleurs-de-lis?* Have the Orleanists been allowed to turn towards that proscribed family which the services of two soldiers — De Joinville and D'Aumale — ennoble, and that great soul, Madame the Duchess of Orleans, encircles with a halo? Have the people — which are not a party, which are *the people,* that is to say, the sovereign,— have the people been offered a chance to vote for that true

Republic before which every monarchy vanishes as the night before the day; that Republic which is the evident and irresistible future of the civilized world; the Republic without dictatorship; the Republic of concord, science, and liberty; the Republic of universal suffrage, of universal peace, and of universal happiness; the Republic that instructs peoples and liberates nationalities; that Republic which, when all is said and done, " will have," as the author of this book says elsewhere,[1] " France to-morrow, and Europe the day after " ? Has this been offered?   No.

Here is how Monsieur Bonaparte has presented the question: At this ballot there have been two candidates,— first candidate, Monsieur Bonaparte; second candidate, the bottomless pit!   France has had her choice.   Admire the address of the man, and his humility somewhat also!   Monsieur Bonaparte has selected as his rival in this affair, who?   M. de Chambord?   No.   M. de Joinville?   No.   The Republic? Still less.   Monsieur Bonaparte, like those pretty Creoles who use the presence of some hideous Hottentot as a foil to their beauty, has selected as his competitor in this election a phantom, an apparition, a sort of Nuremberg socialism, with teeth and claws and burning coals for eyes; the ogre of Tom Thumb, the vampire of the Porte-Saint-Martin, the hydra of Théramène, the big sea-serpent of the " Constitutionnel," kindly lent by its shareholders for the occasion; the dragon of the Apocalypse, the Tarasque, the Drée, the Gra-ouilli, a scare-crow.   Assisted by some Ruggieri or other, Monsieur Bonaparte has produced on this pasteboard monster certain blood-red effects by means of Bengal fire, and said to the scared voter: " There is nothing possible except this or me.   Choose!   Choose between Beauty and the Beast: the Beast is communism; the Beauty is my dictatorship.   Choose!   There is no middle course!   Society overthrown, your house burned, your granary pillaged, your cow stolen, your wife violated, your field confiscated, your children massacred, your wine drunk by others, yourself

[1] Littérature et Philosophies mêlées.   1830.

eaten alive by that huge, gaping mouth you see there, or
me the emperor! Choose! Me or Croquemitaine!" The
bourgeois, frightened and therefore a child, the peasant, ignorant and therefore a child, have preferred Monsieur Bonaparte to Croquemitaine. Let us say, nevertheless, that out
of ten million of voters it would appear that five hundred
thousand preferred Croquemitaine. After all, Monsieur
Bonaparte had only seven million, five hundred thousand
votes.

In this fashion, then, freely as is seen, knowingly as is
seen, what Monsieur Bonaparte has the goodness to call
universal suffrage has voted. Voted what? A dictatorship,
an autocracy, a slavery, a Republic that is the domain of
a despot, a France that is the domain of a pasha, fetters
on every hand, a seal on every mouth, silence, abasement, and
fear, with the spy as the soul of all! To a man,— to
you! — have been given omnipotence and omniscience!
This man is made the supreme constituent, the legislator, the
alpha of right, the omega of power! It has been decreed
that he is Minos, that he is Numa, that he is Solon, that
he is Lycurgus! In him are incarnated the people, the
nation, the State, and the law! And for ten years! What!
do I, a citizen, vote not only my own self-effacement, my
own forfeiture, my own surrender, but the surrender for
ten years of universal suffrage by the new generations over
which I have no right, over which you the usurper force me
to be a usurper also? For that matter, let us say, in passing, that this would of itself be sufficient to brand this monstrous election as null and void, if every kind of nullity
was not already amalgamated with it, heaped and piled upon
it. What! it is this that you compel me to do! You compel me to vote that all is ended, that there is no longer anything, that the people is a negro! You say to me:
"Whereas thou art sovereign, thou shalt give thyself a master; whereas thou art France, thou shalt become Haiti!"
What abominable derision!

Such is the vote of the 20th of December, that sanction,

as M. de Morny says, that absolution, as Monsieur Bonaparte says.   Truly, in a little time from now,— in a year,
in a month, in a week perhaps,— when all we see at present will have vanished, we shall be somewhat ashamed of
having done, though it were for a minute, to this infamous
semblance of a vote called the ballot of seven million, five
hundred thousand, the honour of even discussing it.   It is
however the only basis, the only prop, the only rampart of
the prodigious power of Monsieur Bonaparte.   This vote is
the excuse of cowards; this vote is the buckler of dishonoured
consciences.   Generals, magistrates, bishops, all kinds of prevarication and complicity shelter their ignominy behind this
oath.   France has spoken, they say, — *vox populi, vox Dei;*
universal suffrage has voted; a ballot covers everything.
That a vote! that a ballot!   Spit on it, and pass by.

3.   *That the figures be genuine.*   I admire these figures,
— 7,500,000.   They must have produced a fine effect
through the fog of the 1st of January, written in letters of
gold three feet long, on the front of Notre Dame.   I admire
these figures.   No one was refusing Monsieur Bonaparte
good measure.   After what he had done on the 2d of December, he had a right to something better than that.   Who
was preventing him from putting it at eight millions, nine
millions, a round number?   As to myself, I have been de-
ceived in my expectations.   I reckoned on unanimity.   *Coup
d'état,* you are modest.

What!   You have done all we have just recalled or related; you have taken an oath, and perjured yourself; you
were the guardian of a constitution, and you have destroyed
it; you were the servant of a republic, and you have betrayed
it; you were the agent of a legislative assembly, and you
have crushed it to pieces; you have made of the military
countersign a poniard to slay military honour; you have
used the flag of France to wipe off mud and shame; you
have handcuffed the generals of Africa; you have made the
representatives of the people ride in prison vans; you have
filled Mazas, Vincennes, Mount Valérien, and Saint-Pélagie

with men whose persons were inviolable; you have shot on
the barricade of the law the legislator clad with that scarf
which is the law's sacred and venerable emblem; you have
given to a colonel we could name a hundred thousand francs
for trampling his duty under his feet, and to each soldier
ten francs a day; you have expended in four days forty
thousand francs' worth of brandy on each brigade; you
have entirely covered the carpet of the Elysée with the gold
of the Bank of France, and have said to your friends,
"Take;" you have killed M. Adde in his home, M. Belval
in his, M. de Couvercelle in his, M. Debaecque in his, M.
Labilte in his, M. Monpelas in his, M. Thirion de Montauban in his, you have massacred on the boulevards and elsewhere, fusiladed we know not where nor whom, committed
a great number of murders of which you have the modesty
to acknowledge only a hundred and ninety-one; what! you
have changed the ditches round the trees of the boulevards
into tanks filled with blood; you have shed the blood of the
child along with the blood of its mother, and mixed with
all this blood the champagne of your gendarmes,— you have
done all these things, you have taken all this trouble, and
when you ask the nation. "Are you content?" you obtain
only 7,500,000 *yeas!* In good truth, you are not repaid.
This is the return for devoting oneself to "saving a society!" O ingratitude of Nations!

In reality, three millions of mouths have answered *no!*
Who was it, then, who said that the savages of the South
Sea used to call the French the *oui-oui?*

Let us speak seriously. For irony grows wearisome when
dealing with such a tragic business as this. People of the
coup d'état, no one believes in your seven million, five hundred thousand votes. Come now, a little fit of frankness
will do no harm. Confess that you know you are all black-
legs; cheating then is natural to you. In your balance-sheet
of the 2d of December you count too many votes,— and not
enough of dead bodies. 7,500,000! What are those figures really, now? Where do they come from? Where do

they start from? What do you wish us to do with them? Seven millions, eight millions, ten millions, what difference does it make! We grant you everything, and we dispute everything with you. You have the seven millions *plus* the five hundred thousand; the sum *plus* the balance,— so you say, Prince; you swear to it. But who proves it? Who counted it? — Baroche. Who examined it? — Rouher. Who checked it? — Pietri. Who added it? — Maupas. Who audited it? — Troplong. Who published it? — Yourself. Which means that baseness has counted, platitude has examined, trickery has checked, falsehood has added, venality has audited, and lying has published. Good! Whereupon Monsieur Bonaparte ascends the Capitol; orders M. Sibour to give thanks to Jupiter; makes the Senate put on a livery of blue and gold, the Legislative Body one of blue and silver, his coachman one of green and gold; lays his hand on his heart, and declares that he is the product of universal suffrage, and that his " legitimacy " has jumped from the ballot-urn.

This urn is a juggler's cup.

CHAPTER IV

WHO REALLY VOTED FOR MONSIEUR BONAPARTE

WE declare, then, purely and simply, that on the 20th of December, 1851, eighteen years after the 2d, M. Bonaparte has rummaged with his hand in the conscience of every individual, and from every individual has stolen his vote. Others filch a pocket-handkerchief; he filches an empire.

Let us however be understood. Do we mean to imply, that no one really voted for Monsieur Bonaparte; that no one voluntarily said *yes*; that no one freely and knowingly

accepted this man? Not at all. Monsieur Bonaparte had
for him the vulgar rabble of functionaries, the twelve hundred thousand parasites on the budget and their connections
and underlings,— the corrupt, the compromised, the crafty,
— and in their train the fools, a no inconsiderable mass.
He had for him the cardinals, the bishops, the canons, the
curés, the vicars, the archdeacons, the deacons, the sub-dea-
cons, the prebendaries, the vestrymen, the sacristans, the
beadles, and the " religious " men so-called. Yes, we have
no difficulty in acknowledging that Monsieur Bonaparte had
for him all those bishops who cross themselves after the fashion of Veuillot and Montalembert, and all those religious men
(a precious race, somewhat antique, but very much increased
and recruited since the terror of the property-owners in
1848) who pray in these terms: " O my God! send up my
Lyons railway shares! Sweet Lord Jesus, let me gain twenty-five per cent on my Rothschild-Naples certificates! Holy
Apostles, sell my wines! Blessed martyrs, double my rents!
Holy Mary, Mother of God, Virgin immaculate, Star of the
Sea, deign to cast a favourable eye on my little business at
the corner of Rue Tirechappe and Rue Quincampoix! Tour
of Ivory, grant that the shop opposite me turn out ill! "

All these have really and incontestably voted for Monsieur
Bonaparte: first category, the functionary; second category,
the fool; third category, the religious voltairian-proprietor-
manufacturer.

Let us say at once that in the human intellect — and the
bourgeois intellect in particular — there are some singular
enigmas. We know this, and have no desire to conceal it,
that from the shopkeeper to the banker, from the petty
trader to the stock-broker, a good number of men engaged
in commerce and manufactures in France,— that is to say,
a good number of those men who know the meaning of a
well-placed confidence, of a deposit faithfully guarded, of a
key put into safe hands,— have voted, after the 2d of December, for Monsieur Bonaparte. If you had happened to
meet one of these men of trade, you might very likely have

exchanged with him some such dialogue as the following: —
" Have you voted for Louis Bonaparte to be President of
the Republic? "
" Yes."
" Would you take him for your cashier? "
" No, certainly not! "

CHAPTER V

A CONCESSION

AND that is the ballot! We must repeat this, we must
insist on this, we must not grow weary. " I cry out
a hundred times the same things," says Isaias, " that they
may be heard once." That is the ballot, that is the vote,
that is the sovereign decree of " universal suffrage," which
gives the shelter of a shadow, which gives a title of authority and a diploma of government to those men who hold
France to-day; who command, administer, judge, reign, with
their hands in gold up to the elbows, and their feet in blood
up to the knees!

Now, to have done with the thing let us make a concession
to Monsieur Bonaparte. Let there be no more cavilling.
His ballot of the 20th of December was free, was enlightened; all the newspapers printed what they pleased. Who
have said the contrary? Calumniators only. Electoral meetings were opened; the walls disappeared under their placards;
the pedestrians of Paris swept with their feet a regular snow,
on the boulevards and on the streets, of white ballots and blue
ballots, yellow ballots and red ballots; all who wished spoke,
all who wished wrote; the figures were genuine; it was not
Baroche who counted; it was Barême; Louis Blanc, Guinard,
Felix Pyat, Raspail, Caussidière, Thoré, Ledru Rollin, Etienne Arago, Albert, Barbès, Blanqui, and Gent have been the

examiners; they too were the very persons who published the seven million five hundred thousand votes. We grant all this; we yield all this. And then? What conclusion does the *coup d'état* draw from it?

What conclusion does it draw from it? It rubs its hands. It does not ask better; this is enough. It concludes that all is well, that all is finished, that all is ended, that there is nothing more to say, that it is " absolved."

Stop right there! In regard to the free vote, the genuine figures form but the material side of the question; there remains the moral side. " Oh, there is, then, a moral side? " Why yes, Prince! It is this side that is precisely the true side, the grand side of this question of the 2d of December. Let us examine it.

CHAPTER VI

THE MORAL SIDE OF THE QUESTION

IT is first necessary, Monsieur Bonaparte, that you should get a little information as to what the human conscience really is. There are two things in this world — learn this novel fact — which are called good and evil. This will be a revelation to you; but it is necessary for you to know it. To lie is not good, to betray is bad, to assassinate is worse. It does not matter whether this thing is useful or not, it is forbidden. " By whom? " you will say to me. We shall explain it to you further on; but to continue. Man — again learn this singular circumstance — is a thinking being, free in this world, responsible in the next. A strange thing,— and which must surprise you surely,— he was not made solely for enjoyment, solely in order to satisfy all his fancies, to set all his appetites in motion at random, to crush whatever is before him when he walks, be it blade of grass or sworn oath, to devour whatever comes in his way when he is hungry. Life is not his prey. For example: in order to pass from nothing a year to twelve hundred thousand francs a year, he is not permitted to take an oath which he has no intention of keeping; and in order to pass from twelve hundred thousand francs a year to twelve millions, he is not permitted to break the laws and Constitution of his country, to rush from an ambuscade on a sovereign Assembly, to slaughter Parisians, to deport ten thousand persons, and to proscribe forty thousand more. I must continue my task of enabling you to dive into this strange mystery. Most undoubtedly it is agreeable to have a man's lackeys wear white-silk stockings; but in order to arrive at this grand result he is not permitted to suppress the glory and thought of a people, to overturn the central tribune of the civilized world, to impede the progress of the human race, and to shed oceans of blood. This is forbidden. " By whom? " you will repeat,— you who do not see before you a single person who forbids you anything. Patience. You shall know immediately.

What! here you are disgusted, and I understand it. When a man has on one side his interest, his ambition, his fortune, his pleasures, a fine palace to retain possession of in the Faubourg Saint Honoré, and on the other the jeremiads and squalling of a lot of women who have lost their sons; of families who have lost their fathers; of children who have no longer bread; of a people whose liberties have been confiscated; of a society from under which its support, the laws, has been torn away,— what! when all this squalling is on one side and interest on the other, that he should not be permitted to disdain this hurlyburly, to let all these people " vociferate " away, to march over every obstacle, and go quite naturally in the direction where he sees his fortune, his pleasure, and his fine palace in the Faubourg Saint Honoré,— this is going a little too far. What! he would have to trouble his head about something that occurred three or four years ago, no one knows any longer when or where,— about a day of December, when it was very cold and rained, and it became necessary for him to leave his room in a certain inn, in order to procure

a better lodging; and so he pronounced, with reference to
something or other, no one any longer knows what, in a hall
very badly lit, before eight or nine hundred imbeciles who
believed him, these eight letters, " Je le jure! " What! when
a man is contemplating " a great act," must he pass his time
asking himself what will be the result of it; bother himself as
to whether so and so will rot in prison ships, or die of hunger
in Cayenne, or be bayoneted here, or foolish enough to get
himself killed there? Must he be disturbed because some are
exiled and others ruined, and because those who are shot and
massacred, who rot in hulks and starve in Africa, happen to
be honest men who have done their duty? It would be a nice
state of affairs if all this was to be an obstacle in his path.
Why, imagine it! you have certain appetites; you have no
money, you are a prince; chance has placed power in your
hands, you use it; you authorize lotteries, you have gold ingots exposed in the Jouffroy thoroughfare; the pocket of
every one is accessible, and you draw out whatever you can;
you share with friends, with devoted companions to whom you
owe gratitude; and to fancy that when the public is indiscreet
enough to interfere, when that infamous thing, liberty of the
press, would meddle with the matter, and the law imagines it
has something to do with it,— that then you should quit the
Elysée, abandon power, and, like an idiot, take your seat
between two gendarmes on a bench of the Sixth Chamber!
Nonsense! Is it not a simpler course to sit on the throne of
the Emperor? Is it not a simpler course to crush the liberty
of the press? Is it not a simpler course to crush justice? Is
it not a shorter course to put the judges under your feet?
They ask no better; indeed, they are all ready!

And this is not permitted? And this is forbidden? Yes,
Monseigneur, this is forbidden. " Who does not permit it?
Who forbids it? " Monsieur Bonaparte, a man may be the
master; he may have eight million votes for his crimes and
twelve million francs for his amusements; he may have a senate and M. Sibour in it; he may have armies, cannon, fort-
resses, Troplongs lying flat on their bellies, Baroches creeping

on all fours; he may be a despot, he may be all-powerful: but one who is shrouded in obscurity, who is a stranger to you, rises up before you and says, " Thou shalt not do this thing!" This mouth speaking in the shadow, whom we hear not, see not,— this unknown one, this insolent one, is the human conscience!

This, then, is the human conscience. It is some one, I repeat, whom we see not, and who is stronger than an army, more numerous than seven million five hundred thousand votes, higher than a senate, more religious than an archbishop, more learned in law than M. Troplong, quicker to outstrip justice than M. Baroche, and who *thee's* and *thou's* your Majesty.

CHAPTER VII

AN EXPLANATION TO MONSIEUR BONAPARTE

LET us try to probe somewhat these strange things. Learn this fact, then, Monsieur Bonaparte: that which separates man from the brute is the notion of good and evil,— of that good and that evil about which I spoke to you just now. That is the abyss. The animal is a complete being. The greatness of man consists in this, that he is incomplete; that he feels himself, in a multitude of directions, beyond the finite; that he perceives something beyond himself and on this side of himself. This something beyond man and on this side of man is the mystery; it is (to employ those weak human expressions that never express more than one aspect of a thing) the moral world. In this moral world man is steeped as much as in the material world; nay, more. He lives in what he feels more than in what he sees. Creation may beleaguer him, want may assail him, enjoyment may tempt him, the beast that is in him may torment him; his perpetual aspirations towards another world hurl him irresistibly beyond creation, beyond want, beyond enjoyment, beyond the beast. Always, everywhere, at every moment, he has a glimpse of the superior world; and with this vision he fills his soul, and by it he rules his actions. He does not feel himself perfected in the life here below. He bears in himself, so to speak, a mysterious exemplar of the world anterior and ulterior,— of the perfect world, with which, unceasingly and in spite of himself, he is comparing this imperfect world, himself, his infirmities, his appetites, his passions, and his actions. When he recognizes that he is approaching that ideal model, he is joyous; when he recognizes that he is removing from it, he is sad. He understands thoroughly that there is nothing useless, and that nothing in this world can be destroyed. Justice and injustice, good and evil, good works and bad deeds, fall into the gulf but are not lost, depart into the infinite to the trouble or the benefit of those who accomplish them. After death they are found again, and the total reckoning is determined. To be lost, to fade away, to be annihilated is no more possible for the moral atom than it is for the material atom. Hence that great and twofold sentiment in man of his liberty and of his responsibility. He can be good or he can be wicked. That is an account he will have to settle. He can be guilty; and that — it is a striking fact, and one upon which I insist — is his greatness. Such is not the case with the brute. For it there is nothing but instinct,— to drink when thirsty; to eat when hungry; to procreate in due season; to sleep when the sun sets, to wake when it rises; to do the contrary if it be a beast of night. The animal has but a sort of obscure individuality, which no moral glimmer enlightens. All its law, I repeat, is instinct. Instinct is a species of rail along which irresistible nature drags the brute. No liberty, no responsibility; consequently no other life. The brute does neither good nor evil; it is uninformed. The tiger is innocent.

Now, if perchance you were innocent like the tiger? At certain times we are tempted to believe that, not having any inward monitor more than he, you have no more responsibility. In truth, there are hours when I pity you. Who knows? You are perhaps only a blind, unhappy force. Monsieur Louis Bonaparte, the notion of good and evil you have not. You are perhaps the only man in all humanity who has not this notion. This shuts you off from the human race. Yes, you are formidable. It is what constitutes your genius, we are told. I agree that in any case it is what at the present moment constitutes your power.

But do you know what is born of that kind of power?

The fact? Yes. The right? No. Crime tries to deceive history as to its true name; it comes and says, " I am success." Thou art crime! You are crowned and masked. Off with your mask! Off with your crown! Ah, you have your labour for your pains, for your appeals to the people, your plebiscites, your ballots, your additions, your executive commissions proclaiming the sum total, your streamers with these figures on gilt paper,— 7,500,000! You will get nothing from this scenic display. As to certain things the universal sentiment cannot be put on a wrong scent. The human race, taken in the mass, is an honest man. Even in your environment you are judged. There is not a person in your household, gold-laced or embroidered, not a groom of your stables or a groom of your senate, who does not say quite low what I say aloud. What I proclaim they whisper,— that is all the difference. You are omnipotent; they bow before you,— nothing more. They salute you, their cheeks flushing with shame. They feel that they are vile, but they know that you are infamous.

And now, as you are ready to give chase to all those you call " the revolted of December," since it is on them that you let slip your dogs; since you have instituted a Maupas and created a Ministry of Police especially for this,— I denounce to you that rebel, that revolter, that insurgent, *the conscience of each individual!* You give money, but it is the *hand* that receives it, not the conscience. The conscience! While you are about it, inscribe it on your list of exile. It is a stubborn opponent, that,— obstinate, tenacious, and inflexible,— an opponent that causes trouble everywhere. Hunt me that out of France: you will be tranquil then. Would you know how it treats you, even among your friends? Would you know in what terms a worthy chevalier of Saint Louis, eighty years old, a great adversary of " the demagogues," and a partisan of yours, defended himself for voting for you? " He is a wretch," he said; " but *he is a necessary wretch.*" No! there are no necessary wretches. No! crime is never useful. No! crime is never good. Society saved by treason, blasphemy! — leave such sayings as that to the archbishops. Nothing good has evil for its basis. God does not impose on humanity the necessity of wretches. There is nothing necessary in this world but justice and truth. If this old man looked less on life and more on the tomb, he would have seen this. These words are surprising in the mouth of an old man; for a light from God enlightens those who are approaching the grave, and shows them the truth. Never do righteousness and crime meet. The day they could be united, the words of human speech would change their meaning, all certitude would vanish, and darkness would overspread society. When by some chance (this has occasionally been seen in history) it happens, for a moment, that crime has the force of law, something trembles in the very foundations of humanity. " Jusque datum sceleri!" exclaims Lucian, and this verse traverses history like a cry of horror.

Then, by the confession of those who voted for you, you are a wretch: I omit the " necessary." Make your best of the situation.

" Well, be it so," you will say. " Why, that is the case exactly; one can get himself ' absolved ' by universal suffrage."

" Impossible! "

" What! impossible? "

Yes, impossible. I shall now force you to lay your finger on the point in question.

CHAPTER VIII

AXIOMS

YOU were captain of artillery at Berne, Monsieur Louis Bonaparte; you have necessarily a tincture of algebra and geometry. Here are some axioms of which you have probably an idea.

Two and two make four.

Between two given points the straight line is the shortest.

The part is less than the whole.

Now, get seven million five hundred thousand votes to declare that two and two make five, that the straight line is the longest road, that the whole is less than its part; get it declared by eight millions, by ten millions, by a hundred millions of votes, you will not have advanced a step. Well, then, now you are going to be surprised. There are axioms in probity, in honesty, in justice, as there are axioms in geometry; and the truths of morality are no more at the mercy of a vote than are the truths of algebra. The notion of good and evil cannot be resolved by universal suffrage. It is not given to a ballot to make the false become the true and the unjust the just. The human conscience cannot be put to the vote.

Do you understand now? You see that lamp, that little obscure light forgotten in a corner, lost in the shadow: look at it, admire it! It is hardly visible; it burns in solitude. Get seven millions five hundred thousand mouths to blow upon it at the same time, you will not extinguish it; you will not even make the flame quiver. Get the hurricane to blow upon it,— the flame will continue to mount straight and pure up to heaven.

This lamp is conscience. This flame is that which in the night of exile sheds a light on the paper on which I write at the present moment.

CHAPTER IX

WHERE MONSIEUR BONAPARTE HAS BEEN MISTAKEN

THUS then, whatever be your figures, controverted or not, extorted or not, true or false, it little matters. Those who live with their eyes fixed on justice will say, and keep on saying that crime is crime, that perjury is perjury, that treason is treason, that murder is murder, that blood is blood, that dirt is dirt, that a rascal is a rascal, and that he who thinks he is copying Napoleon in miniature is copying Lacenaire at full length. They say this, and they will repeat it in spite of your figures, because seven million five hundred thousand votes weigh nothing against the conscience of the honest man; because ten millions, a hundred millions, the unanimity even of the human race voting *en masse* would not count before this atom, this particle, of God,— the soul of the just man; because universal suffrage, which has entire sovereignty over political questions, has no jurisdiction over moral questions.

I leave aside for the moment, as I said just now, your methods in connection with the ballot,— the bandages over the eyes, the gag in every mouth, the cannon on the public squares, the sabres drawn, the spies swarming, silence and terror leading the vote to the urn like a malefactor to the station-house,— I leave aside this. I suppose (I tell you again) universal suffrage to be free; true, pure, real, universal suffrage sovereign of itself as it ought to be; the journals in every hand, men and acts questioned and examined, placards covering the walls, free speech everywhere, light everywhere! Well, to such universal suffrage as this submit peace and war, the effective force of the army, public credit, public relief, the budget, the penalty of death, the irremovability of judges, the indissolubility of marriage, divorce, the civil and political status of women, gratuitous instruction, the constitution of the commune, the rights of labour, the salary of the clergy, free trade, railroads, the currency, fiscal questions, colonization,— all the problems whose solution does not bring with them its own abdication, for universal suffrage can do everything except abdicate,— submit these to it, and it will resolve them, doubtless with error, but with the totality of certitude which human sovereignty includes; it will resolve them authoritatively. Now, try to get it to settle the question whether John or Peter has done well or ill in stealing an apple from an orchard. There it halts; there it fails. Why? Is it because this is a lower question? No; it is because it is a higher one. All that constitutes the organization proper to societies, whether they be considered as territory, as commune, as state, as country,— all political, financial, and social matters depend on universal suffrage, and obey it; the smallest atom of the least moral question defies it. The ship is at the mercy of the ocean, but not the star.

It has been said of M. Leverrier and of you, Monsieur Bonaparte, that you were the only two men who believed in your star. In fact, you do believe in your star; you search for it above your head. Well, this star which you seek for outside yourself, other men have within themselves. It shines under the vault of their skulls; it enlightens and guides them; it shows them the lineaments of life; it points out to them in the darkness of human destiny the good and the evil, the just and the unjust, the real and the false, ignominy and honour, righteousness and felony, virtue and crime. This star, without which the human soul is only night, is moral truth. Missing this light, you have been at fault. Your ballot of the 20th of December is for the thinker but a sort of monstrous artlessness. You have applied what you call " universal suffrage " to a question that does not admit of universal suffrage. You are not a statesman, you are a malefactor. That which has reference to you does not concern universal suffrage.

Yes, artlessness; I insist on this. The bandit of the Abruzzi, his hands hardly washed, and the blood still between his nails, goes to the priest for absolution. You, you have gone for absolution to a vote, only you have forgotten to confess; and while saying to the vote, "Absolve me," you have pressed the muzzle of your pistol against its temples. Ah, desperate wretch! to "absolve" you, as you say, is beyond the power of the people; it is beyond the power of humanity. Listen!

Nero, who had invented the society of the 10th of December, and who like you engaged it to applaud his comedies, and even (like you again) his tragedies,— Nero, after gashing the womb of his mother with a knife, might also, like you too, have convoked his universal suffrage. Nero, who resembled you again in this, that he was not troubled by the license of the press,— Nero, pontiff and emperor, surrounded by judges and priests prostrate before him, could, laying one of his bloody hands on the dead body of his mother and raising the other towards heaven, have called all Olympus to witness that he had not shed this blood, and have adjured his universal suffrage to declare before the face of gods and men that he, Nero, had not slain this woman. His universal suffrage, operating pretty much like yours, with the same enlightenment and with the same liberty, could have affirmed by seven million five hundred thousand votes that the divine Cæsar Nero, pontiff and emperor, had done no harm to this woman who was dead. Yet know this, Monsieur! Nero would not have been thereby "absolved;" it would have sufficed if one voice, one single voice on the earth, the humblest and obscurest, had arisen amid that profound night of the Roman empire, and cried out in the darkness, "Nero is a parricide!" for the echo, the eternal echo of the human conscience to repeat for ever and ever, from people unto people and from century unto century, "Nero has slain his mother!" Well, this voice uttering its protest in the shadow is mine. I cry out to-day, and do not doubt the universal conscience of humanity cries with me: "Louis Bonaparte has assassinated France! Louis Bonaparte has slain his mother!"

BOOK VII

THE ABSOLUTION

𝕾𝖊𝖈𝖔𝖓𝖉 𝖋𝖔𝖗𝖒

THE OATH

CHAPTER I

TO AN OATH ADD AN OATH AND A HALF

WHAT is Louis Bonaparte? He is perjury alive; he is mental reservation incarnate; he is felony in flesh and bones; he is false swearing wearing a general's hat and getting itself called Monseigneur.

Well! what is this man of the ambuscade asking of France now? An oath. An oath! Surely, after the 20th of December, 1848, and the 2d of December, 1851; after the inviolable Representatives of the people had been arrested and hunted; after the republic had been confiscated; after the *coup d'état*, — a cynical and downright roar of laughter at the oath from this malefactor was the thing to look forward to. It might have been expected that this Sbrigani would say to France: "See here! it is true! I gave my word of honour. It is funny, isn't it? Let us not speak of these follies any further."

No, he wants an oath. So come hither, mayors, gendarmes,

judges, spies, prefects, generals, police agents, gamekeepers, commissaries of police, functionaries, senators, councillors of State, legislators, clerks,— all the herd: the thing is decided, he wills it; this idea has come into his head; it is his desire, it is his good pleasure. Make haste and form in line then, you from your record office, you from under the eye of your corporal, you from the bureau of the minister. File off, you senators, to the Tuileries, into the Hall of the Marshals; you, spies, to the Prefecture of Police; you, first presidents and *procureurs-généraux*, into his antechamber. Come hither, riding, driving, walking, in robe or scarf, costume or uniform, draped, gilded, spangled, broidered, plumed with sword at side, cap on head, band on neck, girdle on stomach; come on, some before the bust of plaster, others before the man himself. Good! you are there,— you are all there; no one is missing. Now look him well in the face; enter into yourselves; dive into your consciences, your sense of decency, your loyalty, your religion; take off your gloves, raise your hands, and plight your faith to his perjury, and swear fidelity to his treason! Is it done? Yes. Ah, what an infamous farce! And Louis Bonaparte takes this swearing quite seriously. It is really true that he believes in my pledge, in thine, in yours, in ours, in theirs; he believes in everybody's pledge except his own. He insists on those around him swearing, and he enjoins them to be loyal. Messalina is pleased to surround herself with maids. Grand! it is his will that a body have some honour paid him; you understand this, Saint-Arnaud; you will pay heed, Maupas!

Let us nevertheless get to the bottom of the thing; there are oaths and oaths. The oath you take freely, solemnly, in the face of God and men, after receiving a confidential mandate from six millions of your fellow-citizens, in full National Assembly, to the Constitution of your country, to law, to right, to the people, to France,— such an oath is nothing, binds you to nothing, can be laughed at, and torn one fine morning by the heel of your boot; but the oath you take under cannon, under the sabre, under the eye of the police, to keep the position by which you live, the grade which is your only property; the oath you take to save your bread and the bread of your children to a knave, a rebel, to the violator of the laws, the murderer of the Republic, a backslider from all justice, to the man who has himself broken his oath,— oh, that oath is sacred! Let us not jest. The oath taken to the 2d of December, nephew of the 18th Brumaire, is sacro-sanct!

What astonishes me is the folly of it all. To receive as sterling coin and hard cash all these *juro's* of the official plebs; never even to dream that all scruples have been got rid of, and that there cannot be in this a single word of sound currency! A man happens to be a prince and a traitor at the same time, and he imagines that the example given from the summit of the State will not be followed! Think of it! To sow lead and fancy that gold will be harvested! Not even to perceive that in such cases all consciences mould themselves after the conscience above them, and that the false oath of the prince makes base money of all oaths!

CHAPTER II

A DIFFERENCE IN VALUES

AND then of whom are these oaths asked? Of that prefect? — he has betrayed the State. Of that general? — he has betrayed the flag. Of that magistrate? — he has betrayed the law. Of all those functionaries? — they have betrayed the Republic. A curious thing, and one calculated to make the philosopher ponder, is this heap of traitors from which issues this heap of oaths!

Now, let us dwell on the lovely feature of the 2d of December. Monsieur Bonaparte Louis believes in the oaths that are pledged to him! When M. Rouher takes off his glove and says, " I swear!" when M. Suin takes off his glove and says,

" I swear! " when M. Troplong places his hand on his breast, over the spot where senators have the third button and other men the heart, and says, " I swear! "—then Monsieur Bonaparte feels the tears in his eyes, adds up with emotion all these loyal souls, and contemplates these beings with tenderness. He trusts! he believes! O depth of candour! In truth, the innocence of scoundrels is sometimes a source of astonishment to honest men.

One thing nevertheless surprises the benevolent observer, and vexes him a little. It is the capricious and disproportionate fashion in which the oaths are paid for; it is the inequality of the values which Monsieur Bonaparte puts on the merchandise. For instance, if M. Vidocq were still Chief of the Police Department, he would have six thousand francs a year. M. Baroche has eighty thousand. It follows therefore that the oath of M. Vidocq would bring him in only sixteen francs sixty-six centimes a day, while the oath of M. Baroche brings him in two hundred and twenty-two francs twenty-two centimes a day. This is evidently unjust. Why this difference? An oath is an oath; an oath is composed of a glove taken off and eight letters.[1] What is there then in the oath of M. Baroche more than there is in the oath of M. Vidocq? You will tell me that this arises from the different nature of their functions; that M. Baroche presides over the Council of State, while M. Vidocq would only be chief of the Police Department. I answer that this is mere chance; that M. Baroche would probably excel in directing the Police Department, and that M. Vidocq might have made a very good president of the Council of State. That is not a reason.

Has the oath, then, different qualities? Is it like Masses? Are there also Masses at forty sous and Masses at ten sous? Has a person oath enough for his money? Is there, then, in this commodity of the oath the superfine, the extra-fine, the fine, and the demi-fine? Are some of a higher grade than others? Are they firm of texture, less mixed with oakum and cotton, better dyed? Are there oaths quite new, that have

[1] Je le jure!

never been used, and oaths worn out, patched, threadbare? In fine, is there a choice? Let us be told if there is. The answer is worth waiting for. It is we who foot the bills.

Having made this observation in the interest of the tax-payers, I ask pardon of M. Vidocq for making use of his name. I acknowledge that I had not the right to do so. In fact, M. Vidocq would perhaps have refused the oath.

CHAPTER III

THE OATH OF THE LETTERED AND THE LEARNED

MONSIEUR BONAPARTE wanted Arago to swear,— a detail of much value this! Know, then, that astronomy must take an oath! In all well-regulated States France or China — everything is a public function, even science. The mandarian of the Institute holds his office from the mandarian of the police. The great telescope owes liege homage to Monsieur Bonaparte. An astronomer is a species of policeman of the heavens; the observatory is a sentry-box, like any other. The good God up yonder requires to be watched a little now and then; sometimes he does not seem to submit completely to the constitution of the 14th of January. The sky is full of disagreeable allusions, and requires to be kept well in hand. The discovery of a new sun-spot constitutes evidently a case within the domain of the censorship; the prediction of a high tide may be seditious; the announcement of an eclipse may be a treason. We are a little whimsical (*lune*) at the Elysée; a free astronomy is almost as dangerous as a free press. Does any one know what is taking place during these nocturnal *têtes-à-tête* of Arago with Jupiter. If it were Leverrier, it would be all very well; but a member of the provisional Government! Be on your guard, M. Maupas! Look out that the Board of Longitude does not conspire with the stars, and above all with these wild contrivers of celestial *coups d'état* called comets. And then, as we have said already, a Bonaparte must of necessity be a fatalist. The great Napoleon had a star; the little one ought to have at least a nebula. Astronomers have certainly something of the astrologer about them too. Take your oaths, gentlemen.

It is hardly necessary to say that Arago refused.

One of the virtues of the oath to Louis Bonaparte is that according as you refuse it or give it, this oath takes from you or renders back to you your talents, your merits, your aptitudes. You are professor of Greek and Latin: take the oath! if not, you are banished from your chair; you no longer know Greek or Latin. You are professor of Rhetoric: take the oath! otherwise, tremble! The story of Théramène and the dream of Athalie are forbidden to you; you shall wander around for the rest of your days without ever having the chance of resuming them. You are professor of philosophy: take the oath to Monsieur Bonaparte; if not, you become incapable of comprehending the mysteries of the human conscience and explaining them to young people. You are professor of medicine: take the oath to Monsieur Bonaparte; except you do, you no longer know how to feel the pulse of your fever patients. But if all the good professors go away in this style, there will no longer be any good pupils. In medicine, particularly, this is a serious matter; what will become of the sick? Of whom,— the sick? Much we care about the sick! The important point is that medicine take the oath to Monsieur Bonaparte. Besides, either seven million five hundred thousand votes have not any meaning, or it is better to have one's leg cut off by a sworn ass than by a refractory Dupuytren.

Ah, you may well laugh; but all this is heart-rending. You are a young, rare, and noble intellect, like Deschanel; you are a man of firm and upright soul, like Despois; a grave and energetic philosopher, like Jacques; an eminent writer, a popular historian, like Michelet,— take the oath or starve! They refuse. The silence and the shadow to which they have stoically returned know the rest.

CHAPTER IV

SOME CURIOUS FEATURES

ALL morality is denied by such an oath, all shame drained to the dregs, all decency braved. No reason why we should not see incredible things: we see them. In such and such a town,— in Evreux,[1] for example,— the judges who took the oath have judged the judges who refused. Ignominy seated on the tribunal orders honour to be seated on the stool of repentance; the conscience that has been sold " censures " the conscience that has remained honest; the prostitute whips the virgin.

[1] The President of the Tribunal of Commerce at Evreux refused the oath. Let the " Moniteur " speak: —
" M. Verney, ex-President of the Tribunal of Commerce of Evreux, was summoned to appear last Friday before the judges of the Court of Misdemeanours of Evreux, on account of the acts that took place on the 29th of April last, in the consular sessions-hall. M. Verney was charged with the offence of contempt against the government. The Judges of First Instance dismissed M. Verney, but censured him by judgment. An appeal a minima was had by the Procureur of the Republic. Decree of the Court of Appeal of Rouen: · Whereas the prosecution has for sole object the repression of the offence of contempt against the government; whereas this offence resulted, according to the prosecution, from the last paragraph of the letter written by Verney to the Procureur of the Republic at Evreux, on the 26th of April last, and which was conceived as follows: " But it would be too serious a matter to claim longer that which we believe to be the right. The magistracy itself will thank us for not exposing the robe of the judge to a surrender to force, as your dispatch announces; " whereas, however blamable may have been the conduct of Verney in this affair, the court cannot see in the terms of this part of his letter the offence of contempt against the government, since the order, in virtue of which force had to be employed to prevent the judges from sitting who refused to take the oath, did not emanate from the government; whereas, there is no ground since then for applying the penal law to him,— for these reasons the court confirms the judgment appealed from, without costs.' "
The Court of Appeal of Rouen has for First President M. Franck-Carré, ex-Procureur-General to the Court of Peers in the Boulogne prosecution, the same who addressed these words to Monsieur Louis Bonaparte: " You have tampered with the soldiers and distributed money to buy treason."

With that oath you march from one surprise to another. Nicolet is but a bumpkin compared to Monsieur Bonaparte. When Monsieur Bonaparte made his tour of his lackeys, his accomplices, and victims, and pocketed the oath of each, he turned with amiable simplicity to the valiant chiefs of the army of Africa and used pretty nearly this language: " By the way, you know I had you arrested at night in your beds by my people; my spies entered your homes with drawn swords; they have been even decorated by me for this feat of arms. I had you threatened with a gag if you uttered a cry; you were seized by the collar by my prison wardens. I had you shut up in Mazas in the cell of the thieves, and in Ham in my own cell; you have still on your wrists the marks of the cords with which I had you tied. Good-day, gentlemen, and may God have you in his holy keeping! Swear fidelity to me." Changarnier looked at him steadily and answered, " No, traitor! " Bedeau answered, " No, forger! " Lamoricière answered, " No, bandit! " Charras slapped his face. At the present moment the face of Monsieur Bonaparte is red, not from shame, but from that slap.

Another singularity of the oath: In the casemates, in the bastiles, in the prison ships, in the African penal settlements, there are prisoners by thousands. Who are these prisoners? We have said already,— republicans, patriots, soldiers of the law, the innocent, the martyred. We get a glimpse of their sufferings; generous voices have proclaimed them; we ourselves in the work specially devoted to the 2d of December, shall completely tear away the veil. Well, would you wish to know what is happening there now? Occasionally some of these unfortunates, worn out by their sufferings, bending under the weight of their misery; without shoes, without bread, without clothing, without a shirt, and eaten alive by vermin; poor workmen torn from their shops, poor peasants torn from their ploughs; bewailing a wife, a mother; bewailing their children, their bereaved families without food and perhaps without shelter,— some of these unfortunates we say, sick, dying, in their despair and utter distress weaken and consent to " ask pardon." Then a letter, ready prepared and addressed " Monseigneur le prince président," is brought to them to sign. We publish this letter, it is recognized as genuine by M. Quetin-Bauchart : —

" I, the undersigned, declare upon my honour that I accept with gratitude the pardon which has been offered me by Prince Louis Napoleon, and bind myself to take no more part in secret societies, to respect the laws, and to be faithful to the government which the country has given itself by the vote of the 20th and 21st of December, 1851."

Let there be no misunderstanding as to the meaning of this grave fact. This is not clemency granted; it is clemency begged. The formula " Ask us to pardon you " signifies " Grant us our pardon." The assassin, bending over his victim, with uplifted knife, cries to him : " I have stopped and seized thee, flung thee to the ground, despoiled and robbed thee ; and now, pierced with wounds, thou art under my heel, thy blood flowing through twenty gashes ; say that thou *repentest*, and I shall not kill thee outright." This *repentance* of the innocent, exacted by the guilty, is simply the external form taken by his inward remorse. He imagines that in this way he is fortified against his own crime. To whatever expedients he may recur in order to dull the edge of his iniquity, though he have the little bells of the seven million five hundred thousand votes rung perpetually in his ear, the man of the *coup d'état* has a vague and dim perception of a morrow, and struggles against the inevitable future. He feels the need of a legal purgative, a discharge, withdrawal, quittance. He asks it of the vanquished, and when necessary tortures them in order to obtain it. At the bottom of the conscience of each prisoner, of each of the deported, of each of the proscribed, Louis Bonaparte feels that there is a tribunal, and that this tribunal is drawing up his indictment ; he trembles ; the executioner has a secret dread of the victim, and under the figure of a pardon granted by him to the victim he gets his acquittal signed by that judge. He thus hopes to deceive France, who also is a living conscience and an attentive tribunal ; and that when the day for the sentence comes, seeing him absolved by his victims, she too will pardon him. He is mistaken. Let him break through a wall in some other direction, he will not escape through this.

CHAPTER V

THE 5TH OF APRIL, 1852

THIS is what was seen in the Tuileries on the 5th of April, 1852: Towards eight in the evening the antechamber was filled with men in red robes, grave, majestic men, speaking in low tones, holding their black velvet caps, adorned with gold lace, in their hands. Most of them were white-haired. They were the presidents and councillors of the Court of Cassation, the first presidents of the Courts of Appeal, and the *procureurs-généraux,*— all the high magistrature of France. These men had been introduced into this antechamber and left there by an *aide-de-camp;* they came and went, backwards and forwards, talking to one another, pulling out their watches, waiting for the touch of a bell. At the end of an hour they perceived they had not even chairs to sit on. One of them, M. Troplong, went into another antechamber where the servants were, and complained; they brought him a chair. At last a folding-door opened; they entered helter-skelter into a salon. A man in a black coat was standing there, with his back to the chimney-piece. What business had those men in red robes with this man in a black coat? He was Monsieur Bonaparte and they had come to take the oath to him. He nodded to them; they bent down to the ground, as was proper. In front of Monsieur Bonaparte, a few yards from him, was M. Abbattuci, once a Liberal deputy, now Minister of Justice of the *coup d'état.* Proceedings were then begun. M. Abbattuci delivered a discourse, and Monsieur Bon-

aparte made a speech.   The prince, looking at the carpet, uttered a few drawling and disdainful words, he spoke of his
" legitimacy."   After which the magistrates swore, each lift-
ing his hand one after the other.   While they were swearing,
Monsieur Bonaparte, with his back half turned away from
them, chatted with the *aides-de-camp* near him.   When it was
finished, he turned his back on them completely, and they left,
shaking their heads, ashamed and humiliated,— not because
they had committed an act of baseness, but because they had no
chairs in the antechamber!   As they were leaving, the following dialogue was heard:—

" That," said one of them, " was an oath we had to take."
" And which we must keep," returned another.
" Like the master of the house," added a third.

All this is the very essence of humiliation.   Let us pass on.
Among these first presidents who swore fidelity to Louis
Bonaparte, there was a certain number of ex-peers of France,
who, as peers, had condemned Louis Bonaparte to perpetual
imprisonment.   But why look so very far back?   Let us pass
on still; this is a little better.   Among those magistrates, there
were seven whose names are Hardouin, Moreau, Pataille,
Cauchy, Delapalme, Grandet, Quesnault.   These seven men
composed, before the 2d of December, the High Court of Justice; the first, Hardouin, was president, the two last deputies,
the four other judges.   These men had received and accepted
from the Constitution of 1848 a mandate conceived in the following terms: —

" ARTICLE 68.   Every measure by which the President of the Republic
dissolves the National Assembly, prorogues it, or places an obstacle in
the way of the exercise of its mandate, is a crime of high treason.
" The judges of the High Court shall immediately meet under penalty
of forfeiture, convoke juries in the place they designate, to proceed to
the trial of the President and his accomplices; they shall themselves
name the magistrates charged with filling the functions of the public
ministry."

On the 2d of December, in presence of the flagrant outrage, they had begun the trial and named a procureur-general,

M. Renouard, who accepted the mission of prosecuting Louis Bonaparte for the crime of high treason.   Let us join this name Renouard to the seven others.   On the 5th of April the whole eight were in the antechamber of Louis Bonaparte. What they did there we have seen.

Here it is impossible not to pause.   There are certain sad ideas on which we must have the strength to dwell, there are cesspools of ignominy which we must have the courage to sound.

Look at yon man.   His birth was an accident, a misfortune; it took place in some hole, some kennel, some cave, no one knows where or from whom.   He emerged from the dust to fall into the mud.   He has not had father nor mother, except as far as was necessary for his existence; after this all was taken from him.   He has crawled about as well as he was able; he has grown up barefooted, bareheaded, in rags, without a glimmer of knowledge as to why he was living.   He does not know how to read; he does not know that there are laws above his head,— he hardly knows that there is a heaven.   He has no home, no roof, no family, no belief, no book.   He is a blinded soul; his understanding has never opened; for the understanding opens only to the light as the flowers open in the daytime, and he is in night.   Still, he must eat; society has made a brute beast of him, hunger has made a wild beast of him.   He watches the passer-by from the corner of a wood, and robs him of his purse.   He is taken and sent to jail.   It is well.

Now look at that other man.   His is not the red uniform; it is the red robe.   He believes in God, reads Nicole, is a Jansenist and devotee, goes to confession, and receives the consecrated bread.   He is well-born, as it is said; he does not want for anything, has never wanted for anything; his family, has lavished on his infancy the most anxious care, he has had lessons, advice, masters, instruction in Greek and Latin literature.   He is a grave and scrupulous personage, and so he has been made a magistrate.   Seeing this man spend his days in meditating on all the great texts, sacred and profane, in the study of the law, in the practice of religion, in the contemplation of justice and injustice,— seeing this, society has intrusted to his guardianship its most august and venerable possession, the book of the law. It has made him the judge and chastiser of treason. It has said to him: " A day may come, an hour may strike, when the head of the material force of the nation will trample on the law and the right; then shalt thou, the man of justice, rise up and strike with thy wand the man of power." For this reason, and in the expectation of that perilous and supreme day, it heaps benefits upon him, and clothes him with purple and ermine. That day comes at last, that unique and solemn hour, that grand hour of duty. The man with the red robe begins to stammer forth the words of the law; suddenly he perceives that justice does not prevail, that treason is in the ascendant. And then this man who has spent his life in imbuing his mind with the pure and holy light of justice; this man who is nothing if he is not the despiser of iniquitous success,— this lettered man, this scrupulous man, this religious man, this judge to whom has been confided the guardianship of the law and in some sort of the universal conscience, turns towards the triumphant perjurer, and with the very mouth, the very voice with which he would have said if the traitor had been conquered, " Criminal, I condemn you to the galleys! " he says, " Monseigneur, I swear fidelity to you! " Take a balance, put in one scale the judge and into the other the felon, and tell me to which side it leans.

CHAPTER VI

SWEARING ON ALL SIDES

S UCH are the things which have been seen in France on the occasion of the oath to Monsieur Bonaparte. There has been swearing here, swearing there, swearing on all sides, — at Paris, in the provinces, at sunrise, at sunset, in the north

and in the south. During one entire month France has been
a scene of arms stretched out and hands uplifted; with the
final chorus, " Let us swear! " etc. The ministers have sworn
before the President, the prefects before the ministers, the
herd before the prefects. What does Monsieur Bonaparte do
with these oaths? Does he make a collection of them?
Where does he put them? It has been noticed that the oath is
seldom refused except by unpaid functionaries,— councillors-
general, for example. The oath has in reality been taken to
the budget. On the 29th of March a certain senator was
heard to protest in a loud voice that his name had been passed
over, which must have happened through some sort of for-
tuitous decency. M. Sibour,[1] archbishop of Paris, has
sworn; M. Franck-Carré,[2] procureur-general to the Court of
Peers in the Boulogne affair, has sworn; M. Dupin, president
of the National Assembly on the 2d of December,[3] has sworn.
Great God! it is enough to make one wring one's hands with
shame!

And yet an oath is a holy thing. The man who takes an
oath is no longer a man; he is an altar on which God descends.
Man, that infirmity, that shadow, that atom, that grain of
sand, that drop of water, that tear fallen from the eyes of
destiny; man, so little, so feeble, so uncertain, so ignorant, so
perplexed; man, who walks in bewilderment and in doubt,
knowing little of yesterday and nothing of the morrow, seeing
just enough of his path to take a step forward, the rest all
darkness,— trembling if he look before him, sad if he look
behind him; man, enfolded in the immensities and obscurities
of time, space, being, and lost in them,— having a gulf in
himself, his soul, and a gulf outside himself, heaven; man,
who at certain hours bends with a sort of sacred horror under
all the forces of Nature,— under the roaring of the sea, the
moaning of the trees, under the shadow of the mountains,
under the radiance of the stars; man, who cannot raise his

[1] As Senator.
[2] As First President of the Court of Appeal of Rouen.
[3] As Member of his Municipal Council.

head during the day without being blinded by the light, nor during the night without being crushed by the infinite; man, who knows nothing, sees nothing, understands nothing, who may be borne off to-morrow, to-day, in a moment, by the passing wave, by the rustling breeze, by the pebble that falls, by the hour that strikes;— yet on a given day man, that quivering, shuddering, wretched being, the toy of chance, the plaything of the expiring minute, draws himself up on a sudden before the enigma called human life, feels that there is in him something greater than the abyss, honour; stronger than fatality, virtue; deeper than the unknown, faith,— and alone, feeble, and naked he says to all this formidable mystery which holds and encompasses him, " Do with me what thou wilt, but I will do this and I will not do that!" and proud, serene, tranquil, creating by one word a fixed point in this sombre instability which fills the horizon, as the sailor casts an anchor into the ocean he casts his oath into the future.

O oath! admirable confidence of justice in itself! sublime permission to make a solemn averment granted by God to man! It is ended; it exists no longer. One more glory of the soul faded away into space!

BOOK VIII

PROGRESS CONTAINED IN THE *COUP D'ETAT*

––––––

CHAPTER I

THE QUANTITY OF GOOD CONTAINED IN THE EVIL

AMONG us democrats many sincere spirits have been stricken with stupor by the events of the 2d of December. Some have been disconcerted, others discouraged, many dismayed; some of those whom I have seen have cried out, "Finis Poloniæ!" As to myself, I,— since at certain moments it becomes necessary to say *I*, and to speak in presence of history as a witness,— I have seen this event without anxiety, and I proclaim the fact. I say more,— there are moments when the 2d of December finds me a satisfied observer.

When I succeed in abstracting myself from the present; when it is in my power to turn away my eyes for a moment from all these crimes, from all the blood spilt, from all the victims, from all the proscribed, from the death-rattle on the convict-ship, from the frightful prisons of Lambessa and Cayenne where death is quick, from that exile where death is slow, from that vote, that oath, from that enormous blot of shame staining France and widening every day; when, forgetting for some minutes these painful thoughts,— thoughts that habitually possess my soul,— I succeed in shutting myself up in the austere coldness of the statesman, and considering no longer the fact but the consequences of the fact;—

then, among many results doubtless disastrous, I see real, considerable, nay immense progress; and at that moment, while I am always one of those whom the 2d of December rouses to indignation, I am no longer one of those whom it grieves. With my eyes fixed on certain aspects of the future, I arrive at this conclusion: the proceeding is infamous, but the fact is good.

Efforts have been made to account for the unaccountable victory of the 2d of December in a hundred fashions. A balance has been taken between the different sorts of resistance possible, and they have been set off one against the other. The people have been afraid of the *bourgeoisie*, the *bourgeoisie* has been afraid of the people; the Faubourgs have hesitated before the restoration of the majority,— fearing, wrongly for that matter, that their victory would bring back to power that Right which was so profoundly unpopular; the shopkeepers have recoiled before the Red Republic, the people did not understand, the middle classes shuffled. Some have said, " What kind of persons are we likely to send to the Legislative Palace? " Others have said, " What kind of people are we likely to see in the Hôtel de Ville? " In fine, the harsh repression of 1848, the insurrection crushed by cannon, the casemates, the banishments, the transportations,— it was a living and terrible memory; and then, If the rappel could have been beaten! if a single legion had turned out! if M. Sibour had been M. Affre, and had thrown himself in front of the balls of the pretorians! if the High Court had not let itself be dispersed by a corporal! if the judges had done as the Representatives, and the red robes as well as the scraves had been seen on the barricades! if a single arrest had failed! if a regiment had hesitated! if the massacre on the boulevard had not occurred, or had fared ill for Monsieur Bonaparte! etc. All this is true; and nevertheless that has been which ought to have been. Let us repeat that beneath this monstrous victory and in its shadow a vast and certain progress has been accomplished. The 2d of December succeeded because — I say again — from more than one point of view it was perhaps good that it should succeed. All explanations are just and all explanations are vain. The invisible hand is concerned in all this; Providence has made the event. It was in fact necessary that *order* should reach its logical conclusion. It was well that it should be known, and known forever, that in the mouth of the men of the past this word " order " means false swearing, perjury, robbery of the public funds, civil war, councils of war, confiscation, sequestration, deportation, transportation, proscription, fusilades, police, censorship, dishonour of the army, negation of the people, the abasement of France, the senate mute, the tribune prostrate, the press crushed, the political guillotine, the butchery of liberty, the strangling of right, the violation of the laws, the sovereignty of the sabre, massacre, treason, and ambuscade. The spectacle before our eyes is a useful spectacle. The things seen in France since the 2d of December are the orgies of *order*.

Yes, Providence is concerned with this event. Think again of this; that for fifty years the Republic and the Empire filled all imaginations,— the one with its reflection of terror, the other with its reflection of glory. In the Republic men saw only 1793,— that is to say, the formidable necessity of revolutions, as fiery furnaces; in the Empire they saw only Austerlitz. Hence, a prejudice against the Republic and a prestige in favour of the Empire. Now, what is the future of France? Is it the Empire? No! it is the Republic.

It was necessary to change this situation,— to destroy the prestige of what cannot be revived, and destroy the prejudice against what must be. Providence has done it; it has destroyed two mirages. February came, and took from the Republic its terror; Louis Bonaparte came, and took from the Empire its prestige. Henceforth, 1848 (fraternity) is superimposed on 1793 (terror); Napoleon the Little is superimposed on Napoleon the Great. Two great things — of which the one frightened, the other dazzled — retire from the field: '93 is seen no longer except through its justification, and Napoleon is seen no longer except through his caricature; the senseless dread of the guillotine is dissipated, the vain popularity of the Empire has vanished. Thanks to 1848, the Republic no longer alarms; thanks to Louis Bonaparte, the Empire no longer fascinates. The future has become possible. These are the secrets of God.

Moreover, the word " Republic " is not enough; it is the *thing* republic that is wanted. Well, we shall have the thing with the word. Let us develop this point.

CHAPTER II

THE FOUR INSTITUTIONS OPPOSED TO THE FUTURE

WHILE waiting for the marvellous but ultimate simplifications which the union of Europe and the democratic federation of the continent must one day bring to pass, what will be in France the form of the social edifice which the thinker sees dimly at present, whose vague and luminous lineaments he traces through the darkness of dictatorships? This form will be as follows:—

The commune sovereign, administered by an elected mayor; universal suffrage everywhere, subordinate to the national unity only in what touches general interests: so much for the administration. Syndicates and trades-councils regulating the private differences of associations and industries; the jury, magistrate of the fact, instructing the judge, himself the magistrate of the law; the judge elected: so much for the judiciary. The priest excluded from everything except the Church; living with his eye fixed on his book and on heaven; a stranger to the budget, ignored by the State, known only by his followers; having no longer authority, but having liberty: so much for religion. War confined to the defence of the territory; the nation a national guard divided into three bands, and able to rise like one man: so much for power. The law everywhere, the right everywhere, the vote everywhere; the sabre nowhere.

Now, to this future, to this magnificent realization of
the democratic ideal, what were the obstacles?   There were
four obstacles, and they were these:—
A permanent army.
A centralized administration.
A paid clergy.
An irremovable magistracy.

CHAPTER III

SLOWNESS OF NORMAL PROGRESS

WHAT these obstacles are, what they were even under the
Republic of February, even under the Constitution
of 1848; the evil they produced, the good they prevented, the
past which they perpetuated, the excellent social order which
they delayed,— these the political writer saw imperfectly, the
philosopher knew, the nation was ignorant of.   These four
institutions — enormous, ancient, and solid, buttressed one
upon the other, intermingled from their base to their summit,
growing like a forest of huge old trees, their roots under our
feet and their branches over our heads — were stifling and
crushing all the scattered germs of new France.   Where there
should have been life, movement, association, local liberty,
communal spontaneity, there was administrative despotism;
where there should have been the intelligent vigilance, armed
if needful, of the patriot and the citizen, there was the passive
obedience of the soldier; where the living Christian faith might
have gushed forth, there was the Catholic priest; where there
should have been justice, there was the judge.   And the future was there under the feet of the suffering generations,
which could not emerge from earth and were waiting.
Was this known among the people?   Was it suspected?
Was it surmised?   No, far from it.   In the eyes of the

greatest number, and of the middle classes in particular, these four obstacles were four supports. The magistracy, the army, the administration, and the clergy were the four virtues of order, the four social forces, the four holy pillars of the ancient French formation. Attack that if you dare! I do not hesitate to say that in the state of blindness to which the best minds were a prey, with the methodical march of normal progress, with our assemblies (which no one will suspect me of disparaging, but which when they are at once honest and timid, as often happens, are willing to be governed by their average; that is to say, by mediocrity), with the commissions of initiative, the delays and repeated ballotings,— if, in this state the 2d of December had not come with its astounding demonstration, if Providence had not interfered, France would have been condemned indefinitely to endure an irremovable magistracy, a centralized administration, a permanent army, and a paid clergy.

Certainly it is not I who will seek to contest, much less to depreciate, the power of the press and the power of the tribune, these two great combined forces of civilization. But see, nevertheless, what efforts of every kind and in every sense and under every form have been required for the tribune and the newspaper, for books and eloquence, to succeed even in shaking the universal prejudice in favour of these four fatal institutions. What gigantic struggles would be needed, then, to overthrow them; to brandish the evidence before all eyes; to overcome the resistance of the interested, the passionate, and the ignorant; to enlighten thoroughly public opinion, the public conscience, the official powers; to make this fourfold reform penetrate first into ideas and then into the laws! Reckon up the discourses, the writings, the articles in the journals; the projects of law, the counter-projects; the amendments, the amendments on amendments; the reports, the counter-reports; the facts, incidents, polemics, discussions, affirmations, denials, the storms; the steps forward, the steps backward; the days, weeks, months, years; the quarter of a century, the half century!

CHAPTER IV

WHAT THE ASSEMBLY MIGHT HAVE DONE

LET us imagine seated on the benches of an assembly the most fearless of thinkers,— a brilliant intellect; one of those men who when they stand on the tribune feel that there is a tripod beneath them, feel their body expand instantaneously, become giants, tower above the massive appearances that mask realities, and see the future above the high and sombre walls of the present. This man, this orator, this seer, would bid his country take heed; this prophet would enlighten statesmen. He knows where the rocks are; he knows that society will crumble precisely because of these four false reports,— administrative centralization, the permanent army, the irremovable judge, the salaried priest; he knows this, he wishes all to know it; he ascends the tribune, and he says: " I warn you of four great public perils. Your political system bears within itself that which will slay it. It is necessary to transform, root and branch, the administration, the army, the clergy, and the magistracy; to suppress here, retrench there, renew everything, or perish through these four institutions which you take for elements of duration, but which are elements of dissolution."

Murmurs. He exclaims: " Do you know what your centralized administration can become in the hands of a perjured executive power? An immense treason carried into effect at the same time over the whole surface of France by all functionaries without exception."

The murmurs break out again, and with more violence; the audience cries, " Order ! " the orator continues: " Do you know what your permanent army may one day become? An instrument of crime. Passive obedience is the bayonet eternally levelled at the heart of the law. Yes, even here, in this France which is the instructor of the world; in this land of the tribune and the press; in this fatherland of human thought,— an hour may strike when the sabre will rule; when you, inviolable legislators, will be seized by the collar by corporals; when our glorious regiments will be transformed, to the profit of a man and the shame of a people, into gilded hordes and pretorian bands; when the sword of France will be something which strikes from behind, like the poniard of a *sbirro;* when the blood of the first city in the world will bespatter the gold epaulets of your generals."

The murmurs become a clamour. Cries of " Order! " are heard on all sides. The speaker is apostrophized by every one, " You have just insulted the administration; now you outrage the army! " The President calls the speaker to order. The speaker resumes: " And if haply the day should come when a man having the five hundred thousand functionaries who constitute the administration, and the four hundred thousand soldiers who compose the army, in his hand; if a day should come when this man would tear the Constitution to pieces, violate all laws, infringe all oaths, break through all rights, commit all crimes,— do you know what your irremovable magistracy would do,— that protector of right, that guardian of the laws,— do you know what it would do? It would hold its peace! "

The last words of the speaker are lost in the clamour. The tumult becomes a tempest. " This man respects nothing! After the administration and the army, he drags the magistracy in the mud! The censure! the censure! " The speaker is censured, and the censure is recorded on the minutes. The President declares that if he continue the Assembly will be consulted and he shall be silenced. The speaker continues: " And your paid clergy, and your salaried bishops: the day when some pretender or other employs the magistracy, the administration, and the army in all these criminal deeds; the day when all these institutions drip with the blood shed by the traitor and for the traitor,— placed between the man who commits these crimes and the God who orders them to hurl an anathema at the criminal, do you know what your bishops will do? They will fall prostrate, not before God, but before this man!"

Is it possible to form any idea of the fury, the hooting, the jeers, the imprecations, with which such words would be received? Is it possible to imagine the cries, the apostrophes, the menaces, the entire body rising as one man, and the tribune scarcely protected from violence by the efforts of the ushers? The speaker has profaned all the holy arks in succession, and at last touches the holy of holies, the clergy! And then what does he really suppose? What a heap of impossible and infamous hypotheses is this? Hear Baroche bellow and Dupin thunder! The speaker would be again called to order, censured, compelled to apologize, excluded from the Chamber for three days, like Pierre Leroux and Emile de Girardin; perhaps —who knows? — expelled like Manuel. And on the next day the indignant *bourgeoisie* would say, "Well done!" and from all quarters the journals of order would shake their fists at the "calumniator;" and even in his own party, on his own bench in the Assembly, his best friends would abandon him and say, "It is his own fault; he has supposed chimeras and absurdities!" And after this generous and heroic effort, it would be discovered that the four institutions attacked had become more venerable and impeccable than ever, and that instead of advancing, the question had retreated.

CHAPTER V

WHAT PROVIDENCE HAS DONE

BUT Providence acts differently. It puts the thing under your eyes, illuminated on all sides, and says, "See!"

One fine morning a man arrives; and what a man! — the first comer, the last comer, without a past, without a future, without genius, without glory, without prestige. Is he an

adventurer? Is he a prince? This man has quite frankly
filled his hands with money, bank-notes, railway shares, places,
decorations, sinecures; this man bows to his functionaries and
says, " Functionaries be traitors!" The functionaries become
traitors. All,— without exception? Yes, all. He addresses
the generals and says, " Generals, massacre!" The generals
massacre. He turns towards the irremovable judges and
says: " Magistrates, I break the Constitution; I perjure myself; I dissolve the sovereign Assembly, I arrest the inviolable
Representatives; I pillage the public treasury, I sequestrate;
I confiscate; I banish whoever displeases me, or as my fancy
dictates; I shoot down without notice, I fusilade without a
trial; I commit all that men have agreed to call crime, I violate
all that men have agreed to call right: behold the laws, they
are under my feet!"

" We shall pretend not to see," say the magistrates.

" You are insolent!" replies the providential man. " To
turn away your eyes is to insult me. I intend you to assist
me. Judges, to-day you shall congratulate me,— me, who am
force and crime,— and to-morrow you shall try those who resisted me, those who stand for honour, right, and law, and you
shall condemn them."

The irremovable judges kiss his boot, and set about examining into the *affair of the troubles*. Into the bargain,
they take an oath to him.

Next he perceives the clergy in a corner, endowed, gilded,
crossed, coped, and mitred, and says to them: " Ah, you are
there, archbishop! Come here; you shall bless all this for
me." And the archbishop intones his *magnificat*.

CHAPTER VI

WHAT THE MINISTERS, THE ARMY, THE MAGISTRACY, AND THE CLERGY HAVE DONE

AH, what a striking thing, and what a lesson! " Erudimini! " Bossuet would say. The ministers fancied they were dissolving the Assembly; they have dissolved the administration. The soldiers have fired on the army and slain it. The judges imagined they were judging and condemning some innocent persons: they have judged and condemned to death the irremovable magistracy. The priests believed they were chanting a hosanna over Louis Bonaparte: they have chanted a *De profundis* over the clergy.

CHAPTER VII

FORMS OF THE GOVERNMENT OF GOD

WHEN God wishes to destroy a thing, he makes the thing itself his agent. All the bad institutions of this world end in suicide. When they have weighed long enough on men, Providence sends to them, as the sultan does to his viziers, the bowstring by the hand of a mute: they execute themselves. Louis Bonaparte is the mute of Providence.

CONCLUSION

FIRST PART

PETTINESS OF THE MASTER, SHABBINESS OF THE SITUATION

I

BE tranquil! history has him in its grip. Still, if to be laid hold of by history flatters the vanity of Monsieur Bonaparte; if he chance to have (and really it looks like it) any mental illusion as to his value as a political scoundrel,— let him discard it. He must not imagine that because he has piled horror on horror he will ever be able to hoist himself up to the level of the great bandits of history. We have done wrong, perhaps, in some pages of this work to draw a parallel between him and these men. No; although he has committed great crimes, he himself remains paltry. He will never be anything but the nocturnal strangler of liberty; he will never be anything but the man who intoxicated soldiers,— not with glory, as did the first Napoleon, but with wine; he will never be anything but the pygmy tyrant of a great people. The stature of the individual is entirely incompatible with greatness, even in infamy. As a dictator he is a buffoon; as emperor, he will be grotesque. That will finish him. It will be his destiny to make the human race shrug its shoulders. Will his punishment be the less harsh on account of this? No; disdain in no way lessens resentment. He will be hideous, and he will continue ridiculous,— nothing more. History while laughing at him smites him. Even the indignation of those most indignant cannot get him out of this position. Great thinkers take a delight in chastising great despots, and sometimes enlarge them a little to render them worthy of their wrath; but what can the historian do with such a personage as this? The historian can only lead him to posterity by the ear. The man once stripped of his success, the pedestal taken away, the tinsel and the glitter and the big sword removed, the poor little skeleton left naked and shivering,—can anything be imagined more beggarly and pitiful?

History has its tigers. Historians, the immortal guardians of ferocious animals, exhibit this imperial menagerie to the nations. Tacitus alone, that great belluarius, has caught and imprisoned eight or ten of those tigers in the iron cages of his style. Gaze on them! they are terrific and superb; their spots form a part of their beauty. Look! yonder is Nimrod, the hunter of men; this is Busiris, the tyrant of Egypt; this is Phalaris, who roasted living men in his brazen bull, in order to make the bull bellow; this is Ahasuerus, who tore the skin from the heads of the seven Maccabees and then had them roasted alive; this is Nero, who burned Rome and covered the Christians with wax and pitch and lit them as torches; this is Tiberius, the man of Capreæ; this is Domitan; this is Caracalla; this is Heliogabalus; that other is Commodus, who to his other horrible merits has added that of being the son of Marcus Aurelius; those are the czars, those others the sultans; those are the popes (among them notice the tiger Borgia); yonder is Philip called the Good, as the furies were called the Eumenides; yonder is Richard III., sinister and deformed; that is Henry VIII., with his huge belly and broad face, who killed two of his five wives and ripped up one; this is Christiern II., the Nero of the North; that is Philip II., the demon of the South. They are appalling; hearken to their roars, observe them one after another. The historian leads them before you; he drags them to the edge of their cage, opens their mighty jaws, show you their teeth, and their claws. You may say of each, " That is a royal tiger." In fact, they have been caught on all the thrones of earth. History conducts

them through the ages; she will not let them die; she takes
care of them.   They are her tigers; she does not mix them
with the jackals; she puts and keeps apart the filthy beasts.

Monsieur Bonaparte will be, with Claudius, with Ferdinand
VII. of Spain, with Ferdinand II. of Naples, in the cage of
the hyænas.   There is a little of the brigand about him, but
much more of the trickster.   He always gives you the impression of the poor blackleg-prince who lived by his wits in England; his present prosperity, his triumph, his empire, and his
self-importance generally, do not affect you in the least; the
purple mantle trails over boots down at the heels.   Napoleon
the Little,— nothing more, nothing less; the title of this book
is a good one.   The meanness of his vices is injurious to the
greatness of his crimes.   Just consider.   Pedro the Cruel
massacred but did not steal; Henry III. assassinated but did
not swindle; Timur crushed children under the feet of his
horses, pretty much as Monsieur Bonaparte has exterminated
women and old men on the boulevard, but he did not lie.
Listen to the Arabian historian:—

"Timur-Beg, Sahebkeran (master of the world and of the century,
master of the planetary conjunctions), was born at Kesch in 1336; he
butchered one hundred thousand captives.   When he was besieging Siwas,
the inhabitants, to move him, sent a thousand little children bearing each
a Koran on its head, and crying, 'Allah! Allah!'   He had the sacred
books removed with respect, and the children crushed under the hoofs
of his horses.   He used seventy thousand human heads, together with
cement, stone, and brick, in building towers at Herat, Sebzvar, Tekrit,
Aleppo, and Bagdad.   He detested falsehood; when he pledged his
word, he could be trusted."

Monsieur Bonaparte does not reach this stature.   He is
without the dignity which the great despots of the East and
West blend with their ferocity.   He lacks the majestic proportions of the Cæsars.   To be the counter-part and semblance
of all those executioners who have tortured humanity for four
thousand years, a man must not be a cross between a general
of division and a mountebank on the Champs Elysée; he must
not have been a policeman at London; he must not have wiped
from his face, with eyes cast down, in the open Court of Peers,

the scornful insults of M. Magnan; he must not have been called pickpocket by the English journals; he must not have been menaced with Clichy; he must not, in a word, be a scamp.

Monsieur Louis Napoleon, you are ambitious, you aim high, but you must be told the truth. Now, what do you wish we should do in this matter? It is all very well for you to realize, by overthrowing the tribune, the wish of Caligula after your own fashion, " Would that the human race had but a single head, that I might cut it off at one stroke; " it is all very well for you to banish republicans by thousands, as Philip III. expelled the Moors, and as Torquemada hunted the Jews; it is all very well for you to have casemates like Pedro the Cruel, prison-ships like Hariadan, dragonnades like Père Letellier, and dungeons like Ezzelino III., to be a perjurer like Ludovico Sforza, a murderer and assassin of his subjects like Charles IX.;— it is all very well for you to act in this manner: you do so in vain. When we hear your name, you can never make us connect it with theirs in our minds; you are but a rascal. Not every one who wishes to be a monster attains his wish.

II

FROM every aggregation of men, from every city, from every nation, there is evolved of necessity a collective force. Place this collective force at the service of liberty, let it be regulated by universal suffrage, and the city becomes a commune, the nation a republic.

This collective force is not, of its own nature, intelligent. Belonging to all, it belongs to none; it floats, so to speak, outside the people. Until the day when, according to the true social formula, " The least government possible," this force can be used as an agent for the maintenance of good order on the streets and highways, for paving the roads, lighting the lamps, and looking after malefactors; until that day, this collective force, being at the mercy of many hazards and ambitions, requires to be guarded and defended by jealous, clearsighted, and well-armed institutions. It may be enslaved by tradition; it may be surprised by cunning. A man may rush upon it, seize it, bridle it, and tame it, and use it to ride over his fellow-citizens. A tyrant is that man who, sprung from tradition like Nicholas of Russia, or from cunning like Louis Bonaparte, secures for his profit and disposes of as he wishes the collective force of a people. If that man is by his birth what Nicholas was, he is the social enemy; if he has done what Louis Bonaparte has done, he is the public robber. The first has nothing to do with the regular and legal tribunals, with the articles of the codes. Behind him vengeance is lying in wait, hatred is watching; Orloff is in his palace and Mouravieff among his people; he may be assassinated by some one of his army or poisoned by some one of his court; he runs the risk of barrack conspiracies, military secret societies, domestic plots, sudden and obscure maladies, terrible strokes, grand catastrophes. The second must go simply to Poissy. The first has the wherewith to die in purple, to end pompously and royally, as monarchies and tragedies end. The second must live,— live between four walls, behind gratings which allow the people to see him, sweeping yards, making hair-brushes or cloth slippers, emptying tubs, with a green cap on his head and sabots on his feet and straw in his sabots.

Ah, leaders of the old parties, men of absolutism! in France you voted *en masse* among the seven million five hundred thousand votes; outside of France you applauded, and you took this Cartouche for the hero of order. He is ferocious enough to he so, I acknowledge; but look at his stature! Be not ungrateful to your real colossuses: you have been too ready to get rid of your Haynaus and your Radetzkys. Above all, meditate on that parallel that will present itself so naturally to your minds. What is this Lilliputian Mandrin in comparison with Nicholas, Czar and Cæsar, Emperor and Pope,— his power one half Bible and the other half knout; who damns and condemns; who puts eight hundred thousand soldiers and two hundred thousand priests through the exercise; who holds in his right hand the keys of paradise and in his left hand the keys of Siberia; who possesses as his own private property sixty millions of men,— their souls as if he were God, their bodies as if he were the grave!

III

IF there were not before long an abrupt, imposing, and striking termination; if the present situation of the French nation were prolonged and extended,— the great injury, the terrific injury, would be the moral injury.

The boulevards of Paris, the streets of Paris, the fields and towns of twenty departments in France, have been strewn on the 2d of December with citizens killed and dying; fathers and mothers have been butchered on the threshold of their homes, children sabred, the hair of women matted with blood and their bosoms torn by grape-shot; suppliants have been massacred in their houses, others shot in heaps in their cellars, others dispatched by bayonets under their beds, others laid low on their own hearths; the marks of bloody hands are still imprinted here on a wall, there on a door, there on an alcove. After the victory of Louis Bonaparte, Paris tramped for three days through a reddish mud,— a cap filled with human brains has been seen hanging from a tree on the Boulevard des Italiens. I who write these lines have seen among other victims on the night of the 4th, near the Mauconseil barricade, and old man with while hair extended on the pavement, his breast perforated by a musket-shot and his collar-bone broken; the gutter of the street that flowed under him carried away his blood. I have seen, have touched with my hands, have aided in undressing, a poor child of seven years killed, I was told, in the Rue Tiquetonne; he was pale, his head moved backward and forward on his shoulders while we were taking off his clothes; his eyes, half-shut, were fixed, and on leaning over near his mouth it seemed as if you could hear him feebly murmur from his half-open lips the word "mother!"

Well! there is something more poignant than that murdered child, more lamentable than that old man dabbled with blood, more horrible than that rag stained with human brains,

more frightful than those pavements red with carnage, more
irreparable than those men and women, those fathers and
mothers, butchered and assassinated: it is the vanished honour
of a great people!   Certainly, those pyramids of dead bodies
seen in the cemeteries after the wagons which came from the
Champ de Mars had discharged their burdens, those immense
open trenches filled hastily in the morning before the twilight
brightened into day, brought terror to the hearts of the witnesses; but it is more frightful still to think that at the present moment the peoples of the earth are in doubt, and that for
them France, that great splendour of morality, has disappeared!

More heart-rending than the heads cloven by the sabre,
than the breasts riddled with bullets; more disastrous than violated houses, than murder filling the streets, than blood spilt
in the gutters,— is the thought that now among all nations it is said: " That nation of nations, that people of the
14th of July, that people of the 10th of August, that people
of 1830, that people of 1848, that race of giants which
crushed bastiles, that race of men whose visage shone with
light; that fatherland of mankind, which produced heroes and
thinkers who made all revolutions and gave birth to all births;
that France whose name meant liberty, that soul of the world
which radiated over Europe, that light — well! some one has
walked over it, and has extinguished it.   France is no more; it
is ended.   Look! darkness everywhere!   The world is groping on all fours!"

Ah, it was so great!   Where are those times, those glorious
times, filled with storms, but splendid; when all was life, when
all was liberty, when all was grandeur; those times when the
French people, awake, standing in the shadow before all, its
brow lighted by the dawn of the future which had already
arisen for it, said to other peoples still torpid and afflicted
and hardly stirring their chains in their sleep: " Be tranquil!
I am doing the work of all, I am digging the soil for all, I am
God's worker "?   Oh, the anguish of it all!   Behold that
lethargy where there was such power; behold that shame where

there was such pride; behold that superb people which once
held up its head, and bends it now!

Alas! Louis Bonaparte has done more than kill persons; he
has made souls shrink, he has made smaller the heart of the
citizen. It is necessary to belong to the race of the indomi-
table and the invincible, to persevere in the rugged path of re-
nunciation and of duty. Some horrible gangrene of material
prosperity is menacing public honesty with destruction and
rottenness. Oh, what happiness, after all, to be banished, to
be fallen, to be ruined! Is it not so, brave workmen? Is it
not so, honest peasants, hunted out of France, without an
asylum and without shoes? What happiness to eat black
bread, to sleep on a mattress on the ground, to be out at elbows, but to be beyond this, and able to meet those who say,
"You are a Frenchman!" with the answer, "I am proscribed!"

And what a miserable spectacle is the delight of self-interest
and of cupidity as they gorge themselves at the trough of the
2d of December! "Let us live! Let us do business,— job
in zinc shares and railway shares. Let us get money: it is
ignoble, but, faith! it is excellent. A scruple lost is a louis
gained; so let us sell our souls at this rate!" And so men
run, jostle one another, dance attendance, and drain all shame
to the dregs. If a railway concession in France or lands in
Africa cannot be obtained, a place is asked for. A crowd of
fearless and devoted beings besiege the Elysée and throng
around the man. Junot, near the first Napoleon, braved the
splashes from the howitzer-shell in the sand; those near the
second brave the splashes of mud. What care they if they
share his ignominy, provided they share his fortune. There
is a struggle as to who shall be first in this cynical traffic in
one's self; and among these people there are young men, with
pure and limpid eyes and all the appearances of ingenuous
youth, and there are old men who have only one fear,—
namely, that the place solicited may not reach them in time,
and they may die before succeeding in dishonouring themselves. One would surrender himself for a prefecture, another

for a receivership, another for a consulship; this one wants a tobacconist's shop, that one an embassy. All want money,— some more, some less; for it is of the salary they are think- ing, not of the office. Each has his hand outstretched; all offer themselves for sale. One of these days an assayer of consciences will be appointed, just as there is an assayer of coin.

What! they have come to this? What! those very men who supported the *coup d'état;* those very men who were frightened by the red ogre and the *Jacquerie* trash in 1852; those very men who found that this crime was good, because, according to them, it extricated from peril their incomes, their money-boxes, their quittances and receipts,— these same men do not understand that the material interest which alone floated amid an immense moral shipwreck would be, after all, but a poor and worthless waif, and that that situation is in- deed frightful and monstrous of which it may be said, " All is saved, except honour "? The words " independence," " en- franchisement," " progress," " popular pride," " national self- respect," " French greatness," can no longer be uttered in France. Hush! these words make too much noise; we must walk on the tips of our toes, and speak low. We are in the chamber of a sick man. What is that man? He is the chief, he is the master; everybody obeys him. Everybody respects him, then? No, everybody despises him. Oh, what a situa- tion!

And military honour,— where is it? Let us no longer speak, if you wish, of what the army did in December, but of what it is undergoing at the present moment, of him who is at its head, and of him who is above its head. Do you think of this? Does it think of it? O Army of the Republic! — army that had for captains generals paid four francs a day! army that had for chiefs Carnot, austerity; Hoche, honour; Marceau, disinterestedness; Kléber, devotion; Joubert, prob- ity; Desaix, virtue; Bonaparte, genius! — O French army! poor unhappy army! misled and misguided by these men of to-day! What will they do with it, where will they conduct it, in what will they employ it? What parodies are we destined to see and hear? Alas! what sort of men are those who command our regiments and who govern? The master — we know him. This general would have been " attached " on the 3d of December; it is why he *made* the 2d. This other is the " borrower " of the twenty-five millions from the Bank; this other is the man of " the Gold Ingots." " A friend " of this other said to him before he was minister: " You are bilking us with your shares in the affair in question; if there is swindling, I must be in it, however! " Another, who has the epaulets, has just been convicted of fraud. Another, who also has the epaulets, received on the morning of the 2d of December a hundred thousand francs " for eventualities; " he was only a colonel, if he had been a general he would have had more. Another, who is a general, was a body-guard of Louis XVIII., and stood as sentinel behind the king at Mass; he was dismissed for cutting off a gold acorn from the throne and putting it in his pocket; he was, in consequence, expelled from the guards. (Surely, to these men a column might be raised, *ex ære capto*, with the money taken.) Another, who is a general of division, appropriated fifty-two thousand francs, to the personal knowledge of Colonel Charras, out of the funds used for the construction of the villages of Saint-André and Saint-Hippolyte near Mascara. Another, who is commander-in-chief, was nicknamed at Ghent, where he was known, General *Cinq-cent-francs*. Another, who is Minister of War, owes it to the clemency of General Rulhière that he was not brought before a council of war. Such are the men. It doesn't matter. Forward! beat drums, sound trumpets, wave flags! Soldiers! from the height of the pyramids the forty thieves are gazing on you!

Let us get ahead with this painful question, and examine it in all its aspects.

The mere spectacle of such good fortune as that of Monsieur Bonaparte placed on the summit of the State would suffice to demoralize a people. There always is, and that through the fault of social institutions, which ought, above

all, to enlighten and civilize,— there always is among a popu-
lation as numerous as that of France a class which is ignorant, which suffers, which covets, which struggles, placed between the bestial instinct that urges to take and the moral
law that invites to labour.   In the painful and distressed condition in which it still exists, this class to keep upright and
honest needs all the pure and holy light which is found in the
Gospel; it needs that the spirit of Jesus on the one hand, and
the spirit of the French Revolution on the other, should address
it in the same manly language, and show forth unceasingly,
as the only beacon worthy of the eyes of man, the lofty and
mysterious laws of human destiny,— abnegation, devotion,
self-sacrifice, labour which conducts to material happiness,
probity which conducts to interior happiness.   Even with
this perpetual teaching, at once human and divine, this class,
so worthy of sympathy and fraternity, often succumbs; suffering and temptation are stronger than virtue.   Now, do
you understand the infamous counsels which the success of
Monsieur Bonaparte gives to this class?   A poor man in
rags, without resources, without labour, is there in the
shadow, at the corner of the street, seated upon a post; he is
meditating and at the same time resisting a bad action; now he
wavers and now he is strong; he is hungry, and he would like
to steal; to steal, he must have a false key, he must climb a
wall; then, the false key made, and the wall climbed, he reaches
the money-box; if any one awakens, if he is hindered, he will
have to kill; his hair stands on end, his eyes grow wild; his
conscience, the voice of God, revolts, and cries to him: " Stop!
it is wrong! these are crimes! "   At that moment the head of
the State passes by; the man sees Monsieur Bonaparte in the
uniform of a general, with the red ribbon, and lackeys in gold-
laced liveries, riding at full gallop towards his palace in a
carriage drawn by four horses.   The wretch, halting in presence of his crime, drinks in greedily this splendid vision; and
the serenity of Monsieur Bonaparte, and his gold epaulets
and the red ribbon and the livery and the palace and the carriage with four horses say to him, " Succeed! "   He hangs

on to this apparition; he follows it; he runs to the Elysée.
A splendidly arrayed crowd is following in the wake of their
prince; all kinds of carriages pass through this gate, and he
gets a glimpse of men happy and joyous.   Yonder is an ambassador; the ambassador looks at him and says, " Succeed! "
Yonder is a judge; the judge looks at him and says, " Succeed! "   Yonder is a bishop: the bishop looks at him and says,
" Succeed! "   So for him henceforth the whole moral law
consists in getting clear of the police.   To rob, pillage, stab,
assassinate, is bad only when you are stupid enough to allow
yourself to be taken.   Every man who meditates a crime
has a constitution to violate, an oath to infringe, an obstacle
to destroy.   In a word, take your measures well; be clever,
succeed.   The only guilty actions are those that miscarry.
You put your hand in the pocket of some passer-by, in the
evening, at nightfall, in a lonely place; he seizes you, you
surrender; he takes you prisoner, and leads you to the station:
you are guilty, to the galleys!   You do not surrender; you
have a knife about you,— you plunge it into the throat of the
man; he falls, he is dead; now take his purse and get off.
Bravo! it is a thing cleverly done.   You have shut the victim's mouth, the only witness that could speak; you will have
no further trouble.   If you had only robbed the man, you
would have done wrong; kill him, and you are right.

Succeed! that is everything.   Ah, this is a thing to be
dreaded.   On the day when the human conscience becomes
abashed, on the day when success makes right, all is over.
The last flickering ray of morality ascends again to heaven;
darkness is in the soul of man.   All that is left you is to devour one another,— ferocious beasts!

To moral degradation is joined political degradation.
Monsieur Bonaparte treats France as a conquered country.
He effaces republican inscriptions; he cuts down the trees of
liberty and makes fagots of them.   There was in the Place
Bourgogne a statue of the Republic,— he uses a pickaxe on
it; there was a figure of the Republic, crowned with ears of
wheat, on the coinage,— Monsieur Bonaparte puts the pro-

file of Monsieur Bonaparte in its place. He has his bust crowned and harangued in the public markets, as Gessler had his cap saluted. The bumpkins of the faubourgs were accustomed to sing in chorus, when returning from work in the evening; they sang the grand republican songs,— the " Marseillaise," the " Chant du Départ." They were ordered to cease; the denizens of the faubourgs must no longer sing; obscene and bacchanalian ditties are alone permitted.

This triumph has been so great that Monsieur Bonaparte is no longer embarrassed about things. Yesterday there was a certain amount of caution; the fusilade took place at night. This was horrible enough, but it evinced some degree of shame. To-day there is a public display; fear has vanished; the guillotine is erected in broad daylight. Who are guillotined? Who? The men of the law, and justice is there! Who? The men of the people, and the people are there! This is not all. There is one man in Europe who horrifies Europe; he has sacked Lombardy, erected gibbets in Hungary, and flogged a woman under the gibbet on which her husband and son hung strangled. The terrible letter in which this woman relates the foul deed, and says, " My heart has become stone," is still remembered. Last year this man thought he would visit London as a tourist, and being in London he had a fancy to enter a brewery,— the brewery of Barclay and Perkins. There he was recognized; a voice murmured, " It is Haynau!" " It is Haynau!" repeated the workmen. There was a frightful roar; the crowd made a rush on the wretch, tore out fistfuls of his infamous white hair, spat in his face, and flung him outside. Well! this old epauletted bandit, who still feels on his cheek the terrible buffet of the English people, has been invited, it is announced, to visit France at the invitation of " Monseigneur the Prince President." It is but just. London outraged him; Paris owes him an ovation. It will be a reparation. Be it so; we shall witness it. Haynau was received with curses and hooting at the Perkins Brewery; at the Saint Antoine brewery he should be presented with flowers. The Faubourg

Saint Antoine will receive orders to be good. The Faubourg Saint Antoine, mute, motionless, and impassive, will see Louis Bonaparte, the butcher of the boulevard, giving his arm to Haynau, the flogger of women; will see them pass along its old revolutionary streets,— the one in French uniform, the other in Austrian,— triumphant, and chatting like two old friends.

Go on! continue! heap insult upon insult! disfigure this France prostrate on the pavement! render her unrecognizable! crush the face of the people with repeated blows of your heel! Oh, grant me, find out for me, invent, discover for me any way, short of the dagger (which I will not have: a Brutus for this man! shame! shame! he does not deserve even Louvel),— find me any means whatever of casting down this man and delivering my country; of casting down this man,— this man of craft, this man of falsehood, this man of success, this man of woe! Any means, the first at hand, — pen, sword, paving-stone, riot, by the people or by the soldier,— yes, whatever it be, provided it be loyal and open, I lay hold of it, we all lay hold of it, we the proscribed, if it can restore liberty; deliver the Republic, raise our country out of shame, and send back into the dust, into his past oblivion, into the slums from which he emerged, this imperial ruffian, this pickpocket prince, this vagabond of kings, this traitor, this circus-rider, this radiant ruler, unshaken, satisfied, crowned by his happy crime; who comes and goes and walks peacefully through shuddering Paris, and who has everything in his favour,— the Bourse, the shop, the magistracy, all influences, all guarantees, all invocations, from the *Nom de Dieu* of the soldier to the *Te Deum* of the priest! Truly, when one keeps his eyes fixed too long on certain aspects of this spectacle there are times when a kind of giddiness seizes the firmest minds.

Still, does this Bonaparte do himself justice? Has he any glimmer, any idea, any perception, any suspicion whatever of his infamy? Really, one is compelled to doubt it. Yes, sometimes to hear the lofty phrases that escape him, his incredible appeals to that posterity which will shudder with anger when it comes across him,— to listen to him speaking with entire self-possession of his " legitimacy " and of his " mission," a person would be almost tempted to believe that he has succeeded in having a high consideration for himself, and that his head is turned to such a degree that he no longer knows what he is nor what he does. He believes in the adhesion of the proletariat; he believes in the good-will of kings; he believes in the *fête* of the eagles; he believes in the harangues of the Council of State; he believes in the benedictions of the bishops; he believes in the oath he has had sworn to himself; he believes in the seven million, five hundred thousand votes! He speaks now, finding himself in the temper of Augustus, of " amnestying " the proscribed. Usurpation amnestying right! treason amnestying honour! cowardice amnestying courage! crime amnestying virtue! He is so brutalized by success that he finds all this quite natural.

Strange effect of intoxication! singular optical illusion! He sees something glorious, splendid, radiant, in that thing of the 14th of January; in that constitution soiled with mud, stained with blood, adorned with chains drawn amid the hootings of Europe by the police, the Senate, the Legislative Body, and the Council of State, all shod anew! He takes for a triumphial chariot, and will have it driven as such under the Arc d'Etoile, that hurdle on which he stands, hideous, with scourge in hand, dragging after him the bloody corpse of the Republic!

SECOND PART

MOURNING AND FAITH

I

PROVIDENCE, by the mere fact of universal life, leads on to maturity men, things, events. In order that an old world fade away, it is sufficient for civilization, ascending majestically toward her solstice, to illuminate ancient institutions, ancient prejudices, ancient laws, and ancient manners. Her radiance burns up the past and devours it. Civilization enlightens (this is the visible fact), and at the same time consumes (this is the mysterious fact). Under its influence, that which should decline declines, and that which should grow old grows old, slowly and without shock; wrinkles come to things condemned, be they castes, or codes, or institutions, or religions.

This travail of decrepitude is in some sort its own work, — fertilizing decrepitude under which germinates the new life. Destruction goes on gradually; deep crevices which we do not see branch out in the shadow and reduce to dust the interior of that venerable formation which still seems massive from the outside; and then suddenly, some fine day, that antique pile of worm-eaten facts which compose decaying societies becomes unsightly; the edifice cracks, splits, and leans forward. After this nothing can hold together. Let one of those giants peculiar to revolutions arise; let this giant raise his hand, and all is over. There has been such an hour in history, when a blow of Danton's elbow would make Europe crumble. 1848 was one of those hours. Old Europe, feudal, monarchic, and papal, staggered. But a Danton was lacking. The fall did not take place.

It has been often said, in the threadbare phraseology employed in such cases, that 1848 had opened a gulf. No.

The corpse of the past was stretched over Europe; it is still so now. 1848 opened a ditch, and was proceeding to throw that corpse into it; it is that ditch that was taken for a gulf. In 1848, all who clung to the past, all who lived on the corpse, saw that ditch close by them. Not only were the kings on their thrones, the cardinals under their birettas, and the captains on their war-horses thrown into agitation; but whoever had any interest whatever in this thing that was about to disappear; whoever cultivated a social fiction for his profit, and leased or rented an abuse; whoever was the guardian of a falsehood, the door-keeper of a prejudice, or the framer of a superstition; whoever utilized the people for his own ends and ground it down with usury, with taxes, and with lies; whoever sold with false weights,— from those who alter a balance to those who falsify a Bible, from the bad trader to the bad priest, from those who manipulate figures to those who coin miracles,— all, from the Jewish banker, who is somewhat of a catholic, to the bishop, who is somewhat of a Jew,— all the men of the past leaned their heads towards one another and trembled. That yawning ditch into which all their fictions, their treasury, were so near falling,— fictions that weighed over man for so many centuries,— they resolved to fill up. They resolved to wall it in, to pile stones and rocks on it, and on the heap to erect a gibbet, and to hang on that bloody and gloomy gibbet the great criminal — Truth! They resolved to have done once for all with the spirit of enfranchisement and emancipation, and to tread down and crush forever the ascending forces of humanity.

The undertaking was a serious one. What it was we have already indicated, more than once, in this book and elsewhere. To undo the labours of twenty generations; to take the nineteenth century by the throat and slay in it three centuries,— the sixteenth, the seventeenth, and the eighteenth (that is to say, Luther, Descartes, and Voltaire,— religious inquiry, philosophical inquiry, universal inquiry); to crush throughout Europe that immense vegetation of free thought,

— a great oak here, a blade of grass there; to marry the knout and the holy-water sprinkler; to put more of Spain in the South and more of Russia in the North; to resuscitate all that could be resuscitated of the Inquisition, and stifle all that could be stifled of intelligence; to stupefy youth,— in other words, to brutalize the future; to force the world to be present at the *auto-da-fé* of ideas; to overturn the tribunes, to suppress the journal, the public poster, books, utterances of every sort,— a cry, a murmur, a whisper; to create silence; to hunt down thought in the printer's case, in the composing-stick, in the leaden letter, in the stereotype plate, in the lithograph, in the theatre, in the mouth of the actor, in the copy-book of the school-master, in the pack of the pamphlet-hawker; to preach to man material interest as his faith, his law, his aim, and his God; to say to the people " Eat, and think no longer; " to displace the brain of man and put it in his stomach; to extinguish individual initiative, local life, national aspirations, all the profound instincts that urge man towards rectitude, to annihilate that *ego* of nations which is called fatherland; to destroy nationality among divided and dismembered populations, constitutions in constitutional states, the Republic in France, liberty everywhere, and everywhere to stamp out human effort: in a word, to close up that abyss which is named " progress " — such was the vast, enormous plan, extending over Europe, which no person conceived singly, for not one of those men of the old world had the genius to do so, but which all followed.

As to the plan itself, as to this immense idea of universal repression, whence did it come? Who can say? It was in the air; it appeared in the direction of the past; it lit up certain souls; it pointed out certain paths; it was like a glare of light issuing from the tomb of Machiavelli. At certain times of human history, when certain things are being plotted, when certain things are being done, it seems as if the old demons of humanity — Louis XI., Philip II., Catherine de Medicis, the Duke of Alba, Torquemada — are somewhere there in a corner, seated around a table and holding council. Yet, when we look and search, instead of the colossuses of old we see abortions; where we imagine the Duke of Alba, we find Schwartzenberg; where we imagined Torquemada, we find Veuillot. The ancient European despotism continues its march with these little men, and never ceases; it resembles the Czar Peter when travelling,—"We take relays of horses where we find them," he wrote, "and when we have no more Tartar horses we take asses." To attain this end,— the repression of everything and of every one,— it was necessary to tread a dark, tortuous, hard, and difficult road: it has been trodden. Some of those who entered it knew what they were doing.

Parties live on words. These men, these ringleaders, who were terrified and united by 1848 had, as we have said before, found their words,— " religion," " family," " property." Certain obscure phrases of what is called " socialism " they turned to account with that vulgar adroitness which suffices to impress timidity. It was necessary " to save religion, property, the family, the flag!" they said; and the rabble rout of scared interests flocked to their side. They coalized, faced around, formed a square. They crowded together; and this crowd was composed of diverse elements. The proprietor entered it because his income had diminished; the peasant, because he had to pay the forty-five centimes; such a one who did not believe in God believed it necessary to save religion because he was compelled to sell his horses. The force which this crowd contained was released and made available. With it repression became the order of the day everywhere, and by means of everything,— by law, by arbitrary power, by assemblies, by tribunes, by the jury, by the magistracy, by the police; in Lombardy by the sabre, in Naples by the dungeon, in Hungary by the gibbet. To muzzle intellects, to fetter minds again (slaves escaped for a moment), to prevent the disappearance of the past, to prevent the birth of the future, to perpetuate the power of kings, and of all powerful, privileged, and fortunate personages,— everything became good, everything became just, everything became legitimate. For the necessities of the struggle a moral ambuscade against liberty was contrived and spread over the world,— put in action by Ferdinand at Palermo, Antonelli at Rome, Schwartzenberg at Milan and Pesth, and later on, by the men of December at Paris, those wolves of the human race.

There was among the peoples one people which was a sort of eldest brother in the family of the oppressed, which was like a prophet in the tribune of mankind. This people took the initiative in all the movements of humanity. It said, "Come!" and all followed. As a complement to the fraternity of men which is in the Gospel, this nation taught the fraternity of nations. It spoke by the voice of its writers, of its poets, of its philosophers, and its orators as by a single mouth; and its words went to the extremities of the world, to settle like tongues of fire on the brows of all nations. It presided at the Divine Supper of human intelligence; it multiplied the bread of life to those who wandered in the desert. One day a storm encompassed it; it walked over the abyss and said to the frightened peoples, "Why fear ye?" The waves of the revolutions it raised grew calm under its feet, and far from engulfing, glorified it. Nations sick, suffering, and feeble pressed around it. This one limped; the chain of the Inquisition, riveted on her limbs for three hundred years, had lamed her: it said, "Walk!" and she walked. This other was blind; the old Roman papism had filled her eyes with fog and with night: it said to her, "See!" and she opened her eyes and saw. It said: "Throw away your crutches; that is to say, your prejudices. Throw away your bandages; that is to say, your superstitions. Stand up erect, raise your heads, look at the heavens, contemplate God! The future is yours, O peoples! You have a leper,— ignorance; you have a plague,— fanaticism; there is not one of you that does not bear one of those frightful maladies which is termed a despot. March on, forward! break the bonds of evil! I am your deliverer, your physician!" Through all the earth there was a grateful shout from the peoples, which these words were restoring to health and strength.   On one day it approached dead Poland; it lifted its finger and cried, " Arise! " and dead Poland arose.

This people the men of the past, whose fall it prophesied, dreaded and hated.   By craft, and tortuous patience and audacity, they seized and succeeded in garroting it at last.   For more than three years the world has witnessed a gigantic execution, a frightful spectacle.   For more than three years the men of the past, the scribes and pharisees, the publicans and the high-priests, are crucifying, in presence of the human race, the Christ of the peoples,— the French people. Some have furnished the cross, others the nails, others the hammer.   Falloux has placed on her brow the crown of thorns; Montalembert has pressed the sponge of gall and vinegar on her lips; Louis Bonaparte is the wretched soldier who has pierced her side and forced from her the last cry, " Eli! Eli! Lamma Sabacthani! "

And now it is all over.   The French people is dead.   The great tomb is opened to receive it for three days.

II

LET us have faith.   Let us not be cast down.   To despair is to desert.

Let us look to the future.   The future!   We know not what storms separate us from the port, but the far-off and radiant port is before our eyes.   The future, we repeat, is the Republic for all; let us add,— the future is peace with all.

Let us not adopt the vulgar caprice of calumniating and dishonouring the age in which we live.   Erasmus called the sixteenth century " the excrement of the times," —*fex temporum*.   Bossuet styled the seventeenth century " a bad and petty age."   Rousseau branded the eighteenth century with these words: " This great rottenness in which we live."   Posterity has taken these illustrious men to task; it has said to Erasmus, " The sixteenth century is great; " it has said to

Bossuet, " The seventeenth century is great; " it has said to Rousseau, " The eighteenth century is great." Moreover, even if the infamy of these ages were real, these men would still have been in the wrong. The thinker must accept with simplicity and calmness the environment amid which Providence has placed him. The splendour of human intelligence, the elevation of genius, is not less striking by contrast than by harmony with the times. A stoical and thoughtful man is not lessened by external degradation. Virgil, Petrarch, and Racine are great in their purple; Job on his dunghill is greater still.

But we who are men of the nineteenth century can say that the nineteenth century is not a dunghill. Whatever may be the shame of the moment; whatever be the blows dealt us by the backward and forward motion of events; whatever be the apparent desertion or the momentary lethargy of minds, — none of us democrats will deny the magnificent epoch in which we live, the virile age of humanity. Let us proclaim it aloud, proclaim it in downfall and defeat. This century is the grandest of centuries! And do you know why? Because it is the mildest. This century, the immediate issue of the French Revolution and its first-born, is freeing the slave in America, raising the pariah in Asia, extinguishing the suttee in India, and tramping out the last embers of the stake in Europe. It is civilizing Turkey; getting the spirit of the Gospel even into the Koran; elevating woman; subordinating the right of the stronger to the right of him who has more justice on his side; suppressing pirates; diminishing penalties; improving the sanitation of prisons; throwing the branding-iron into the sewer; condemning the penalty of death; taking away the ball from the legs of criminals; abolishing torture; discrediting and stigmatizing the sword; rendering harmless its Dukes of Alba and its Charles IX.'s, and tearing from tyrants their claws. This age proclaims the sovereignty of the citizen and the inviolability of life; it crowns the people and consecrates the man. In art is has genius of all kinds,— writers, orators, poets, historians, publicists, philosophers, painters, sculptors, and musicians; majesty, grace, power, strength, splendour, depth, colour, form, and style.   It steeps itself at once in the real and the ideal, and bears in its hands the two thunderbolts,— the true and the beautiful.   In science it accomplishes all miracles; it makes a saltpetre out of cotton, a horse out of steam, a workman out of Volta's battery, a messenger out of the electric fluid, a painter out of the sun.   It opens on two infinities two windows, the telescope and the microscope,— the one on the infinitely great, the other on the infinitely little; and it finds in the abyss of the insects as well as in the abyss of the stars a proof that God is! It suppresses duration, it suppresses distance, it suppresses suffering; it writes a letter from London to Paris, and receives a reply in ten minutes; it cuts off a thigh from a man, and the man sings and smiles.   There is one more progress to be realized, and it is drawing near to it,— a progress that is nothing in comparison with the other miracles which it has already performed: it has but to find the means of guiding in a mass of air a lighter bubble of air.   It has already the bubble of air,— it holds it imprisoned; it has but to find the impulsive force, to make the vacuum before the air-balloon, to burn the air before it as the fusee does the powder before it: it has only to resolve in any fashion whatever this problem, and it will resolve it,— and do you know what will happen then? That very instant frontiers vanish, barriers are effaced; the entire Chinese wall around thought, around commerce, around industry, around nationalities, around progress, falls down. In despite of censorships, in despite of indexes, it rains books and journals on all sides; Voltaire, Diderot, Rousseau, fall in hail-showers on Rome, Naples, Vienna, St. Petersburg; the human word is manna, and the serf picks it up in the furrows; fanaticisms die, oppression is impossible.   Man was crawling along the earth,— he is free; civilization becomes a cloud of birds, and flies and whirls around and perches at the same time on all points of the globe.   Stay! do you see her yonder? She is passing! Level your cannon, old despotisms,— she disdains you; you are but the ball, she is the lightning. No more hatreds, no more self-interests devouring one another, no more wars; a new life made up of harmony and light prevails and tranquillizes the world; the fraternity of nations traverses space and communicates in the eternal azure; men meet one another in the heavens!

While watching for this last progress, observe the point to which this century has conducted civilization already. Once there was a world in which men walked with slow steps, with bent back and with bowed head; in which Count de Gouvan had himself waited on at table by Jean Jacques; in which the Chevalier de Rohan had Voltaire cudgelled; in which Daniel de Foe was put in the pillory; in which a town like Dijon was separated from a town like Paris by the necessity of making a will, by robbers at all the corners of the woods and a ride of ten days in a coach; in which a book was a kind of infamy and filth, which the executioner burned on the steps of the Palace of Justice; in which superstition and ferocity gave each other the hand; in which the Pope said to the Emperor, "Jungamus dexteras, gladium gladio copulemus;" in which crosses were met at every step from which hung amulets, and gibbets from which hung men; in which there were heretics, Jews, and lepers; in which houses had loop-holes and battlements; in which the streets were closed by a chain, the rivers by a chain, the camps even by a chain (as at the battle of Tolosa), the cities by walls, kingdoms by prohibitions and penalties; in which except authority and force, always in the closest union, all was divided, severed, kept apart, alienated, set at variance, hating and hated, scattered and dead,— men dust, power a block of iron. To-day there is a world in which all is living, united, interlinked, and incorporated,— a world in which reign thought, commerce, and industry; in which political ideas, becoming more and more fixed, are tending towards an amalgamation with science,— a world in which the last scaffolds and the last cannon are hastening to cut off the last heads and vomit forth the last shells,— a world in which distance

has disappeared; in which Constantinople is nearer to Paris
than Lyons was a hundred years ago; in which America
and Europe throb with the same heart-beat,— a world of
universal dissemination and of universal love, whose brain is
France, whose arteries are railways, and whose fibres are electric wires. Do you not see that to expound such a situation
is to explain everything, to demonstrate everything, and to
resolve everything? Do you not feel that the old world had
of necessity an old soul,— tyranny; and that on the new
world a young soul is about to descend necessarily, irresistibly, divinely,— liberty?

  This was the work the nineteenth century had done among
men and was gloriously continuing,— the nineteenth century,
that century of decline, that century of decay, that century
of abasement, as say the pedants, the rhetoricians, the imbeciles, and all that filthy brood of bigots, rogues, and knaves
who sanctimoniously bespatter glory with their gall, who declare Pascal a madman, Voltaire a coxcomb, and Rousseau a
brute, and whose triumph would set a dunce's cap on the
human race!

  You speak of the Lower Empire? Do you do so seriously?
Had the Lower Empire behind it John Huss, Luther, Cer-
vantes, Shakspeare, Pascal, Molière, Voltaire, Montesquieu,
Rousseau, and Mirabeau? Had the Lower Empire behind it
the taking of the Bastille, and the Federation, Danton,
Robespierre, and the Convention? Had the Lower Empire
America? Had the Lower Empire universal suffrage? Had
the Lower Empire the two ideas of country and humanity,—
country, the idea which enlarges the heart; humanity, the
idea which enlarges the horizon? Do you know that under
the Lower Empire Constantinople was falling into ruin, and
at its capture had no more than thirty thousand inhabitants?
Has Paris come to this? Because you have seen a pretorian
onslaught successful, you declare you are in the Lower Empire. It is easy to say it, and cowardly to think it. But
reflect for a moment, if you can. Had the Lower Empire
the mariner's compass, the voltaic pile, the printing-press,

the journal, the locomotive, the electric telegraph? — so
many wings which bear man aloft, and which the Lower Empire had not. Where the Lower Empire crept, the nineteenth
century soars. Do you really believe what you are saying?
What! we will again see the Empress Zoe, Romanus Argy-
rus, Nicephorus, Logothetes, Michael Calafates? Folly! Do
you imagine that Providence is an echo of itself? Do you
believe that God is eternally repeating the same thing?

Let us have faith! Self-mockery is the beginning of baseness. Let us affirm the truth. It is by such affirmation we
become good; it is by such affirmation we become great. Yes,
the enfranchisement of intelligence, and the consequent enfranchisement of peoples, was the sublime task the nineteenth
century was accomplishing in 'co-operation with France; for
the double providential travail of the time and of the men, of
maturity and of action, was blended in the common work,
and the great nation was the beacon of the great epoch.

O my country! it is now, when we behold thee bleeding,
lifeless, with drooping head and closed eyes, and open mouth
that no longer speaks; with the marks of the whip on thy
shoulders, and the imprint of the nails of the boots of thy
executioners on thy entire body, naked and soiled, and like
unto the dead; the object of hatred and, alas! object of derision,— it is now, O my country! that the heart of the proscribed overflows with love and respect for thee! Thou liest
motionless. The men of despotism and of oppression laugh,
and delight in the haughty delusion that thou art to be
feared no more. Fleeting will be their joy. The nations
who are in darkness forget the past and see only the present
and despise thee. Pardon them; they know not what they
do. Despise thee! Great God! despise France? And who
are they? What language do they speak? What books
have they in their hands? What names do they know by
heart? What posters are pasted on the walls of their theatres! What form have their arts, their laws, their manners,
their garments, their pleasures, their fashions? What is the
great date for them as for us? '89! If they take France

out of their soul, what is left them?   O peoples! though
Greece were fallen, and fallen forever, would she be despised?
Is Italy despised?   Can France be despised?   Gaze on those
paps! she is your nurse.   Gaze on that womb! she is your
mother.   If she sleeps, if she is in a lethargy, silence and
hats off!   If she is dead, on your knees!

The exiles are scattered; the winds of destiny disperse men
as a handful of ashes.   Some are in Belgium, in Piedmont,
in Switzerland, where they have no liberty; others are in London, where they have no shelter.   One is a peasant, torn from
his natal vineyard; another is a soldier, having but the frag-
ment of the sword broken in his hand; another a workman,
ignorant of the language of the country, without clothing
and without shoes, he knows not where he will get to-morrow's
meal; another has quitted a wife and children, the darlings
of his heart, the object of his toil, the joy of his life; another
has an old white-haired mother weeping his absence, another
an old father who will die without again beholding him; another has left behind him his love, the adored being who will
forget him,— yet they stand erect, they clasp one another's
hands, and they smile.   There is no one who does not stand
aside respectfully as they pass by; there is no one who does
not contemplate with deep emotion, as one of the grandest
spectacles afforded to mankind, all these serene consciences,
all these broken hearts.   They suffer and are silent; in them
the citizen has immolated the man; they look adversity calmly
in the face; they do not cry out even under the pitiless
scourge of misfortune, " Civis Romanus sum! "   But at evening, the season of meditation, when all in the foreign town
is arrayed in sadness (for that which seems cold in the day-
time becomes funereal in the twilight),— at night, when sleep
comes not, souls the most stoical become the prey of sorrow
and dejection.   Where are the little children!   Who will give
them bread; who will give them their father's kiss?   Where
is the wife; where is the mother; where is the brother; where
are they all?   And those songs, heard in the evening in the
mother-tongue,— where are they?   Where is the wood, the

tree, the pathway, the eaves full of nests, the belfry encircled by tombs? Where is the street, where the suburb, the lamp lit before the door, the friends, the workshop, the accustomed toil! And the furniture sold at public auction, the sale invading the sanctuary of home! Oh, what eternal farewells! Destroyed, dead, cast to the four winds of heaven, is that moral being called the family hearth, made up not only of gossip and tenderness and embraces, but of fixed habits, the visits of friends, the laugh of this one, a shake of the hand from that one, a view from a certain window, the spot where such a piece of furniture rested, the arm-chair where the grandfather sat, the carpet on which the first-born played! Fled are the objects which had received the impress of your life! vanished the visible form of your remembrances! There are certain familiar and obscure phases of sorrow that bend the courage of the proudest. The orator of Rome blenched not as he stretched his neck to the knife of the centurion Lenas, but he wept at the thought of his house demolished by Clodius.

The proscribed are silent; or if they complain, it is among themselves. They know one another, and are doubly brothers, having the same country, and being victims of the same proscription; and so they retail their miseries, brother to brother. He who has money shares it with those who have none; he who has firmness gives a portion to those who lack. Recollections are interchanged, aspirations, hopes. With outstretched arms they turn in the darkness to that which they have left behind. Oh, how happy yonder are those who no longer think of us! Each suffers, and at moments each becomes incensed. On all memories are engraved the names of all the executioners. Each has something which he curses,— Mazas, the prison-ship, the casemate, the informer who betrayed him, the spy who lay in wait for him, the gendarme who arrested him, Lambessa where there is a friend, Cayenne where there is a brother. But there is one thing which they all bless; it is France! Ah, a complaint, a word against thee, France! No, no! never has the fatherland a stronger hold

on the heart than in exile. They will do their whole duty
with tranquil soul and steadfast perseverance. No longer to
behold thee is their sorrow; never to forget thee, their joy.
But oh, the sadness of it all! And after eight months it is
still in vain we tell ourselves that things are as they are.
That yonder is the spire of Saint-Michel and not the Pantheon, that Sainte-Gudule is before our eyes and not Nôtre
Dame; we cannot believe it! But it is true; it cannot be denied, and must be acknowledged, though we were to expire
from humiliation and despair, that what is yonder, stretched
prostrate on the earth, is the nineteenth century, is France!

What! it is this Bonaparte who has consummated this dis-
aster? What! it is in the centre of the greatest people of
the world, in the middle of the greatest century of history,
that this man has arisen and triumphed? To make France
his prey, great God! What the lion would not have dared,
the ape has done? what the eagle would have feared to seize
in his talons, the parrot has clutched in its claws! what Louis
XI. would have failed in, what Richelieu would have hurled
himself against in vain, what Napoleon would have been un-
equal to,— in one single day, between the dark and the dawn,
the absurd has become possible; axioms have become chimeras,
and everything that was a lie has become a living fact.
What! the most signal co-operation of men, the most magnificent movement of ideas, the most tremendous concatenation
of events, that which a Titan could not have restrained, that
which a Hercules could not have turned aside, the river of
humanity in its onward flow, with France surging ahead, civilization, progress, intelligence, revolution, liberty,— all has
been brought on one fine morning to a stand, has been absolutely and at a moment's notice, stopped by this mummer, this
dwarf, this stunted Tiberius, this abortion, this nothing!
God was marching onward; Louis Bonaparte, with plume on
head, threw himself across the path and said to God, " Thou
shalt go no farther! " And God has stopped.

And do you imagine that this is so! And do you fancy
that this plebiscite exists; that this Constitution of some day

or other in January exists; that this Council of State and Legislative Body exist? Do you imagine that there is a lackey called Rouher, a valet called Troplong, a eunuch called Baroche, and a sultan, a pacha, a master, named Louis Bonaparte? You do not see, then, that all this is a chimera! you do not see, then, that the 2d of December is only a monstrous illusion, a pause, a halt, a sort of stage curtain behind which God, that wonderful mechanist, is preparing and building up the last act,— the supreme and triumphal act of the French Revolution! You are gazing stupidly at the curtain, at the things painted on that coarse canvas,— the nose of this one, the epaulets of that one, the big sabre of that other; at those peddlers of cologne-water in their gold lace whom you term generals, those baboons whom you style magistrates, those simple creatures whom you dub senators; and you take this medley of caricatures and spectres for realities! And you do not hear, in the shadow beyond, that muffled sound! you do not hear some one moving backward and forward! you do not see that the breathing of that which is behind makes the canvas tremble!

THE END.